John Ashton, James Mew

Drinks of the World

John Ashton, James Mew
Drinks of the World
ISBN/EAN: 9783744662307

Printed in Europe, USA, Canada, Australia, Japan

Cover: Foto ©Andreas Hilbeck / pixelio.de

More available books at **www.hansebooks.com**

DRINKS OF THE WORLD

BY

JAMES MEW,

Author of "Types from Spanish Story," &c., &c.,

AND

JOHN ASHTON,

Author of "Social Life in the Reign of Queen Anne," &c., &c.

ONE HUNDRED ILLUSTRATIONS.

1892.

LONDON:

The Leadenhall Press, 50, *Leadenhall Street, E.C.*
Simpkin, Marshall, Hamilton, Kent & Co., Ltd.

NEW YORK: Scribner & Welford.

"Ingeniosa Sitis."—*Martial, Epig.* xiv. 117.

"J'y ai songé comme un autre, et je suis tenté de mettre l'appétence des liqueurs fermentées, qui n'est pas connue des animaux, à côté de l'inquiétude de l'avenir, qui leur est étrangère, et de les regarder l'une et l'autre comme des attributs distinctifs du chef-d'œuvre de la dernière révolution sublunaire." —*Brillat-Savarin, Physiologie du Goût, Medit.* 9.

"Ac si quis diligenter reputet, in nulla parte operosior vita est, ceu non saluberrimum ad potum aquæ liquorem natura dederit, quo cætera omnia animantia utuntur."—*Pliny, Nat. Hist.* xiv. 28.

"Wine that maketh glad the heart of man."—*Ps.* civ. 15.

"DRINKS"

Dedicated

to

those who know how to use

and thankfully enjoy

the good things

so bountifully provided

by

Dame Nature.

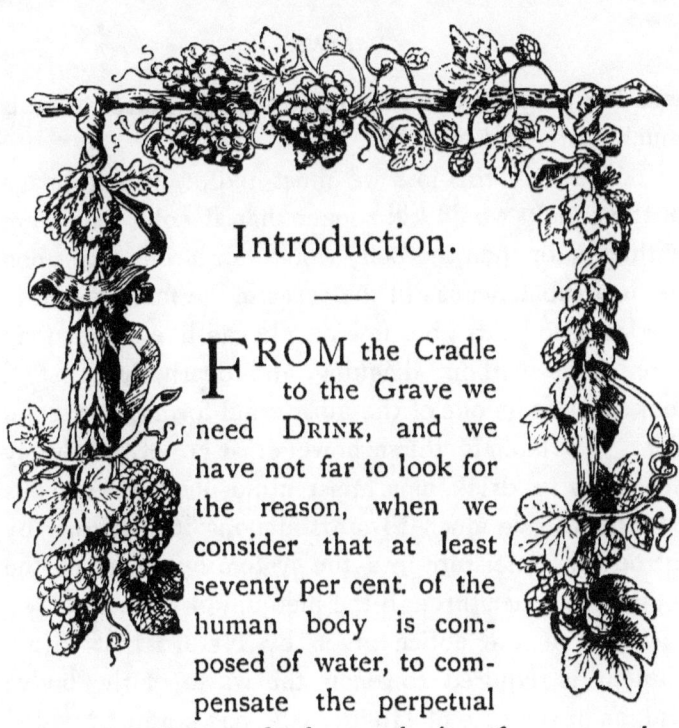

Introduction.

FROM the Cradle to the Grave we need DRINK, and we have not far to look for the reason, when we consider that at least seventy per cent. of the human body is composed of water, to compensate the perpetual waste of which, a fresh supply is, of course, absolutely necessary. This is taken with our food (all solid nutriment containing some water), and by the drink we consume. But, as the largest constituent part of the body is fluid, so, naturally, its waste is larger than that of the solid; this fluid waste being enormous. Besides the natural losses, every breath we exhale is heavily laden with moisture, as breathing on a cold polished surface, or a cold day by condensing the breath, will show; whilst the twenty-eight miles of tubing disposed over the surface of the human body will evaporate, *invisibly*, two or three pounds of water daily. Of course, in very hot weather, or after extreme exertion, this perspiration is much more, and is visible.

To remedy this loss we must DRINK, as a stoppage of the supply would kill sooner than if solid food were withheld, for then the body would, for a time, live upon its own substance, as in the cases of the fasting men of the last two years; but few people can live longer than three days without drinking, and death by thirst is looked upon as one of the most cruel forms of dissolution. To palliate thirst, however, it is not absolutely necessary to drink, as a moist atmosphere or copious bathing will do much towards allaying it,—the one by introducing moisture into the system by means of the lungs, the other through the medium of the skin.

Thirst is the notice given by Nature that liquid aliment is required to repair the waste of the body; and, as in the case of Hunger, she has kindly provided that supplying the deficiency shall be a pleasant sensation, and one calculated to call up a feeling of gratitude for the means of allaying the want. Indeed, no man knows the real pleasures of eating and drinking, until he has suffered both hunger and thirst.

Water, as a means of slaking man's thirst, has been provided for him in abundance from the time of Father Adam, whose "Ale" is so vaunted by abstainers from alcoholic liquors. But Water, unless charged with Carbonic Acid gas, or containing some mineral in solution, is considered by some, as a constant drink, rather vapid; and Man, as he became civilized, has made himself other beverages, more or less tasty, and provocative of excess, and also more or less deleterious to his internal economy. The juice of luscious fruits was expressed, the vine was made to give up its life blood ; and, probably through accident, alcoholic fermentation was discovered, and a new zest was given to drinking. A good servant, Alcohol is a bad master ; but that it satisfies a widely felt craving, probably induced by civilization, is certain, for most savage tribes, emerging from their primitive and natural state, manufacture drinks from divers vegetable substances, more or less alcoholic.

The present volume is intended for that class of the public which is known as "the general reader"; and its object is to interest rather than to inform. Therefore it deals at no great length with what may be termed the *caviare* of the subject, as, for instance, the varied opinions of the medical faculty with respect to the hygienic value of drinks, their supposed uses in health and disease, and their chemical constituents, or analyses. Nor is the question of price discussed, nor long lists of vineyard proprietors given, nor the names of the brewers, nor the number of casks of beer brewed. In short, as few statistics have been introduced as possible. In deference to a maxim not always remembered in books on beverages, "*De gustibus non est disputandum,*" or its English equivalent, abhorred of Chesterfield, "What is one man's meat is another man's poison," the verdicts of enthusiasts and vendors have been, except in rare instances, alike rejected.

Nor has very much been said on the inviting topic of adulteration. It would be almost cruel to disturb the credulity of the good people who drink and pay for gooseberry as Champagne, or *Val de peñas* as curious old Port. It is a pretty comedy to watch the *soi-disant* connoisseur drinking a wine fully accredited with crust, out of a bottle ornamented with fungus and cobwebs of proper consistency—a wine flavoured with *essence* at so much a pound, and stained with *colour*[1] at so much per gallon. There is no need to proclaim upon the housetops the constituents of Hamburg sherry, nor how the best rum is flavoured with " R.E.," or brandy with " Caramel " or " Cognacine."

We have generally avoided the profane use of trade or professional jargon, too often the outcome of ignorance, pretence, and affectation, such as " full," "fruity," " smooth on palate," " round in the mouth," "full of body," " wing," " character," etc. ; nor have we touched, or desired to touch, on the influence of alcohol on man's social or other well-being. Peter the Hermit is fully represented already, and we have no mission to call upon our fellow-countrymen to " rise to the dignity of manhood," and never touch another glass of Madeira.

The authors have followed the example of the illustrious Molière in taking their matter wherever they could find it. The information contained in this work is derived either from other books, oral information, or personal experience. " The sun robs the sea, the

---

[1] These essences and colours are no new thing. Addison spoke of them nearly two hundred years ago in his "Trial of the Wine Brewers" in the *Tatler*. Tom Tintoret and Harry Sippet have left a large family behind them.

moon robs the sun, the sea robs the moon," says Timon of Athens, repeating Anacreon, who adds that the earth robs them all. So preceding authors are indebted to one another, and the present volume to them all. It has been written, it is hoped, without bias or prejudice of any kind ; but, as the drinks containing Alcohol are many more than those in which it is absent, more have been mentioned. That a full record of all drinks should appear, is impossible ; nor could any critic expect it; but an attempt has been made to give a fairly full list, and to render it as pleasant reading as the subject admits.

THE DRINKS OF ANTIQUITY.

EGYPT: Method of Wine-Making—Early Wines—Names of Wines—Ladies and Wine—Beer, etc. ASSYRIA: List of Assur-ba-ni-pal's Wines—Method of Drinking—Different Sorts of Wine. HITTITE: Two Ladies Drinking—Their Appreciation of Wine—The Hittite Bacchus. JUDEA: Mention of Wines in the Old Testament—Wine as an Article of Commerce—Mixed Wines—Wine Vessels.

HAS any man been bold enough to attempt to fix upon the discoverer of Wine? Not to our knowledge. Nor can a date be even hazarded as to its introduction. It was so good a thing, that we may be sure that men very soon came to know its revivifying effects. We do know this: that the oldest records of which we have any cognisance, those of the Egyptians (who were in a high state of civilization and culture when the Hebrews were semi-barbarous nomads), show us that they had wine, and used it in a most refined manner, as we see by the headpiece to this chapter. Here a father is nursing his child, who invites him to smell a lotus flower, another blossom of which his mother is showing him. An attendant proffers wine in bowls wreathed with flowers, and another is at hand with a bowl possibly of water, and a napkin. This wreathing the bowls with flowers shows how highly they esteemed the " good creature," and, also, that they were then at least as civilized as the later Greeks and Romans, who followed the same practice.

We have the Egyptian pictures showing the whole process of wine-making. We see their vines very carefully trained in bowers, or in avenues, formed by columns and rafters; their vineyards were walled in, and frequently had a reservoir of water within their precincts, together with a building which contained a winepress; whilst boys frightened the birds away with slings and stones, and cries. The grapes, when gathered, were put into deep wicker baskets, which men carried either on their heads or shoulders, or slung upon a yoke, to the winepress, where the wine was squeezed out of a bag by means of two poles turned in contrary directions, an earthen pan receiving the juice. But they also had large presses, in which they trod the fruit with their naked feet, supporting themselves by ropes suspended from the roof.

The grape juice having fermented, it was put into earthen jars, resembling the Roman *amphoræ*, which were closed with a lid covered with pitch, clay, mortar or gypsum, and sealed, after which they were removed to the storehouse, and there placed upright. The Egyptians had a peculiar habit, which used also to be general in Italy and Greece, and now obtains in the islands of the Archipelago, of putting a certain quantity of resin or bitumen at the bottom of the amphora before pouring in the wine. This was supposed to preserve it, but it was also added to give it a flavour—a taste probably acquired from their having been used to wine skins, instead of jars, and having employed resins to preserve the skins.

The Egyptians had several kinds of wine, even as early as the fourth dynasty (above 6000 years ago, according to Mariette), when four kinds of wine, at least, were known. Pliny and Horace say that the wine of Mareotis was most esteemed. The soil, which lay beyond the reach of the alluvial deposits, suited the vine, and extensive remains of vineyards near the Qasr Karóon, still found, show whence the ancient Egyptians obtained their wines. Athenæus says, "the Mareotic grape was remarkable for its sweetness;" and he thus describes the wine made therefrom : " Its colour is white, its quality excellent, and it is sweet and light, with a fragrant *bouquet;* it is by no means astringent, nor does it affect the head. . . . Still, however, it is inferior to the Teniotic, a wine which receives its name from a place called Tenia, where it is produced. Its colour is pale and white, and there is such a degree of richness in it, that, when mixed with water, it seems gradually to be diluted, much in the same way as Attic honey when a liquid is poured into it; and besides the agreeable flavour of the wine, its fragrance is so delightful as to render it perfectly aromatic, and it has the property of being slightly astringent. There are many other vineyards in the valley of the Nile, whose wines are in great repute, and these differ both in colour and taste; but that which is produced about Anthylla is preferred to all the rest." He also commends some of the wines made in the Thebaïd, especially about Coptos, and says that they were "so wholesome that invalids might take them without inconvenience, even during a fever."

Pliny cites the Sebennytic wine as one of the choice Egyptian *crûs*, and says it was made of three different sorts of grapes. He also speaks of a curious wine called *Ecbolada*.

Wine took a large part in the Egyptian ritual, and was freely poured forth as libations to the different deities; and in private life women were not restricted in its use. In fact, the ungallant Egyptians have left behind them several delineations of ladies in a decided state of "how came you so?" It was probably put down to the Egyptian equivalent for Salmon.[1] But if they noticed the failings of their womankind, they equally faithfully portrayed their own shortcomings, for we see them being carried home from a feast limp and helpless, or else standing on their heads, and otherwise playing the fool.

Still, wine was the drink of the wealthy, or at least of those, as we should call them, "well to do." They had a beer, which Diodorus calls *zythum*,[2] and which,

[1] See tailpiece, where a servant is coming to the assistance of her mistress.
[2] Jablonski is our authority for supposing it primarily an Egyptian

he says, was scarcely inferior to the juice of the grape. This beer was made from barley, and, hops being unknown, it was flavoured with lupins and other vegetable substances. This old beer was called *hega*, and can be traced back as far as the 4th dynasty. Then they also had Palm wine, and another wine called *baga*, supposed to be made from dates or figs;

and they also made wines from pomegranates and other fruits, and from herbs, such as rue, hellebore,

drink. A *zythum* and a *dizythum* seem to have existed, corresponding, let us say, to our *Single* and *Double X*.

This *zythum* is nearly allied to the *sacera* of Palestine, the *cesia* of Spain, the *cervisia* of Gaul, the *sebaia* of Dalmatia, and the *curmi* or *camum* of Germany. According to Rabbi Joseph, this beer was made ⅓ barley, ⅓ *Crocus Sylvestris*, and ⅓ salt. He adds, " He that is bound, it looseth; and he who is loose, it binds; and it is dangerous for pregnant women."

absinthe, etc., which probably answered the purpose of our modern "bitters."

The Assyrians, who rank next in antiquity to the Egyptians, were no shunners of wine; they could drink sociably, and hob-nob together, as we see by the accompanying illustration.

Their wine cups were, in keeping with all the dress and furniture of the royal palaces, exceedingly ornate; and it is curious to note the comparative barbarism of the wine skin, and the nervous beauty of the wine cups being filled by the effeminate eunuch. The numerous bas-reliefs which, happily, have been rescued, to our great edification, afford many examples of wine cups of very great beauty of form. The inscriptions give us a list of many wines, and among them was the wine of Helbon, which was grown near Damascus, at a village now called Halbûn. It is alluded to in Ezekiel xxvii. 18: "Damascus was thy merchant, by reason of the multitude of the wares of thy making, for the multitude of all riches; in the wine of Helbon, and white wool."

Wm. St. Chad Boscawen, Esq., the eminent Assyriologist, has kindly favoured us with the following illustration and note on the subject of Assyrian wines:—

"This list of wines is found engraved upon a terra-cotta tablet from the palace of Assur-ba-ni-pal, the Sardanapalus of the Greeks, and evidently represents the wines supplied to the royal table. It reads:

Col. I. Wine of the Land of Izalli.
Wine, the Drink of the King (*Daniel* i. 5).
Wine of the Nazahrie.
Wine of Ra-h-ū (*Shepherds' Wine*).
Wine of Khabaru.

Col. II. Wine of Khilbunn or Helbon.
Wine of Arnabani (*North Syria*).
Wine of Sibzu (*Sweet Wine*).
Wine of Sa-ta-ba-bi-ru-ri (*which I think means Wines which from the Vineyard come not*).
Wine of Kharrubi (*Wine of the Carrob or Locust bean*)."

On Phillips's Cylinder (col. i. l. 21-26) is a list of wines which Nabuchodorossor is said to have offered: "The wine of the countries of Izalla, Toúimmon, Ssmmini, Helbon, Aranaban, Souha, Bit-Koubati, and Bigati, as the waters of rivers without number." And among the inscriptions deciphered appear a long list of wines which the Assyrian monarchs are said to have carried into their country as booty, or to have received as tribute.

We see the process of filling the wine cups at a feast. They were dipped into a large vase instead of being filled from a small vessel. Nor were they alone contented with grape wine, they had palm wine, wine made from dates, and beer even as the Egyptians had.

According to the *Abodah Zarah*, a treatise on false worship, there was a mixed drink used in Babylon called *Cuttach*, which possessed marvellous properties. "It obstructs the heart, blinds the eyes, and emaciates the body. It obstructs the heart, because it contains whey of milk; it blinds the eyes, because it contains a peculiar salt which has this property; and it emaciates the body, because of the putrefied bread

which is mixed with it. If poured upon stones, it breaks them; and of it is a proverb, 'That it is better to eat a stinking fish than take *Cuttach*.'" The same treatise also mentions Median beer and Edomite vinegar.

The Hittites had been a powerful and civilized nation when the Jews were in an exceedingly primitive condition, and Abraham found them the rightful possessors of Hebron, in Southern Palestine (Gen. xxiii.), and so far recognised their rights to the soil, as to purchase from them the Cave of Machpelah for "four hundred shekels of silver, current money with the merchant." Their power afterwards waned, as they had left Hebron and taken to the mountains, as was reported by the spies sent by Moses, four hundred years afterwards (Num. xiii.), but they have left behind them carvings which throw some light upon

their social customs. For instance, here is one of two ladies partaking of a social glass together. Unfortunately, we do not know at present the true meaning of their inscriptions, for scholars are yet at variance as to the translation of them. That they thoroughly cherished Wine may be seen from the accompanying illustration, which represents one of their deities, who appears to be a compound of Bacchus and Ceres, and aptly illustrative of the two good things of those countries, Corn and Wine, which, with the Olive and Honey, made an earthly Paradise for the inhabitants thereof. It shows how much they appreciated Wine, when they deified it.

As to the Hebrews, they were well acquainted with wine, and placed Noah's beginning to be a husband-

man, and planting a vineyard, as the earliest thing he did after the subsidence of the flood. Throughout their sacred writings, Wine is frequently mentioned, and intoxication must have been very well known among them, judging by the number of passages making mention of it. A great variety of wines is not named—nay, there are only two specifically mentioned:

the Wine of Helbon, which, as we have seen, was an article of merchandise at Damascus, a fat, luscious wine, as its name signifies; and the wine of Lebanon, which was celebrated for its *bouquet*. "The scent thereof shall be as the wine of Lebanon" (Hos. xiv. 7). It is possible that this *bouquet* was natural, or it might have been artificial, for it was the custom to mix perfumes, spices, and aromatic herbs so as to enhance the flavour of the wine, as we see in Canticles viii. 2:

" I would cause thee to drink of spiced wine of the juice of my pomegranate;" by which illustration we also see that the Hebrews made wines other than those from grapes.

That it was commonly in use is proved, if it needed proof, by the miracle at the marriage at Cana, where the worldly-wise ruler of the feast says, " Every man at the beginning doth set forth good wine; and when men have well drunk, then that which is worse: but thou hast kept the good wine until now." That they drank water mixed with wine may be inferred by the two verses (Prov. ix. 2, 5): "She hath mingled her wine"; "Drink of the wine that I have mingled.' Their wine used to be trodden in the press, the wine being put into bottles or wine skins, specially mentioned in Joshua ix. 4, 13. In later days they had vessels of earthenware and glass, similar to those in the illustration, which were found whilst excavating in Jerusalem.

That the ancient Jews knew of other intoxicating liquors, such as Palm and Date wines, there can be very little doubt.

J. A.

CLASSICAL WINES.

GREEK.[1]

Homer's Wine of the Coast of Thrace—Pramnian Wine—Psithian, Capnian, Saprian, and other Wines—The Mixing of Wines—Use of Pitch and Rosin—Undiluted Wine—Wine Making—Spiced Wines—A Greek Symposium.

THE only wine upon which Homer dilates, in a tone of approval approaching to hyperbole, is that produced on the coast of Thrace, the scene of several of the most remarkable exploits of Bacchus. This wine the minister of Apollo, Maron, gave to Ulysses. It was red and honey sweet, so strong that it was mingled with twenty times its bulk of water, so fragrant that it filled even when diluted the house with perfume (*Od.* ix. 203). Homer's *Pramnian* wine is variously interpreted by various writers.

[1] Information on this subject is given by Sir Edward Barry, *Observations on the Wines of the Ancients*; Henderson, *History of Ancient and Modern Wines*; and Becker's *Charicles*.

The most important wines of later times are those of the islands Chios, Thasos, Cos, and Lesbos, and a few places on the opposite coast of Asia. The *Aminean* wine, so called from the vine which produced it, was of great durability. The *Psithian* was particularly suitable for *passum*, and the *Capnian*, or smoke-wine, was so named from the colour of the grapes. The *Saprian* was a remarkably rich wine, "toothless," says Athenæus, "and sere and wondrous old."

Wine was the ordinary Greek drink. Diodorus Siculus says Dionysus invented a drink from barley, a mead-like drink called βρύτος; but there is nothing to show that this was ever introduced into Greece. The Greek wine was conducive to inebriety, and Musæus and Eumolpus (*Plato, Rep.* ii.) made the fairest reward of the virtuous an everlasting booze—ἡγησάμενοι κάλλιστον ἀρετῆς μισθὸν μέθην αἰώνιον. Different sorts of wine were sometimes mixed together; sea water was added to some wines. Plutarch (*Quæst. Nat.* 10) also relates that the casks were smeared with pitch, and that rosin was mixed with their wine by the Eubœans.

Wine was mingled with hot water as well as with cold before drinking. To drink wine undiluted was looked on as a barbarism. Straining, usual among the Romans, seems to have been the reverse among the Greeks. It is seldom mentioned. The Roman wine was most likely filtered through wool. The Spartans (*Herodotus*, vi. 84) fancied Cleomenes had gone mad by drinking neat wine, a habit he had learned from the Scythians. The proportions of the mixture varied, but there was always more water, and half and half ἴσον ἴσῳ was repudiated as disgraceful.

The process of wine-making was essentially the same among the Greeks and the Romans. The grapes were gathered, trodden, and submitted to the press. The juice which flowed from the grapes before

any force was applied was known as πρόχυμα, and was reserved for the manufacture of a particular species of rich wine described by Pliny (*H. N.* xiv. 11), to which the inhabitants of Mitylene gave the name of πρόδρομος. The Greeks recognised three colours in wines—black or red, white or straw-colour, and tawny brown (κιρρός, *fulvus*). When wine was carried, ἀσκοί, or bags of goat-skin, were used, pitched over to make them seam-tight. The cut below, from a bronze found at Herculaneum (*Mus. Borbon.* iii. 28) exhibits a Silenus astride one of them.

The mode of drinking from the ἀμφορεύς, bottle or amphora, and from a wine skin, is taken from a painting on an Etruscan vase.

A spiced wine is noticed by Athenæus under the name of τρίμμα. Into the οἶνοι ὑγιεινοί, or medical wines, drugs, such as horehound, squills, wormwood, and myrtle-berries, were introduced to produce hygienic effects. Essential oils were also mixed with wines. Of these the μυρρινίτης [1] is mentioned by Ælian (*V. H.* xii. 31). So in the early ages when Hecamede prepares a drink for Nestor, she sprinkles her cup of

Pramnian wine with grated cheese, perhaps a sort of Gruyère, and flour. The most popular of these compound beverages was the οἰνόμελι² (*mulsum*), or honey wine, said by Pliny (xiv. 4) to have been invented by Aristæus. Greek wines required no long time to ripen. The wine drank by Nestor (*Odyss.* iii. 391) of ten year old is an exception.

The sweet wines of the Greeks (the produce of various islands on the Ægean and Ionian Seas) were probably something like modern Cyprus and Constantia, while the dry wines, such as the Pramnian and Corinthian, were remarkable for their astringency, and were indeed only drinkable after being preserved for many years. Of the former of these Aristophanes says that it shrivelled the features and obstructed the digestion of all who drank it, while to taste the latter was mere torture.

¹ This is probably the murrhina of Plautus (*Pseudol.* ii. 4, 50)
² This drink must not be confounded with ὑδρόμελι, honey and water, our mead, or ὑδρομῆλον, our cider

CLASSICAL WINES.

ROMAN.

Falernian, Cæcuban, and other Wines—Galen's Opinion—Columella's Receipt—The Roman Banquet—Dessert Wines—The Supper of Nasidienus—Dedication of Cups—Wines mentioned by Pliny made of Figs, Medlars, Mulberries, and other Fruits.

OF Roman wines the Campania Felix boasted the most celebrated growths. The Falernian, Massican, Cæcuban, and Surrentine wines were all the produce of this favoured soil. The three first of these wines have been, as the schoolboy (not necessarily Macaulay's) is only too well aware, immortalised by Horace, who doubtless had ample opportunities of forming a matured judgment about them.

The Cæcuban is described by Galen as a generous wine, ripening only after a long term of years. The Massican closely resembled the Falernian. The Setine was a light wine, and, according to Pliny, the favourite drink of Augustus, who perhaps grounded his preference on his idea that it was the least injurious to the stomach. Possibly Horace differed from his patron in taste. He never mentions this wine, which is however celebrated both by Martial and by Juvenal

As for the Surrentine, the fiat of Tiberias has dismissed it as generous vinegar. Dr. Henderson has no hesitation in fixing upon the wines of Xeres and Madeira as those to which the celebrated Falernian bears the nearest resemblance. Both are straw-coloured, assuming a deeper tint from age. Both present the varieties of dry and sweet. Both are strong and durable. Both require keeping. The soil of Madeira is more analogous to that of the Campania Felix, whence we may conclude perhaps that the flavour and aroma of its wines are similar to those of the Campania. Finally, if Madeira or sherry were kept in earthen jars till reduced to the consistence of honey, the taste would become so bitter that, to use the expression of Cicero (*Brut.* 83), we should condemn it as intolerable.

The wines of antiquity present disagreeable features; sea water, for instance, and resin already mentioned. Columella advises the addition of one pint of salt water for six gallons of wine. The impregnation with resin has been still preserved, with the result of making some modern Greek wines unpalatable save to the modern Greeks themselves. Columella (*De Re Rustica,* xii. 19) says that four ounces of crude pitch mingled with certain aromatic herbs should be mixed with two *amphoræ,* or about thirteen gallons of wine.

Ancient wines were also exposed in smoky garrets until reduced to a thick syrup, when they had to be strained before they were drunk. Habit only it seems could have endeared these pickled and pitched and smoked wines to the Greek and Roman palates, as it has endeared to some of our own caviare and putrescent game.

To drink wine unmixed was, it has been said before, held by the Greeks to be disreputable. Those who did so were said to be like Scythians. The Maronean wine of Homer was mixed with twenty measures of water. The common proportion in the more polished days of Greece was three or four parts of water to one of wine. But probably Greece, like Rome, had many a Menenius who loved a cup of hot wine with not a drop of allaying Tiber in it. If the condition of Alcibiades in the Platonic symposium was the result of wine so diluted, the wine must have been strong indeed.

The Grecian and Roman banquet began with the *mulsum*, of mingled wine and honey. The dessert wines among the Greeks were the Thasian and Lesbian; among the Romans the Alban, Cæcuban, and Falernian, and afterwards the Chian and Lesbian.

In the triumphal supper of Cæsar in his dictatorship Pliny says Falernian flowed in hogsheads and Chian in gallons. At the well-known Horatian supper of Nasidienus the Cæcuban and indifferent Chian were handed round before the host advised Mæcenas that Alban and Falernian were procurable if he preferred them.

Juvenal and Martial tell us of the complaint of clients, that while the master and his friends drank the best wine out of costly cups, they themselves had to put up with ropy liquors in coarse, half-broken vessels. Human nature has changed little in this respect since those satirists wrote.

The old fashion of dedicating cups to divinities led perhaps to our modern system of drinking healths. Sometimes as many cups were drunk to a person as there were letters in the name of the person so honoured.

It was better then for the bibulous to toast the ancient Sempronia or Messalina than the modern Meg or Kate.

Hydromeli, made of honey and five-year-old rainwater; *oxymeli*, made of honey, sea-salt, and vinegar; *hydromelon*, made of honey and quinces; *hydrorosatum*, a similar compound with the addition of roses; *apomeli*, water in which honeycomb had been boiled; *omphacomeli*, a mixture of honey and verjuice; *myrtites*, a compound of honey and myrtle seed; *rhoites*, a drink in which the pomegranate took the place of the myrtle; *œnanthinum*, made from the fruit of the wild vine; *silatum*, taken, according to Festus, in the forenoon, and made of *Saxifragia major* (Forcellini) or *Tordylium officinale* (Liddell and Scott); *sycites*, wine of figs; *phœnicites*, wine of palms; *abrotonites*, wine of wormwood; and *adynamon*, a weak wine for the sick—are most of them mentioned as drinks in Pliny.[1] This author also mentions drinks made of sorbs, medlars, mulberries, and other fruits, of asparagus, origanum, thyme, and other herbs. Hippocrates praises wine as a medical agent. In his third book the father of medicine gives a description of the general qualities and virtues of wines, and shows for what diseases they are in his opinion advantageous.

[1] Pliny, *Nat. Hist.* xiv. 19, etc.

For more information on wines the reader may consult Sir Edward Barry, Dr. Alexander Henderson, and Cyrus Redding. Henderson, who was, like Barry, a physician, did not always agree with him. Barry's observations, according to Henderson, are chiefly borrowed from Bacci. Those not so borrowed are for the most part "flimsy and tedious."

The vessels and other drinking cups were commonly ranged on an abacus of marble, something like our sideboard. It was large, if Philo Judeus is to be believed. Pliny, speaking of Pompey's spoils in the matter of the pirates, says the number of jewel-adorned drinking cups was enough to furnish nine *abaci*. Cicero charges Verres with having plundered the *abaci*.

When Rome was in the height of her luxury, murrhine cups were introduced from the East. What this substance was, the ruins of Pompeii have never revealed; some maintain it was porcelain, others think it was a species of spar.

Dr. Henderson adopts the opinion of M. de Rozière that these cups were of fluor-spar; but this article is not found in Karamania, from which district of Parthia both Pliny and Propertius agree that they came, though they differ with respect to their nature; its geographic situation seems confined to Europe. The anecdote told by Lampridius of Heliogabalus (502) proves, not the similarity of material, but only the equal rareness and value of vessels of onyx and murrhine.

A writer in the *Westminster Review* for July, 1825, believes them to have been porcelain cups from China;

the expression of Propertius, "*cocta focis*," proves that they were manufactured. In the time of Belon (1555)

AMPHORÆ, RHYTONS, ETC. (*Brit. Mus.*).

the Greeks called them *the myrrh of Smyrna*, from *murex*, a shell. From this it seems that their name was given to the vases from a resemblance of colours to those of the *murex*. Stolberg (*Travels*, ix. 280) says he saw in a collection at Catania a little blue vase, believed to be a *vas murrhinum*.

The modern jars in any of the wine districts of Italy, such as Asti Montepulciano or Montefiascone, thin earthen two-handled vessels holding some twenty quarts, are almost identical with the ancient *amphoræ*. Suetonius speaks of a candidate for the quæstorship who drank the contents of a whole *amphora* at a dinner given by Tiberius. This *amphora* was probably of a smaller size. Wooden vessels for wine seem to have been unfamiliar to the Greeks and Romans; they, however, occasionally employed glass. Bottles, vases, and cups of that material, which may be seen often enough now in collections of antiquities, show the great taste which in these and in other matters they possessed. A few of these are given to illustrate our text. Skins of animals, rendered impervious by oil or resinous gums, were probably the most ancient receptacles for wine after it was taken from the vat. To these there are frequent allusions in Homer and Isaiah. Vessels of clay, with a coating of pitch, were introduced subsequently.

NORTHERN DRINKING.

Beowulf—Ale—Beer—Mead—English Wine—The Mead Hall—Drinking Horns—Tosti and Harold—Pigment, etc.—The Clergy, etc., drinking—Northern Wine drinking—King Hunding—Brewing—Strange Drinking Vessels, and their Use—Punishment of Drunkards.

SAILING from the north, being lured to the south with visions of plunder and luxury, came the Danish and Norwegian Vikings, and, as England was the nearest to them, she received an early visit. With them they brought their habit of deep drinking, which was scarcely needed, as on that score the then inhabitants of England could pretty well hold their own. Their liquors seem to have been ale, *ealu*, beer, *beor*, wine, *win*, and mead, *medo*.

There was a difference between those that drank ale and those that drank beer, as we find in *Beowulf*[1]:—

[1] Line 964, etc.

"Full oft have promis'd,
with beer drunken,
Over *the* ale cup,
sons of conflict,
that they in *the* beer-hall
would await
Grendel's warfare
with terrors of edges:
then was this mead-hall,
at morning tide,
this princely court, stain'd with gore;
when *the* day dawn'd,
all *the* bench-floor
with blood bestream'd,
the hall, with horrid gore;
of faithful *followers* I own'd the less,
of dear nobles,
who then death destroyed.
Sit now to *the* feast,
and unbind with mead
thy valiant breast with *my* warriors
as thy mind may excite.
Then was for *the* sons of *the* Goths
altogether
in *the* beer hall
a bench clear'd;
there the strong of soul
went to sit
tumultuously rejoicing:
the thane observ'd *his* duty,
who in *his* hand bare
the ornamented ale-cup,
he pour'd *the* bright, sweet *liquor:*
the gleeman sang at times
serene in Heorot:
there was joy of warriors,
no few nobles
of Danes and Weders."

In Dugdale's *Monasticon* (ed. 1682, p. 126), in a Charter of Offa to the Monastery of Westbury, three sorts of ale are mentioned. Two tuns full of hlutres aloth (*Clear ale*), a cumb full of lithes aloth (mild ale), and a cumb full of Welisces aloth (Welsh ale), which is again mentioned as *cervisia Walliæ*.

But though beer and ale were the drinks of the common folk, yet they were not despised by their leaders.

> [1] "At times before *the* nobles
> Hrothgar's daughter
> to *the* earls in order
> *the* ale cup bore."

We see the social difference between ale and wine drinkers in one of the Cotton MSS. (*Tib.* A. 3), where a lad having been asked what he drank replied: "Ale, if I have it; Water, if I have it not." Asked why he does not drink wine, he says: "I am not so rich that I can buy me wine; and wine is not the drink of children or the weak-minded, but of the elders and the wise."

The English at that time grew the Vine for wine-making purposes; indeed, very good wine can now be, and is, made from English grapes. Every monastery had its vineyard, and to this day London has six Vine Streets and one Vineyard Walk. The wine-hall seems to have been a different apartment to either the mead, or ale-halls, and of a superior order.

> [2] "*The* company all arose;
> greeted then

---

[1] Line 4044, etc.   [2] Line 1387, etc.

> *one* man another
> Hrothgar Beowulf,
> and bade him hail,
> gave *him* command of *the* wine-hall."

* * * *

> [1] "*He* strode under *the* clouds,
> until he *the* wine-house,
> *the* golden hall of men,
> most readily perceiv'd,
> richly variegated."

The mead-hall seems to have answered the purpose of a common hall, as we see by the following. Speaking of Hrothgar, the poet says:—

> [2] "*It* ran through his mind
> that *he a* hall-house
> would command,
> *a* great mead-house,
> men to make,
> which the sons of men
> should ever hear of;
> and there within
> all distribute
> to young and old,
> as to him God had given,
> except *the* people's share,
> and the lives of men.
> Then I heard *that* widely
> *the* work *was* proclaim'd
> to many *a* tribe
> through this mid-earth
> that *a* public place was building."

Mead was considered a glorified liquor fit for MEN, and is thus sung of by the bard Taliesin:—

---

[1] Line 1432, etc. [2] Line 135, etc.

"That Maelgwn of Mona be inspired with mead and cheer us
  with it,
From the mead-horn's foaming, pure, and shining liquor,
Which the bees provide, but do not enjoy ;
Mead distilled, I praise ; its eulogy is everywhere
Precious to the creature whom the earth maintains.
God made it to man for his happiness,
The fierce and the mute both enjoy it."

Mead was made from honey and water, fermented, and in many languages its name has a striking similarity. In Greek, honey is *methu*, in Sanskrit, *madhu*, and the drink made therefrom in Danish, is *miod*, in Anglo-Saxon, *medu*, in Welsh, *medd*, whence metheglyn —*medd*, mead, and *llyn*, liquor. In *Beowulf* we frequently find mention of the *mead-horns*, and we find it vividly portrayed in the heading of this chapter, which is taken from the Bayeux Tapestry. These horns were generally those of oxen, although some were made of ivory, and were probably used because fictile ware was so easily broken in those drinking bouts in which they so frequently indulged. Another reason was doubtless that they promoted conviviality, for, like the classical *Rhyton*, they could not be set down like a bowl, but must either be nursed, or their contents quaffed.

Many examples of drinking horns remain to us, and illustrations of two are here given : one that of Ulph, belonging to, and now kept at, York Minster, and the other the Pusey horn. These are veritable *drinking horns ;* but there are many other tenure horns in existence, which are hunting horns.

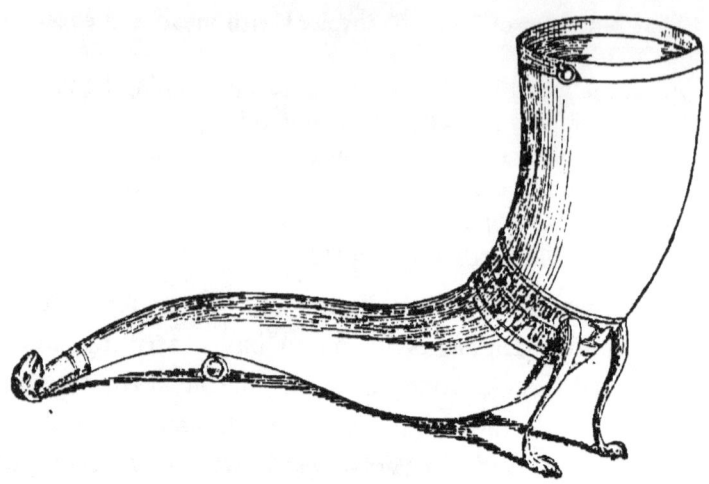

The Pusey Horn.

This horn is an old tenure horn. It was once the custom, when making a gift of land, instead of making out a deed of gift, to present some article of personal use, such as a knife, a drinking or hunting horn, and with it the manor or land, the recipient keeping the present, as a proof that the land was given him. This Pusey horn is said to have been given by King Knut to William Pewse, and on the silver-gilt band, to which are appended dog's legs and feet, is inscribed in Gothic letters—

> "Kyng Knowde geve Wyllyam Pewse
> This horne to holde by thy lond."

It is an ox horn, dark brown, and is $25\frac{1}{2}$ inches long, having a silver-gilt rim, and at the small end a hound's head, also of silver-gilt, which unscrews, thus enabling it to be used either as a drinking or hunting horn.

Ulph's horn is considered of somewhat later date, and is of ivory.

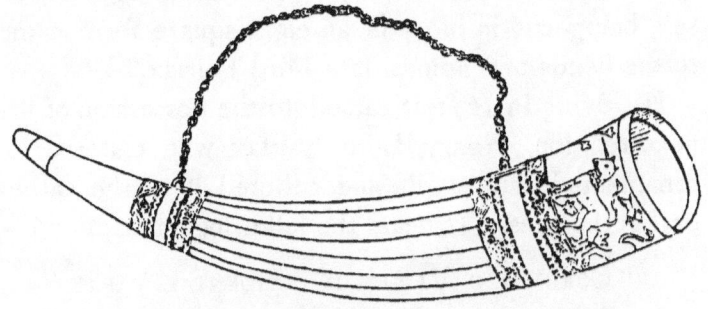

ULPH'S HORN.

Of this horn Dugdale[1] says: "About this time also, Ulphe, the son of Thorald, who ruled in the west of Deira,[2] by reason of the difference which was like to rise between his sons, about the sharing of his lands and lordships after his death, resolved to make them all alike; and thereupon, coming to York, with that horn wherewith he was used to drink, filled it with wine, and before the altar of God, and Saint Peter, Prince of the Apostles, kneeling devoutly, drank the wine, and by that ceremony enfeoffed this church with all his lands and revenues. The figure of which horn, in memory thereof, is cut in stone upon several parts of the choir, but the horn itself, when the Reformation in King Edward the VIth's time began, and swept away many costly ornaments belonging to this church,

---

[1] *Hist. Account of the Cathedral Church of York*, Lond., 1715, p. 7.
[2] That division of the ancient kingdom of Northumberland, which was bounded by the river Humber southwards, and to the north by the Tyne.

was sold to a goldsmith, who took away from it those tippings of gold wherewith it was adorned, and the gold chain affixed thereto; since which, the horn itself, being cut in ivory in an eight square form, came to the hands of Thomas, late Lord Fairfax."

He, dying in 1671, it came into the possession of his next relation, Henry, Lord Fairfax, who restored its ornaments in silver-gilt, and restored it to the cathedral authorities. It bears the following inscription :—

"CORNV HOC, VLPHVS IN OCCIDENTALI PARTE
DEIRÆ PRINCEPS, VNA CUM OMNIBVS TERRIS
ET REDDITIBVS SUIS OLIM DONAVIT.
AMISSVM VEL ABREPTVM.
HENRICVS DOM. FAIRFAX DEMVM RESTITVIT.
DEC. ET CAPIT. DE NOVO ORNAVIT.
A. D. MDC. LXXV."

Most of us know Longfellow's poem of King Witlaf's drinking horn, a story which may be found in Ingulphus, who says that Witlaf, King of Mercia, who lived in the reign of Egbert, gave to the Abbey of Croyland the horn used at his own table, for the elder monks of the house to drink out of it on festivals and saints' days, and that when they gave thanks, they might remember the soul of Witlaf the donor. That they had some horn of the kind is probable, for the same chronicler says that when the monastery was almost destroyed by fire, this horn was saved.

Besides the liquors above mentioned, the Anglo-Saxons had others, as we see in a passage of Henry of Huntingdon (lib. vi.), which is probably an invention, the same story being told by Florence of Worcester, of Caradoc, the son of Griffith, A.D. 1065. However, he says that in 1063, in the king's palace at Winchester, Tosti seized his brother Harold by the hair, in the royal presence, and while he was serving the king with wine; for it had been a source of envy and hatred that the king showed a higher regard for Harold, though Tosti was the elder brother. Wherefore, in a sudden paroxysm of passion, he could not refrain from this attack on his brother.

Tosti departed from the king and his brother in great anger, and went to Hereford, where Harold had purveyed large supplies for the royal use. There he butchered all his brother's servants, and inclosed a head and an arm in each of the vessels containing wine, mead, ale, pigment,[1] morat,[2] and cider, sending a message to the king that when he came to his farm he would find plenty of salt meat, and that he would bring more with him. For this horrible crime the king commanded him to be banished and outlawed.

There is no doubt but that the Anglo-Saxons drank to excess, and thought no shame of it. Many times in Beowulf are we told of their being dragged from the mead-benches by their enemies and slaughtered, and in a fragment of an Anglo-Saxon poem on Judith we read :—

> "Then was Holofernes
> Enchanted with the wine of men :
> In the hall of the guests

[1] A liquor made of honey, wine, and spice.
[2] Honey, diluted with the juice of mulberries.

> He laughed and shouted,
> He roared and dinn'd,
> That the children of men might hear afar,
> How the sturdy one
> Stormed and clamoured,
> Animated and elate with wine
> He admonished amply
> Those sitting on the bench
> That they should bear it well.
> So was the wicked one all day,
> The lord and his men,
> Drunk with wine;
> The stern dispenser of wealth;
> Till that they swimming lay
> Over drunk.
> All his nobility
> As they were death slain,
> Their property poured about.
> So commanded the lord of men,
> To fill to those sitting at the feast,
> Till the dark night
> Approached the children of men."

Even the clergy and monks drank probably more than was good for them, for a priest was forbidden by law to eat or drink at places where ale was sold. But that did not prevent their drinking at home; their benefactors provided well for that, as one instance will show. Ethelwold allowed the Monastery of Abingdon a great bowl, from which the drinking vessels of the brothers were filled twice a day. At Christmas, Easter, Pentecost, the Nativity and Assumption of the Virgin, on the festivals of Saints Peter and Paul, and all the other saints, they were to have wine, as well as mead, twice a day; and taking the number of Saints

in the Anglo-Saxon Calendar, it must have gone hard with them, if this was not almost an every-day occurrence.

The Northern nations did not lose their love of drink as time rolled on, as we may find in the pages of Olaus Magnus. They drank wine, but owing to the extreme cold it was not of native production, but imported. In this illustration we see the vessel that has brought it, and the bush outside, denoting that it was to be sold. They got it from Spain, Italy, France, and Germany, but he says that the wine most in repute was a Spanish wine called Bastard, which Shakspeare mentions more than once, as (1 *Henry IV.* act ii. sc. 4) Prince Henry relating his adventures with a drawer, says, " Anon, anon, sir! Score a pint of Bastard in the Half Moon."

He gives receipts for making Hydromel, or Mead, which was to be made of one part honey, and four of

boiling water, to be well stirred, boiled, and skimmed. Hops were then to be added, then casked, and brewers' yeast added. Then to be strained, and it was fit for drinking in eight days. He tells a pathetic story of King Hunding, who being sorely grieved at the loss of his brother-in-law, Gutthorm, called all his nobility around him to a great feast, and had a large tun, filled with hydromel, placed in the middle of the hall. When his guests were sufficiently inebriated, he threw himself into the liquor, and died sweetly.

Beer had they, made of malt and hops, and he gives

various methods of brewing, and also a list of divers beers and their medicinal qualities.

He also gives an illustration of various drinking

vessels then (16th cent.) in use among the Danes and Swedes, where is here reproduced. Here we see some plain, others ornamental with runes, and some with very curious handles. He says they were mostly of brass, copper, or iron, because in that cold climate the liquor they held had to be warmed over the fire.

An old translation of a portion of his *Historia de Gentibus Septentrionalibus* gives the following account "Of the manner of drinking amongst the Northern People."

"It will not displease curious Readers to hear how the custom is of drinking amongst the Northern People. First, they hold it Religion to drink the healths of Kings and Princes, standing, in reverence of them; and here they will, as it were, sweat in the contention, who shall at one or two, or more draughts, drink off a huge bowl. Wherefore they seem to sit at Table as if they had Crowns on their heads, and to drink in a certain kind of vessel; which, it may be, may cause men that know it not, to admire it. But that were more admirable to see the servants go in a long train, in troops, as Pastours of Harts with horns, that they may drink up those Cups full of beer to the Ghests. And, not content with these Ceremonies, they will strive to shew their Sobriety, by setting such a high Cup full of Beer upon their naked heads, and dance and turn round with it; in like manner they deliver other Cups which they bring in both hands to

the Ghests to drink off, at equall draughts, which are full of Wine, Ale, Mede, Metheglin, or new Wine."

He winds up with a moral dissertation on the punishment of drinkers, and, after detailing the various effects of alcohol on different races, as rendering the Gaul petulant, the German quarrelsome, the Goth obstreperous, and the Finn lachrymose, he suggests that drunkards should be seated on a sharp wedge, compelled to drink a mighty horn of beer, and then be hauled up and down by a rope. J. A.

WINES.

Definition—Various Meanings of Wine—Alcohol—Varieties of Wine—Miller—Professor Mulder—Origin of Wine—Brook of Eshcol—Strabo and Reland—Francatelli's Order of Wines—Classification of M. Batalhai Reis.

IN the matter of wine, as in that of beer, it is perhaps as well to commence with a dictionary description or definition. Ogilvie declares it to be the "fermented juice of the grape, or fruit of the vine." It is, however, also the juice of certain fruits, prepared in imitation of wine obtained from grapes, but distinguished by naming the source whence it is derived, as currant wine, gooseberry wine, etc.; and a third meaning of wine—a meaning with which we have happily little to do—is the effect of drinking wine in excess, or intoxication.[1]

Wines are practically distinguished by their colour, flavour, stillness or effervescence, and what is known as hardness or softness. The differences in quality

[1] In this sense it is apparently used in Gen. ix. 24: "Noah awoke from his *wine*."

depend on the vines, the soils, the exposure of the vineyards, the treatment of the grapes, and the mode of manufacture. The alcohol [1] contained is the leading characteristic. In strong ports and sherries this varies from about 16 to 25 per cent. It is about 7 per cent. in claret, hock, and other so-called light wines. Wine containing about 13 per cent. of alcohol may be assumed to be *fortified*, as it is called, with brandy or other spirit.

The varieties of wine produced are said to be "almost endless." This great number of wines is in some measure owing to an interesting fact mentioned by Miller in his *Organic Chemistry* (3rd ed. p. 187), who tells us that a particular variety of grape, when grown upon the Rhine, furnishes a species of hock; the same grape, when raised in the valley of the Tagus, yields Bucellas, in which the palate of a connoisseur may possibly detect the flavour of hock; whilst in the island of Madeira the same grape produces the wine known as *Sercial*, which, though generally allowed to be a delicious wine, has suggested, it seems, to no skilled palate the flavour either of Bucellas or of hock.

It would therefore be more logical to commence an article on wines with an article on the grapes from which they are produced, but we fear it would be far

[1] From an Arabic word for antimony, applied to the eyes, the name is said to have been transferred to rectified spirits ($C_2 H_6 O$). It is a liquid formed by fermentation of aqueous sugar solutions. *Spirit of Wine* contains about 90 per cent. of alcohol. 55 parts of alcohol and 45 of water form *proof spirit*. Of alcohol, spirits contain 40–50 per cent.; wines, 7–25; ale and porter, 6–8; small beer, 1–2.

less interesting. Of the chemical composition of wine, and of its *uses in health and disease,* on which so many books from the days of old have been already written, we shall, in accordance with our preface, say nothing at all, or very little. Every person who feels himself or herself interested in this latter matter may learn as much as he or she will from the pages of the *Lancet*, while Professor Mulder has probably written enough about the former to satisfy the most anxious student.

The origin of most things is obscure. Treatises have been composed about that of wine. We have no intention of reproducing aught of them in the present work. Let us be content to suppose that wine had its origin, again like most things, somewhere at some time in the East. The date of its introduction into Greece is no more known than that of its introduction into Italy. A traditional credit is due to Saturn, to Noah, and to Bacchus as early wine manufacturers. Certainly in Palestine they had the advantage of fine grapes. On the well-known historic occasion of Moses sending men to search the land of Canaan, in the time of the first ripe fruit, we learn that when they came unto the brook of Eshcol, they cut down from thence a branch with one cluster of grapes and " bare it between two upon a staff." It has been perhaps somewhat hastily assumed that the fruit was therefore necessarily of a large size. There may have been other reasons for this proceeding than an enormity of weight. But if, as is generally imagined, these grapes were unusually fine and large, wine makers would be clearly benefited thereby. In support of this interpretation of the passage in Numbers, Strabo has declared that some of the grapes in the Holy Land measured two feet in length; and Reland has not hesitated to declare, as if unwilling to be outdone by Strabo, that some bunches are of ten pounds weight.

This prefatory matter could make no pretence to completeness if it omitted an instruction for the service of wines, denoting the order in which they should be drank at the dinner table, which has already been given by an adept. Whether the matter is more admirable, or the style, it is difficult to determine.

"I would recommend," says Francatelli, "all *bonvivants* desirous of testing and thoroughly enjoying a variety of delectable wines, without being incommoded by the diversity of those introduced for their learned degustation, to bear in mind that they should be drunk in the following order; viz., " When it happens that oysters preface the dinner, a glass of Chablis or Sauterne is their most proper accompaniment."

After soup of any kind, genuine old Madeira, East India Sherry, or Amontillado are recommended as "welcome stomachics." But you are to avoid, as you value your health, drinking punch after Turtle soup, especially Roman punch. With fish, a large variety of wines, such as Pouilly, Meursault, Montrachet, Barsac, and generally all dry white wines, is allowed. With the entrées you are permitted to drink any variety of Bordeaux or Burgundy.

Second course and dessert wines are given at too great a length to admit of reproduction. About these a "question of the highest importance" arises as to which should be preferred. But here Francatelli remembers a fact which might have spared him his vast labour on this service of wines: that "it is difficult, not to say impossible, to lay down rules for the guidance of the palate." The sanguine person, we are told, will prefer the *genuine* Champagne; the phlegmatic, Sherry or Madeira. The splenetic and melancholy man will be prone to select Roussillon and Burgundy. The bilious will imbibe Bordeaux. In few words, " Burgundy is aphrodisiac, Champagne is captious, Roussillon restorative, and Bordeaux stomachic." By careful attention to the foregoing remarks, the reader will happily be preserved from any serious mistake in the matter of his dinner. But other meals must also be taken into consideration, about which Francatelli preserves a Sibylline and mysterious silence. For instance, luncheon. We learn, however, from another source that there are luncheon sherries and dessert sherries. With lunch the brown, rich, and full-bodied Raro may be suitably drunk; but the pale Solera and the soft yet nutty Oloroso should make their appearance at dessert alone.

M. Batalhai Reis, Consul for Portugal at Newcastle-on-Tyne, in a report on the wine trade of England, has troubled himself thus in the interests of posterity to classify the wines of the world.

CLASS I.—TABLE WINES.

Alcohol and sugar imperceptible. Taste acid and astringent.

Division A. Red.

Group 1. *Acid.* Examples : Inferior Bordeaux and Burgundies, Wines from North of Portugal.

Group 2. *Astringent.* Examples : Superior Bordeaux and Burgundies, Collares from Portugal.

Division B. White.

Group 1. Simple Flavour. Example : Rhine Wines.

Group 2. Complex Flavour. Example : Bucellas of Portugal.

Class II.—Transition Wines.

Alcohol and sugar perceptible. Taste astringent. Flavour complex.

Division A. Red. Examples : Many Spanish and Portuguese wines.

Division B. White. Examples : Many Spanish and Portuguese wines.

Class III.—Generous Wines.

1st Family. Madeira type. Wines of the Canaries, Azores, Lisbon; Carcanellas, Sherry, Marsala, and Cyprian wines.

2nd Family. Port type.

3rd Family. Tokay, Malaga.

4th Family. Chateau Yquem, Johannisberg, Steinberg.

Class IV.—Sparkling Wines.

Group A. Natural.

Group B. Artificial.

This division of the wines of the world is presented to the reader as a literary curiosity. It is at once simple and scientific. In a word, no book on wines can be considered complete without it. In the succeeding pages Wines as Beers are, for convenience of reference, arranged after the alphabetical order of their countries.

AFRICA: Constantias — Rota — Mascara. AMERICA: Catawbas—Muscatel—Chacoli—Mosto. AUSTRALIA: Carbinet—Kaludah—Verdeilho— Conatto. CANARIES: Vedueño — Sack. ENGLAND: Home-made Wines.

AFRICA.

Of this country the most important wines of the present are, perhaps, Pontac, Hanepoot, Frontignac, and Drakenstein. On the wines of the Cape of Good Hope, Dr. Edward Kretschmar is a great authority. *Kokwyn*, made from Muscat grapes, resembles Malaga. The best dry white wines, called Cape Hocks, are produced in the village of *Paarl*. The *Constantias*, so called from the wife of the Dutch governor, Van der Stell, are of three kinds. These excellent sweet wines are too frequently falsified and adulterated before reaching the palate of the English consumer. A red wine, called *Rota*, is made at Stellenbosh. Cape Madeira is a boiled and mixed wine. Stein wine is excellent when old. Red Cape, when drunk in the country, is a " sound, good wine," says Cyrus Redding.[1] The wine of Morocco is chiefly made by the Jews; it is light, acid, and will not keep. In Tetuan a wine is made nearly equal, according to Cyrus Redding, to the Spanish wine of

---

[1] Who would believe this from the specimens tasted in England? Yet we are assured the statement is perfectly true.

Xeres. Palm' wines are, of course, common. The people of Cacongo prepare a wine called *Embeth*, and those of Benin *Pali* and *Pardon*. The Caffres make a wine called *Pombie*, from millet or Guinea corn.[1] In Congo they drink a wine called *Milaffo*, which will not keep beyond three days.

Of the many wines produced at Algiers, the best is probably the white wine of *Mascara*, situated on a slope of the plane of Egbris, 1,800 feet above the sea level. The Arabic name of the place is a corruption of *Umm-al-asakir*, or the Mother of Soldiers. The wine is the principal industry of Algiers. It is eagerly bought up by agents of Bordeaux houses. Wines of inferior quality are made at Boue, Tlemcen, Medeah, and Milianah. The wines of *Oran* are said to resemble the small wines of Languedoc. In ancient times the valley of the Nile produced the wines of Mareotis, Mendes, Koptos, and Arsinoe, and its Delta the liqueur wine of Sebenytus.

AMERICA.

The first attempt to cultivate the vine in North America was made, we are informed by Drs. Thudichum and Dupré, in 1564. Some of its best known wines at the present time are the *Catawbas*[2] (still and

[1] Patterson's *Travels in Caffraria*, p. 92.

[2] One of these inspired Longfellow, who thinks (poetically) the richest wine is that of the West, which grows by the beautiful river, whose sweet perfume fills the apartment, with a benison on the giver:—

"Very good in its way is the Verzenay,
 Or the Sillery, soft and creamy;
But Catawba wine has a taste more divine,
 More dulcet, delicious, and dreamy."

A dreamy taste is something startling even in poetical description.

sparkling), red *Aliso* and *Angelico*. Wine has been made from the vines on the Ohio, said to resemble Bordeaux in quality. In several parts of Mexico, as at Passo del Norte, at Zalaya, and at St. Louis de la Paz, wines are made of tolerable flavour. The red wine of California is agreeable. In Florida, according to Sir John Hawkins, wine was made from a grape like that of Orleans, as far back as 1564. The island of Cuba possesses a "light, cool, sharp wine," according to Redding.

In South America wine was made long ago in Paraguay. A sweet wine resembling Malaga is made at Mendoza, at the foot of the Andes, and is found to improve by transportation some thousand miles across the Pampas. The wines made in Chili and Peru are white and red. The *Muscatel* of Chili is considered to be especially good.[1] The white wine of *Nasca* is inferior. The wine of *Pisco* is highly esteemed. Though the white is held by connoisseurs to be superior to the red wine of Chili, yet it is little drunk in the cradle of its production. *Chacoli* is a wine commonly patronised by labourers. The *Mosto* of *Concepcion* differs from *Mosto asoleado* by the grapes of the latter being sundried for some twenty days.

AUSTRALIA.

Australian wines are pretty well known from our tradesmen's circulars. For instance, there is the *Gouais*, the *Carbinet*, a soft wine like Burgundy, the

[1] Chili has lately taken Paris medals for its wines; it also produces a light and wholesome beer.

Mataro, the *Sauvignon*. There is that "elegant dinner wine," *Kaludah*, the Singleton Red or White *Hermitage*, "noted for its refinement"; the *Tintara Ferruginous*, of "immense power and generous quality"; the *Tokay Imperatrice*; and the *Alexandrian Moscat*, both poetically described as "abounding in memories of the sun which begot them," and possessing the "most beautiful bouquet that can be imagined," with a flavour "resembling the first crush in the mouth of three or four fine ripe Muscatel grapes—the large white oval ones—covered with a light bloom, and attached to a clean, thin stalk."

Drs. Thudichum and Dupré, who are themselves indebted to a publication by Toovey, have given an excellent description of these wines. *Verdeilho* is a wine, like Madeira, of delicate aroma and a full body; *Frontignac* is described as a thin white wine with a slight taste of the Muscat grape, being a fictitious elder flower flavour; *Malbee* is described as made from "claret" grape; *Tavoora* is described as a pure "port" of 1859; *Tintara*, a red, clear wine; *Adelaide*, a pure white wine, mainly from *Riessling* grapes with a *soupçon* of Muscatel, "a little too fiery for greatness." *Wattlesville* is an acidulous white wine. The poor and acid *Chasselas*, the strong-scented *Highercombe*, said to resemble good Sauterne, with many varieties of so-called claret, as *Emu*, *St. Hubert*, and so-called Hock, as *Heron* and *Royal Reserve*, are also imported from Australia. The *Conatto* is a rich liqueur with a flavour of Curaçoa and Rum Shrub combined.

CANARIES.

The Canary Islands have long been celebrated for their wines. The favourite Teneriffe wine is *Vidueño* or *Vidonia*. Canary *sack* is supposed to have been made from the *Malvasia* sweet grape, whereas the modern sack is dry (*sec*). The best vineyards are at Orotava, S. Ursula, Ycod de los Vinos, Buenavista, and Valle de Guerra.

ENGLAND.

British made wines hold no very high rank. A cheap foreign manufacture is, according to some of their vendors, gradually ousting them from the market. But at one time they formed a part of the education of the good housewives of Great Britain. Home wines were chiefly made from plums, apples, gooseberries, bilberries, elderberries, blackberries, currants (red and black), raspberries, cherries, cowslips, parsnips, raisins, greengages, damsons, ginger, oranges, and lemons. Less commonly and in former times we had wines from mulberries, quinces, peaches, apricots, and from the sap of the birch, beech, sycamore, and other trees. Years ago " sweets " or home-made wines were sent from Scotland and Ireland, such as ginger wine and so-called cherry and raspberry whiskies. The flowers of meadow-sweet (*Spiræa ulmaria*) yield a fragrant distilled water, which is said to be used by wine merchants to improve the flavour of their wines. In a little work by Mr. G. Vine on Home-made Wines, the reader will find numerous receipts how to make and keep these wines, with observations on gathering and preparing the fruit, fining, bottling, and storing. A correspondent of the *Gardeners' Chronicle* gives a receipt for *beer wine*, a beverage which has puzzled many connoisseurs. The curious may find it also quoted in Vine's brochure.

The manufacture of home-made wines is familiar. An excellent wine is sometimes made from a mixture of the fruits above mentioned, as, for instance, that from gooseberries and currants. All home-made wines are prone to run into acetous fermentation without the addition of a due proportion of pure spirits. Plums or sloes, with other ingredients, can, it is said, be turned into excellent fruity port, the "very choice" kind, silky, soft, and full bodied. A wine said to be agreeable is also made from the red berries of the mountain ash or service-tree (*pyrus aucuparia*). Birch wine is still made in some parts of England. Morewood gives a long receipt for its manufacture. Like most other wines, it improves greatly with age. This is especially true of parsnip wine. From potatoes which have suffered a sort of malting from frost, a tolerable wine has been obtained. It is said—but there are people who will say anything—that a great portion of the champagne drunk in this country is made from sugar and green gooseberries. Rhubarb wine has been affirmed to be synonymous with British champagne. The reader anxious on this subject may consult Dr. Shannon's elaborate *Treatise on Brewing*. Cowslip wine is all too like some of the Muscatel wines of Southern France, and the wine of the *Sambucus nigra* has been more than once, through some unlucky accident, confused with Frontignac.

FRENCH WINES.

The Great Makers of Champagne—Its Manufacture—Bottling—Treatment—Bordeaux or Claret—Its early Use and Name—Whence it comes—The different Growths—White Wines of the District—Burgundy—Different Growths and Qualities—Other Wines.

CHAMPAGNE.

REIMS and Epernay are the two great centres of the Champagne district; but Reims, from its size and antiquity, must be considered its capital. Here are the establishments of Pommery & Greno, Ernest Moy, Théophile Roederer & Co., Louis Roederer & Co., Henriot & Co., Permet & Fils, De St. Marceaux & Co., Werlé & Co. (successors to the renowned Veuve Cliquot), Heidsieck & Co., De Lossy & Co., G. H. Mumm & Co., Jules Mumm & Co., Piper & Co., and many others of lesser note.

The wines of this district have, for centuries, been famous, and especially beloved of kings and potentates.

Our Henry VIII. had a vineyard at Ay, and, in order to know that he got the genuine article, he had a superintendent of his own on the spot. Francis I., Leo X., and Charles V. of Spain, all had vineyards in the Champagne district. But the wine they obtained thence was not sparkling: that was to come later, and is said to have been the invention of Dom Petrus Perignon, who died in 1715, monk of, and cellarer to, the Royal Monastery of St. Peter's at Hautvilliers. He was especially happy in his blends of wine, and having found out the secret of highly charging the wine, naturally, with carbonic acid, is said to have introduced the cork and string necessary to confine it in its bottles.

Champagne Wine owes its goodness, in the first place, to the soil on which it is grown, which is unique in its mixture of chalk, silica, light clay, and oxide of iron; in the second, to the very great care and delicate manipulation which the wine receives. Every doubtful grape is discarded, and the carts conveying the grapes from the vineyard go at a most funereal pace, so that none of their precious contents should get bruised; for if these little grapes) for they are little larger than currants) get at all crushed, or partly fermented, in carriage, the fruit is rendered absolutely worthless for Champagne purposes.

Very great care, too, is exercised in the pressing. The grapes are laid in carefully stacked heaps upon the floor of the press, where they are left for a time, and then the first gentle, but firm, sustained squeeze is applied. The juice thus extracted is the cream of the grape, and is used only for the finest brands. There are six of these squeezes made, each more powerful than the last; and the result of each is, of course, inferior in quality to its predecessor, till the sixth, called the *rébêche*,[1] is reached, which produces a coarse wine, reckoned only fit to be given to the workmen.

The must begins to ferment more or less quickly, according to the temperature, in the casks, at the end of ten or twelve hours, and the process continues for a considerable time, during which the colour changes from pale pink to a light straw tint. About three months are allowed to elapse, when the fermentation stops through repeated rackings and the cold of the season.

And now the real trouble of the Champagne manufacturer begins. First, there is the blend, which varies in the case of each manufacturer. The produce of the different vineyards is mixed in enormous vats, according to the recipe in vogue in the particular establishment, and to this mixture is added, if necessary, a proportion of some old wine of a superior vintage. A most subtle, carefully educated, and exquisite taste is required to discern when the wine, in this crude state, has acquired the proper flavour and bouquet. Then comes the important point of effervescence—a source of much anxiety to the manu-

---

[1] The *rébêche* is principally sold to people manufacturing cheap Champagnes; by mixing with other wines of very light complexion, they give them body, and make a stuff which can be produced at a very low price.

facturer, for the extremest care is required to regulate the quantity of carbonic acid gas, so that there shall be neither too little nor too much. For if there be too little, the wine will be flat; and if there be too much, the bottles will burst by thousands. An instrument, called a *glucometer*, or *saccharometer*, is used to measure the amount of saccharine matter in the wine at this point; and if the necessary standard be not reached, the deficiency is supplied by the purest sugar candy. To the ordinary palate, at this stage it differs in no respect from still white wine, of somewhat tart flavour, and is now drawn off into other casks to undergo the next treatment in the process; viz., the fining, to make it bright, and remove what is known to connoisseurs of wine as "ropiness."

The wine is now ready for bottling, and the danger to be avoided is the bursting of the bottles, for the pressure of the gas is tremendous; hence it is that the champagne bottle is the most solid and massive in use. The bottling takes place, as a rule, about eight months after the grapes have been first pressed, and the precautions against breakage are of the most minute description. The instant any symptoms of bursting display themselves, the wine has to be removed to a cooler temperature; but even with every precaution, the loss sustained by the bursting of bottles is often very serious indeed, sometimes to an almost ruinous extent. The risk of breakage is generally almost past by the end of October, and the bottles are then kept in the cellars for a period ranging from eighteen months to three years, according to the custom of the establishment.

But even now all is not over, for during this period a sediment, resulting from the fermentation of the wine, has been deposited, which must be removed before the wine is ready for consumption; and very troublesome work it is to get rid of this sediment. The bottles are placed in a slanting direction with the necks downward, and the angle of inclination is altered from time to time till they stand almost perpendicular, whilst every time the position is changed, the bottle is sharply twisted round, so that the sediment may not cling to the sides. Finally, the deposit collects in a ball in the neck of the bottle, from whence it is "disgorged"—literally blown out—when the original cork is removed. A temporary stopper is then inserted until the liqueur, which is to give the wine its distinctive character, dry or sweet, is introduced. This liquor consists of a preparation of the very finest sugar candy, the best Champagne, and the oldest and purest Cognac.

The next process is corking, and, as we all know, champagne corks are not as other corks. They are made larger than the vent of the bottle, and are soaked in water, and very often steamed. They are somewhat expensive, the best corks used costing about threepence each; but it is a very false economy to use common corks, for the gas would escape. The pliant cork is placed in a machine which pinches it and compresses it to the size of the aperture of the bottle, and holds it there till a twenty-pound weight is let drop, on the principle of a pile-driving hammer, and drives the cork in firmly. The powerful leverage used to bring down the edge of the cork for wiring and stringing, imparts the round-shaped top peculiar to champagne corks. The bottles, after being corked and wired, are allowed to rest for two or three months, in order that the wine and the liqueur may properly amalgamate, and are then tinselled and labelled, ready for the consumer; but some of the best wines are kept for years to mature, and are, of course, of far higher value.

A sweet Champagne may be made of any wine, but a dry Champagne must be a good wine, as, if it is not sound, its acidity is detected at once; but this defect would be hidden by the liqueur necessary to make it sweet.

At Epernay, the bulk of the wine is not so good as that coming from Reims, and sells at a lower price; but there are firms there of world-wide note, such as Moet & Chandon, Perrier, Joüet & Co., Mennier Frères, Wachter & Co., etc.

Bordeaux or Claret.

In England we generally call the wines coming from Bordeaux, *Clarets*, the derivation of which cognomen is somewhat obscure; but it seems almost universally accepted that it comes from the French word *Clairet*, which is used even at the present time as a generic term for the *vins ordinaires* of a light and thin quality, grown in the south of France, and was in use from a very early date. The old French poet, Olivier Basselin (who died 1418 or 1419), sings:—

"Beau nez, dont les rubis ont coûté mainte pipe
De vin blanc et clairet . . ."

There was, however, another Claret, a compounded wine, resembling *hypocras*, which Giraldus Cambrensis, who lived in the twelfth century, classes thus: "Claretum, mustum, et medonem" (Claret, must, and mead). And the venerable Franciscan, Bartholomew Glanville,[1] says: "Claretum, ex vino et melle et speciebus aromaticis est confectum" (Claret is made from wine, honey, and aromatic spices). It makes a marked feature in a curious tenure.[2] "John de Roches holds the Manor of Winterslew, in the county of Wilts, by the Service, that when our Lord the King should abide at Clarendon, he should come to the Palace of the King there, and go into the Butlery, and draw out of any vessel he should find in the said Butlery at his choice, as much Wine as should be needful for making (*pro factura*) a Pitcher of Claret (*unius Picheri Claretti*), which he should make at the King's charge, and that he should serve the King with a Cup, and should have the vessel from whence he took the Wine, with all the Remainder of the Wine left in the Vessel, together with the Cup from whence the King should drink that Claret." This refers to a roll of 50 Ed. III., or 1376.

But this is not the Claret of our days, which is the wine produced in the countries watered by the rivers Dordogne and Garonne and the Gironde, at least it should be so; but, in truth, owing to the good railway communication, wine comes to Bordeaux from every

[1] *De Proprietatibus Rerum.* Argent. 1485, lib. xix., cap. 56.
[2] Blount's *Fragmenta Antiquitatis.* Sec. "Grand Serjeantry," No. IV.

part of France, large quantities owing their birth to the banks of the Rhone, from the Herault, Roussillon, etc.; and a judicious blending at Bordeaux, and its

FROM THE "COMPOST ET KALENDRIER DES BERGERES," 1499.

being shipped thence, is a very good title to its being grown in the Médoc; but the quantity shipped to all parts of the world, compared with the acreage of growth, entirely precludes the supposition that it possibly could have been the production of that district.

The nobility of the Médoc wines is small. There are only four *premiers crûs*, but they are magnificent. They are Château Lafitte, Château Latour, Château Margaux, and Château Haut-Brion; and all these, especially the Latour, have a flavour and seductive *bouquet* all their own, which is believed to arise from an extremely volatile oil contained in the grape skins, which, like all ethers, requires time to evolve and mature. But the soil, undoubtedly, has most to do with it, and this must be in a very large degree composed of fragments of rock, small and large, while the smooth round pebbles reflect the rays of the sun and throw them upwards, so as almost to surround the grapes with light and heat. Again, these stones absorbing the sun's rays during the day, give out warmth after sunset, whilst they keep the roots of the vines cool, and prevent to a great degree the evaporation of the natural and necessary moisture of the earth.

But these *premiers crûs* are not always good; for instance, in 1869, Messrs. Fulcher & Baines, wine brokers, sold by auction a very large parcel of Château Margaux for about 30s. per dozen. There was no doubt but that it was genuine wine, bottled at the Château, for the cases and corks were all properly branded; but of such low quality was it, or it deteriorated so rapidly, that when sold again in 1871 the same wine only averaged 18s. per dozen.

DRINKS.

The 2nd Growths are :—

Mouton,	coming from	*Pauillac.*
Rauzan-Segla,	,,	*Margaux.*
Rauzan-Gassies,	,,	,,
Léoville-Las Cases,	,,	*St. Julien.*
Léoville-Poyféré,	,,	,,
Léoville-Barton,	,,	,,
Durfort-Vivens,	,,	*Margaux.*
Lascombes,	,,	,,
Gruard-La rose-Sarg,	,,	*St. Julien.*
Gruard-La rose,	,,	,,
Braune-Cantenac,	,,	*Cantenac.*
Pichon-Longueville,	,,	*Pauillac.*
Pichon-Longueville-Lalande,	,,	,,
Ducru-Beaucaillou,	,,	*St. Julien.*
Cos-Destournel,	,,	*St. Estèphe.*
Montrose,	,,	,,

3rd Growths.

Kirwan,	coming from	*Cantenac.*
Château-d'Issau,	,,	,,
Lagrange,	,,	*St. Julien.*
Langoa,	,,	,,
Château-Giscours,	,,	*Labarde.*
Malescot-St. Exupéry,	,,	*Margaux.*
Cantenac-Brown,	,,	*Cantenac.*
Palmer,	,,	,,
La Lagune,	,,	*Ludon.*
Desmirail,	,,	*Margaux.*
Calon-Ségur,	,,	*St. Estèphe.*
Ferrière,	,,	*Margaux.*
M. d'Alesmeis Becker,	,,	,,

4th Growths.

St. Pierre,	coming from	St. Julien.
Branaire-Duluc,	,,	,,
Talbot,	,,	,,
Duhart-Milon,	,,	Pauillac.
Poujet,	,,	Cantenac.
La Tour-Carnet,	,,	St. Laurent.
Rochet,	,,	St. Estèphe.
Château-Beychevelle,	,,	St. Julien.
La Prieuré,	,,	Cantenac.
Marquis de Therme,	,,	Margaux.

5th Growths.

Pontet-Canet,	coming from	Pauillac.
Batailley,	,,	,,
Grand-Puy-Lacoste,	,,	,,
Ducasse-Grand-Puy,	,,	Pauillac.
Lynch-Bages,	,,	,,
Lynch-Moussas,	,,	,,
Dauzac,	,,	Labarde.
Moulton d'Armailhacq,	,,	Pauillac.
Le Tertre,	,,	Arsac.
Haut-Bages,	,,	Pauillac.
Pédesclaux,	,,	,,
Belgrave,	,,	St. Laurent.
Camensac,	,,	,,
Cos-Labory,	,,	St. Estèphe.
Clerc-Milon,	,,	Pauillac.
Croizet-Bages,	,,	,,
Cantemerle,	,,	Macau.

These are only some of the wines of the Médoc, so that I may be excused from recapitulating the names of the different growths of the Graves, the Pays de Sauternes, the Côtes, the Palus, and those of Entredeux Mers—their name is legion, and it would answer no good purpose. Cocks, in his *Bordeaux and its Wines*, gives a list of 1,900 of the *principal growths*, so that we can have a good choice of names from which to christen our " Shilling Gladstone."

The wines of Bordeaux used to be greatly drank in England until the great wars with France—in the last century, when, of course, their importation was prohibited—but, even then, large quantities were smuggled. They must, however, have been of better quality than the cheap stuff now imported. In Scotland, where an affinity with France always existed, it was a common drink, and very cheap; for in Campbell's *Life of Lord Loughborough* (vi. 29), we find that excellent claret was drawn from the cask at eighteenpence a quart: and its downfall as a beverage in Scotland is thus sung by John Home, probably in allusion to the Methuen Treaty of 1703.

> "Firm and erect the Caledonian stood,
> Prime was his mutton, and his claret good;
> Let him drink port, an English Statesman cried;
> He drank the poison, and his spirit died."

The white wines of these districts are delicious, and are not sufficiently appreciated in England, where we know very little of the Sauternes, Bommes, Barsac, Fargues, St. Pierre de Mons, Preignac, and those of Petits Graves and the Côtes. Chief of all is the wine of Château d'Yquem, of which Vizitelly[1] thus writes :—

"Among the white wines of the Gironde which obtained the higher class reward, two require to be especially mentioned. One, the renowned Château d'Yquem of the Marquis de Lur Saluces, the most luscious and delicately aromatic of wines, which, for its resplendent colour, resembling liquid gold, its exquisite bouquet, and rich, delicious flavour, due, according to the chemists, to the presence of Mannite, is regarded in France as unique, and which, at Vienna, naturally met with the recognition of a medal for progress.

"Mannite, the distinguished French chemist Berthelot informs us, has the peculiar quality of not becoming transformed into alcohol and carbonic acid during the process of fermentation. For a tonneau of this splendid wine twelve years old, bought direct from the Château, the Grand Duke Constantine paid, some few years since, 20,000 francs, or £800. The other wine calling for notice was La Tour Blance, one of those magnificent, liqueur-like Sauternes, ranking immediately after Château d'Yquem, and to some fine samples of which, of the vintages of 1864 and 1865, a medal for merit was awarded.

"The characteristic qualities of Château d'Yquem, which certain *soi-disant* connoisseurs pretend to poohpooh, as a mere ordinary *vin de liqueur*, are due, in no degree, to simple accident. On the contrary, the

[1] *The Wines of the World, Characterized and Classed,* 1875, pp. 16, 17.

THE DILLETANTE SOCIETY.

In this illustration of "the Dilletante Society" we find that Noblemen and Gentlemen such as Lord Mulgrave, Lord Seaforth, Hon. Chas. Greville, Charles Crowle, and the Duke of Leeds, drank their claret out of the black bottle—dispensing with the decanter altogether.

vintaging of this wine is an extremely complicated and delicate affair. In order to insure the excessive softness and rich liqueur character which are its distinguishing qualities, the grapes, naturally excessively sweet and juicy, are allowed to dry on their stalks, preserved, as it were, by the rays of the sun, until they become covered with a kind of down, which gives to them an almost mouldy appearance. During this period, the fruit, under the influence of the sun, ferments within its skin, thereby attaining the requisite degree of ripeness, akin to rottenness.

"On the occasion of the vintage, as it is absolutely essential that the grapes should be gathered, not only when perfectly dry, but also warm, the cutters never commence work until the sun has attained a certain height, and invariably suspend their labours when rain threatens, or mists begin to rise. At the first gathering they detach simply the *graines rôties*, or such grapes as have dried after arriving at proper maturity, rejecting those which have shrivelled without thoroughly ripening, and, from the former, a wine of extreme softness and density, termed *crème de tête*, is produced.

"By the time the first gathering has terminated, other grapes will have sufficiently ripened and rotted, or dried, and both sorts are now detached, yielding the wine called *vin de tête*, distinguished by equal softness with the *crème de tête*, but combined with a larger amount of alcohol, and greater delicacy of flavour. At this point, a delay generally ensues, according to the state of the weather, it being requisite, towards the end of October, to wait while the rays of the sun, combined with the night dews, bring the remainder of the grapes to maturity, when the third gathering takes place, from which the wine, termed *centre*, frequently very fine and spirituous, is produced. Another delay now ensues, and then commences the final gathering, when all the grapes remaining on the stalks are picked, which, when the vintage has been properly conducted, is usually only a very small quantity, yielding what is termed the *vin de queue.*"

However, although it is not given to all of us to be able to afford Château d'Yquem, yet there are many of the other white wines of France, which are within ordinary limits, and which compare more than favourably with the red wines.

Burgundy and other Wines.

Verily there cannot be much amiss with wine that causes a holy man (by profession) to break forth into song as follows :—

> "Nous les boirons lentement,
> Nous les boirons tendrement,
>   Ton Clos Vougeot, ton Romanée :
> Par nous la sainte liqueur,
> Qui nous rechauffe le cœur,
>   Ne sera jamais profanée."

More generous than the wines of Bordeaux, it has been the drink of Kings and Popes, and perhaps no vineyard has a similar honour done it as that of Clos-Vougeot (Napoleon's favourite wine); for when a French regiment marches past that celebrated vineyard, it halts, and presents arms. On the golden slope—the Côte d'Or—is grown this wine of Burgundy, and the *vignerons* divide the district into two parts, the Côte de Nuits and the Côte de Beaune, the first of which produces the finest wines, from Vosne especially, whence come Romanée-Conti, La Tâche, Richebourg, Romanée-St. Vivant, La Grande Rue, Gaudichat, Malconsort, and others; but of all these Romanée Conti is king. Unfortunately the yield of this vineyard is very small, and genuine Romanée is seldom to be met with. But there are plenty of good wines to be bought at moderate prices, those of Chambertin, Volnay, Beaune, Mâcon, and Beaujolais. Chief among the white Burgundies is Chablis; but there are other sorts, not half enough drank in England —Mâcon, Pouilly, Meursault, Chevalier-Montrachet, Montrachet-Ainé, and many other fine white wines. Sparkling Burgundy is not to be despised.

The Côtes du Rhone produce fine wines, too, such as Hermitage, Côte Rôtie, Condrieu, and St. Peray; but of these, perhaps, Hermitage red and white are best known to us.

Much wine is made in the South of France, in the departments of the Hérault, the Gard, the Aude, and the Pyrenées-Orientales, whilst Languedoc has always been famous for its wines, which are very similar to some Spanish varieties. Roussillon is nearly as good as Burgundy, and, after being manipulated at Cette, is often palmed off as "Vintage Port," and the Muscat wines of the Hérault and the Pyrenées-Orientales are particularly luscious, especially those from Lunel.

F

Some wines come from Corsica, but they do not find their way, as such, into the English market; no doubt, though, but we have them in some shape, for the mystifications of the wine trade are stupendous, and, to an outsider, unfathomable.

J. A.

GERMANY : Rhine Wines—Heidelberg Tun—Hock—Steinwein—
Asmannhaüser—Straw Wines—Goethe's Opinion of Wine.
GREECE: Verdea—Vino Santo—The Wine of Night. HUNGARY:
Maszlacz — Tokay — Carlowitz — Erlauer. ITALY : Monte
Pulciano — Chianti — Barolo — Barbera — Montefiascone —
Lachryma Christi, etc. MADEIRA : Malvasia—Tinta—Bual, etc.
PERSIA : Shiraz.

GERMANY.

THE Germans, says Cyrus Redding, like vain men of other nations, have wasted a good deal of idle conjecture on the antiquity of the culture of the vine in their country; and then, as though to show by example that this waste of idle conjecture is not confined to the Germans, Mr. Redding continues the investigation of this important matter himself. In the opinion of an experienced merchant these wines have a "distinct character and classification of their own." Their alcoholic strength is low, averaging about 18 per cent.

To the north of Coblentz the wines are of little comparative value, though a Rhenish wine has been produced at Bodendorf, near Bonn. On the Rhine or its tributary rivers between Coblentz and Mayence, all the most celebrated wines of Germany are grown. The grapes preferred for general cultivation are the Riessling, a small, white, harsh species. The true *Hochheimer*, daily consumed in Germany, is grown to the eastward of Mentz, between there and Frankfort. The wines mellow best in large vessels, an experience which has produced the celebrated Heidelberg Tun, holding some six hundred hogsheads. The distinguishing characteristics of German wine have been

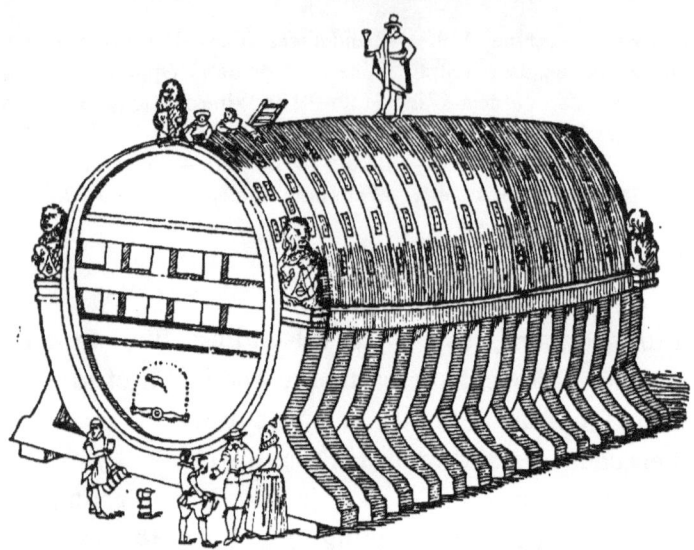

This illustration dates 1608 as "A Sciographie or Modell of that stupendous vessel which is at this day shewed in the Pallace of the Count Palatine of Rhene in the citie of Heidelberg." A model of this Tun was shown at the German Exhibition held in London, 1891. Its capacity was eclipsed by a famous *tonneau*, elaborately ornamented with allegorical figures, etc., which was shown in the French Exhibition of 1889. It would hold 200,000 bottles of Champagne, and came from Epernay. It had to be drawn by a large team, by road, and the French press was full of its imaginary adventures on its journey to Paris.

said to be generosity, dryness, fine flavour, and endurance of age. The dyspeptic will learn with delight that the strong wines of the Rhine are extremely salutary, and contain less acid than any other. It is also averred that they are never saturated with brandy. *Liebfrauenmilch*[1] is grown at Worms. It

[1] This wine is said to profit much by a quiescent state of the air afforded by the town wall.

is full bodied, as is that of *Scharlachberg*. *Nierstein*,[1] *Laubenheim*, and *Oppenheim* are good wines, but *Deidesheimer* is considered superior to them. *Hock*[2] is derived from Hochheim; but nearly every town on the banks of the Rhine gives its name to some lauded vintage. The flavour of Hock is supposed to be improved by thin green glasses. Perhaps, says the judicious Redding, this is mere fancy. The Palatinate wines are cheaper Hocks. Moselles have a more-delicate perfume. The whole eastern bank of the Rhine to Lorich, called the Rheingau, about fourteen miles in extent, has been famous for its wines for ages. Naturally, therefore, it was once the property of the Church. Here is *Schloss-Johannisberger*, once nearly destroyed by General Hoche, where a leading Rhine wine is made. *Steinberger* takes the next rank to *Johannisberger*. *Gräfenberg*, also once ecclesiastical property, produces wine equal to *Rüdesheimer*, which is a wine of the first Rhine growths. *Marcobrunner*, *Roth*, *Königsbach* are excellent drinks. *Bacharach* has lost its former celebrity. The conclusion to which a cele-

---

[1] A wine at Homburg, called *Erlacher*, at about one mark a bottle, is, says Dr. Charnock, frequently superior to the ordinary *Niersteiner*.

[2] "Hock," says one of those wine circulars, which weary alike the postman and the public, "is the English name for the noble vintages of the Rhine, which afford models of what wine ought to be. Their purity is attested by their durability. They are almost imperishable. They increase appetite, they exhilarate without producing languor, and they purify the blood. The Germans say good Hock keeps off the doctor. Southey says it deserves to be called the Liquor of Life. And so Pindar would have called it, if he had ever tasted it." Nothing surely can be added to this description of its virtues.

brated connoisseur has arrived after an exhaustive examination of German wines is this : " On the whole, the wines of *Bischeim, Asmannshauser,* and *Laubenheim* are very pleasant wines ; those of rather more strength are *Marcobrunner, Rüdesheimer* and *Niersteiner,* while those of *Johannisberg, Geissenheim,* and *Hochheim* give the most perfect delicacy and aroma." The Germans themselves say *Rhein-wein, fein-wein ; Necker-wein, lecker-wein ; Franken-wein, tranken-wein ; Mosel-wein, unnosel-wein.*[1]

The red wines of the Rhine are considered inferior to the white. Red *Asmannshaüser* is perhaps the best. Near Lintz *Blischert* is made. Königsbach and Altenahr yield ordinary wines. The most celebrated of Moselle wines is the *Brauneberger,* of which the varieties are numerous. A variety called *Gruenhaüser* was formerly styled the Nectar of the Moselle. The wines of Ahr, of which some are red, resemble Moselles, but will keep longer. Of the wines of the Neckar the most celebrated is *Besigheim.* Baden, Wisbaden, Wangen, and Würtzberg, all grow good wines. Of the last is *Stein-wein,* produced on a mountain so called, and named by the Hospital

---

[1] Thus unfortunately translated, Rhine wine is good, Neckar pleasant, Frankfort bad, Moselle innocent. But Moselle, we have been told, is very far from " innocent." *Unnosel* is without bouquet. *Tranken* means not bad but drinkable, and *lecker* is rather lickerish than good. A sample of the same carelessness occurs on the next page, where *ein weinfask von anderhalb ahm ein pipe* is intended to express *ein Weinfass von anderthalb Ohm, eine Pipe.* It is a pity that an excellent work, to which we, as many writers on wine have like ourselves been deeply indebted, should be marred by these irregularities.

to which it belongs, *Wine of the Holy Ghost. Leisten* wines are grown on Mt. Saint Nicolas. *Straw* wines are made in Franconia. *Calmus*, a liqueur wine, like the sweet wines of Hungary, is made in the territory of Frankfurt. The best vineyards are those of Bischofsheim. Wines of Saxony are of little worth. Meissen and Guben produce the best. Naumburg makes some small wines, like inferior Burgundy. The excellence of the Rhine wines has seldom perhaps been proved more clearly than by one who loved them well. Goethe, in his *Aus einer Reise am Rhein, Main und Neckar*, says: "*Niemand schämt sich der Weinlust, sie rühmen sich einigermaassen des Trinkens. Hübsche Frauen gestehen dass ihre Kinder mit der Mutterbrust zugleich Wein geniessen. Wir fragten ob denn wahr sey, dass es geistlichen Herren, ja Kürfürsten geglückt, acht Rheinische Maass das heisst sechzehn unserer Bouteillen, in vierundzwanzig Stunden zu sich zunehmen? Ein scheinbar ernsthafter Gast bemerkte, man dürfe sich zu Beantwortung dieser Frage nur der Fasteneeredigt ihres Weihbischofs erinnern, welcher, nachdem pr das schreckliche Laster der Trunkenheit seiner G-meinde mit den stärksten Farben dargestellt, also geschlossen habe—*" But for those who understand not the German tongue we will give some of the sermon of this Church dignitary on the Rochusberg in English. "Those, my pious brethren, commit the greatest sin who misuse God's glorious gifts. But the misuse excludes not the use. Wine, it is written, rejoices man's heart. Therefore we are clearly intended to enjoy it. Now perhaps, beloved brethren, there is not one of you who cannot drink two measures of wine without feeling any ill effects therefrom ; he, however, who with his third or fourth measure has so far forgotten himself as to abuse, beat and kick his wife and children, and to treat his dearest friend as his worst enemy, let such an one discontinue to drink three or four measures, which thus render him unpleasing to God and despicable to man. But he who with the fourth measure, nay, with his fifth or his sixth, still maintains his sense in such a manner that he can behave properly to his fellow-Christian, attend to his domestic duties, and obey his spiritual superiors as he ought, let him be thankful in modesty for the gift accorded to him. But let him not advance beyond the sixth measure, for here commonly is the term set to human power and endurance. Rare indeed is the occasion in which the benevolent God has lent a man such especial grace that he may drink eight measures—a grace which He has, however, accorded to me His servant. Let, therefore, every one take only his allotted measure und auf dass ein solches geschehe, alles Ubermaass dagegen verbannt sey, handelt sämmtlich nach der Vorschrift des heiligen Apostels welcher spricht ; Prüfet alles und das Beste behaltet !"

GREECE.

The vinification of Greece is commonly imperfect. Most of its wines become vinegar in summer. Avoid, says a well-known guide-book, the wine of this country, which is generally acid and always impure.[1] The

[1] Colonel Leake described the ordinary country wine as a villainous

"TASTING THE VINTAGE."—*After* Hasenclever.

best Greek wines are those of the islands Ithaca, Zante, Tenos, Samos, Thera (Santorin),[1] and Cyprus. The white wine of Zante, called *Verdea*, resembles Madeira in flavour. The wine of Naxos is of considerable strength, and is greatly improved by age. A quantity of it, known as *Vino Santo*, is exported. Andros was sacred to Dionysus, and a tradition (Plin. ii. 103; xxxi. 13; Paus. vi. 26) says that for seven days during a festival of this god the waters of a certain fountain were changed to wine. The wine did no credit to the god, if it resembled that which this island at present produces. The "Nectar" of *Morta* is bitter and astringent. Dr. Charnock has recommended the *Monthymet* as a good mild wine, and the *Œconomos*. A white wine, called "*the wine of night*," is supplied under the distinctive names of *St. Elie* and *Calliste*; the latter is the better.

HUNGARY.

The wines of Hungary, we are told, "possess considerable body with a moderate astringency." The varieties of wine known as *Ausbruch* and *Maszlacz*,

compound of lime, resin, spirits of wine, and grapes, without body or flavour. Nor were things better in the days of old. Dugald Dalgetty, a German Ensign, writing from Athens in 1687, says, "Would that I could exchange a cask of Athenian wine for a cask of German beer!" The *vin du pays* is impregnated with resin or turpentine now as formerly, whence, according to Plutarch, the Thyrsus of Bacchus is adorned with a pine cone. Pliny says it favours the preservation of the drink.

[1] The island owes this name to its patron saint Irene, martyred here A.D. 304.

including the *Tokays, Rust, Menes,* and many more, are of the most important character. Without the addition of dry berries the so-called natural wine or *Szamorodni* is obtained. The Tokay essence, a very sweet wine, should be also very old. When fifty years in bottle it costs some £3 [1] for a small flask. Ausbruch, also sweet, should be also old. *Maszlacz* is of four different kinds. The *Mezes, Male* or *Imperial*, does not get into trade. *Meograd, Krasso,* and *Villany* from the West of Hungary are good strong wines of the second class. Wines of the third class are very numerous. There is no space to mention more than the red wines: *Baranya, Presburg, Somogy, Vagh-Ujhelyer, Paulitsch,* and *Erdöd,* and the white *Miszla, Balaton, Füred, Hont, Pesth,* and *Weissenburg*. *Samlauer* is one of the best white wines made at a place called Samlau, as *Erlauer* another good wine at Erlau. The most commonly known Hungarian wines of the present are *Oedenburg, Samlau, Neszmely,* and *Carlowitz*.

Italy.

That Italy produces good wines is, says Cyrus Redding, undeniable. She also produces wines that are very bad. The best Italian wines are said to be produced in Tuscany. As Hafiz is the authority for

---

[1] The value attached to this wine is one example among many of the caprice of fashion. The *Muscadine* of Syracuse or the *Lagrima* of Malaga is equal to it in richness, and few people would prefer it to other wines, did they dare to contradict the decision of fashion in its favour, and to have a taste of their own.

Shiraz, so Redi's *Bacco in Toscana* should be consulted for the wines of Italy. *Monte Pulciano* is of a purple hue, sweet and slightly astringent. It is to this wine that Redi gives the palm, calling it *la manna di Monte Pulciano*. The wine of *Chianti*, near Sienna, is well known. *Artiminio*, *Poncino*, *Antella*, and *Carmignano*, though of less reputation, are not greatly inferior. The best *Verdea*[1] comes from Arcetri near Florence. *Trebbiano*, a gold-coloured syrup, is produced, according to Drs. Thudichum and Dupré, from grapes, "passulated on the vine by torsion of the stalk." *Montelcino*, *Rimaneze*, and *Santo Stefano* are Siennese wines. Of Sardinia the chief wines are the so-called *Malvasias*, *Giro*, *Aleatico*, like the *Tinto* of Alicante, and *Bosa*, *Ogliastra*, and *Sassari*. Of Piedmont the principal wines are *Barolo*, *Barbera*, *Nebbiolo*, *Braccheto*. *Asti*, *Chaumont*, *Alba*, and *Montferrat* have had reputation thrust upon them. *Grignolinos* are made from a vine closely related to the *Kadarka* of Hungary, and the *Carmenet* of the Gironde. The wines of Genoa are of small repute. Central Italy furnishes *Montefiascone*,[2] with a delicious

[1] So called from its green colour. It is said to have been a favourite wine of Frederick the Great. It is held now in slighter esteem.

[2] Called *Est Est* from the writing under the bust of the valet of the bibulous German bishop Defoucris, who drank himself to death, upon which his valet composed his epitaph.

' *Est est* ' *propter minium* ' *est*,'
Dominus meus mortuus est.

Reverence for antiquity is our sole excuse for there production of these wretched lines. *Monte Pulciano* has also the credit of having killed a Churchman. Other wines doubtless have had the same honour.

aroma, *Albano*, resembling *Lacryma Christi*, and *Orvieto*. The principal wine of Naples, from the base of Vesuvius, is *Lacryma Christi*, a rich, red, exquisite drink, affirmed by some adventurous fancies to be the *Falernian* of Horace. "O Christ!" said a Dutchman who drank, "why didst Thou not weep in my country?" *Gallipoli, Tarento, Baia, Pausillipo*, yield good wines. The islands in the Bay of Naples all produce wine; that of *Caprea* is of good ordinary quality, both white and red. Calabria furnishes many good wines. *Muscadenes* and dry wines are made at Reggio. *Asprino*, a white foamy wine, with a pleasant sharpness, is a favourite of the Campagna. *Carigliano* is a Muscadine, with a flavour of fennel. Dr. Charnock speaks highly of the wine of Capri, and of Orvieto, a delicate white wine of Rome. The disagreement of travellers about the merits of wines arises principally, of course, from a diversity of tastes, but also in the matter of Italian wines, from the fact that different wines bear the same names in different countries. There is, for instance, a *vino santo* and a *vino greco* in Naples. A Veronese wine, *vino debolissimo e di niuna stima*, is also called *vino santo*, and an excellently good wine at Brescia. It is the same with half a dozen of the most noted wines of Italy. *Modico*, a fine white wine from the place of that name near Salerno, was apparently a favourite of the noted School of Salernum. The best known wines out of Italy are the *Barola, Barbera*, and the rest which may be found on the wine-list of every *padrone* of an Italian restaurant; the *Inferno* of the Valtellina; the *Lam-*

brusco of Modena; the *Chianti* of Tuscan—a wine grown on the estate of Baron Ricasoli, not thought so much of in Italy as in England; and the *Lacryma Christi* of Naples. Most Italian wines are bottled in flasks, in the old Roman style, with oil[1] on the top, and wool over the oil.

MADEIRA.

Wine is first mentioned as a product of Funchal, the capital of Madeira, in the fifteenth century. In 1662, when Charles II. married the Infanta Catherine of Bragança, English merchants began to settle in Madeira. The principal varieties of Madeira are *Malvasia*, *Bual*, *Sercial*, *Tinta*, and *Verdelho* (the *Verdea* of Tuscany). In England, Madeira is now within the reach of all. At the beginning of this century, it was known only to connoisseurs. The "fine rich old *Boal*" is fairly familar, and if we may trust the wine merchants, the "Very Superior Old," variously described as full, soft, golden, delicate, and mellow, is gradually winning its way into public favour, since that same "soft fulness," added to a delicious and yet pungent flavour, produces a drink "altogether superior" to the best Sherry.

PERSIA.

The ancient, most famous wines of this country were those of Chorassan, Turan, and Mazanderan. These

---

[1] "Let no man," says the Talmud, "send his neighbour wine with oil upon its surface."—*Chulin*, fol. 94, col. 1.

places still produce wines; but their characteristics and reputation have, it is affirmed, become blended in the wine of Shiraz, in the province of Ferdistan, on the Persian Gulf. Chardin, the Frenchman, describes this wine as of excellent quality, but of course not so fine as the French wines. The German, Kämpfer, puts Shiraz on the same level with the best Burgundy and Champagne. He who wishes to learn the nature of the wine of Shiraz should consult the *Diwan* of Hafiz. How far this poet speaks of wine literally understood, and how far of spiritual delights, is a matter for commentatorial investigation. Persian wine is frequently mixed with *raki* and saffron, and the extract of hemp. *Sherbet*, made of fruit juices and water, is English rather than Oriental.

PORTUGAL: Peso da Regoa—Four Methods of Cultivation of Vine—White and Black Ports—The *Quintas*—Tarragona—Charneco. RUSSIA: Kahetia—Gumbrinskoé. SICILY: Marsala. SPAIN: Malaga—Sherry—Amontillado. SWITZERLAND: Chiavenna—St. Gall—The Canton of Vaud. CIDER: Derivation—Ainsworth—Gerard—Bacon — Evelyn — Turberville — Macaulay—Phillips. PERRY.

PORTUGAL.

One hundred and fifty years ago, in the small town of Peso da Regoa, then called Regua only, near the confluence of the Corgo with the Douro, lived a single fisherman, in a hut which he had himself constructed. When the Oporto Wine Company was established, their warehouses were erected here, and an annual fair for the sale of wine was established.

Peso da Regoa—the Peso comes from an adjoining village—is now a thriving town, and may be considered the capital of the Alto Douro district (*Paiz Vinhateiro do Alto Douro*), whence are sent to England and elsewhere those wines which are here known as Port. The wine district is bounded by Villa Real on the north, Lamego on the south, S. João da Pesqueira on the east, and Mezãofrio on the west. It is unwholesome, and but thinly populated. Those who list may draw from this fact a divine prohibition of the bibbing of Port.

The vine is cultivated in Portugal in four ways. (1) By being trained round oaks or poplars *de enforcado*, as the Romans *ulmisque adjungere vites*. (2) By the terrace system, the best as (1) is the most picturesque. (3) By bushes in rows, with the intermediate ground ploughed. (4) By the trellis or *de ramada*. The first liquor drawn from the *lagar*, or press, the result of the weight of the grapes alone, is called *Lacryma Christi*. After that a gang of men jump into the *lagar*, and dance to the sound of the fife or bagpipe. The weather is warm, the work is hard; the result is better conceived than expressed.

Of white ports the best are *Muscatel de Jesus* (the testimony to religious influence in this and the *Lacryma Christi* is extremely touching), considered the prince of all, the *Dedo de Dama*, the *Ferral Branco, Malvazía* (our Malmsey),[1] *Abelhal, Agudelho, Alvaraça, Donzellinho, Folgozão, Gonveio,* White *Mourisco, Rabo da Ovelha,* and *Promissão.* Of the black ports the finest is *Touriga,* and the sweetest *Bastardo.* Other dark ports are *Souzão,* the darkest of all, *Aragonez, Pegudo,* besides *Tintas,* whose names are legion. Other wines grown here, or in the immediate vicinity, are *Alvarilhão,* a kind of claret, *Alicante, Muscatel, Roxo,* and *Malvazia Vermelha.* Great quantities of wine are produced in the *quintas* outside the line of demarcation, and some of these wines are equal to those made in the wine district of the *Alto Douro* itself. Red wines transformed into French clarets at Bordeaux, are exported in large quantities. A wine from Tarragona, known as "Spanish Red," or superb Catalan, is sent yearly to

[1] Malmsey wine is also a product of Funchal, in Madeira. The first so-called wine was shipped for Francis I. of France. The word is probably a corruption of *Malvasia* or *Monemvasia* (μόνη ἐμβασία, or single entrance), a Greek island from which the grape may have been brought by the Florentine Acciajoli in 1515.

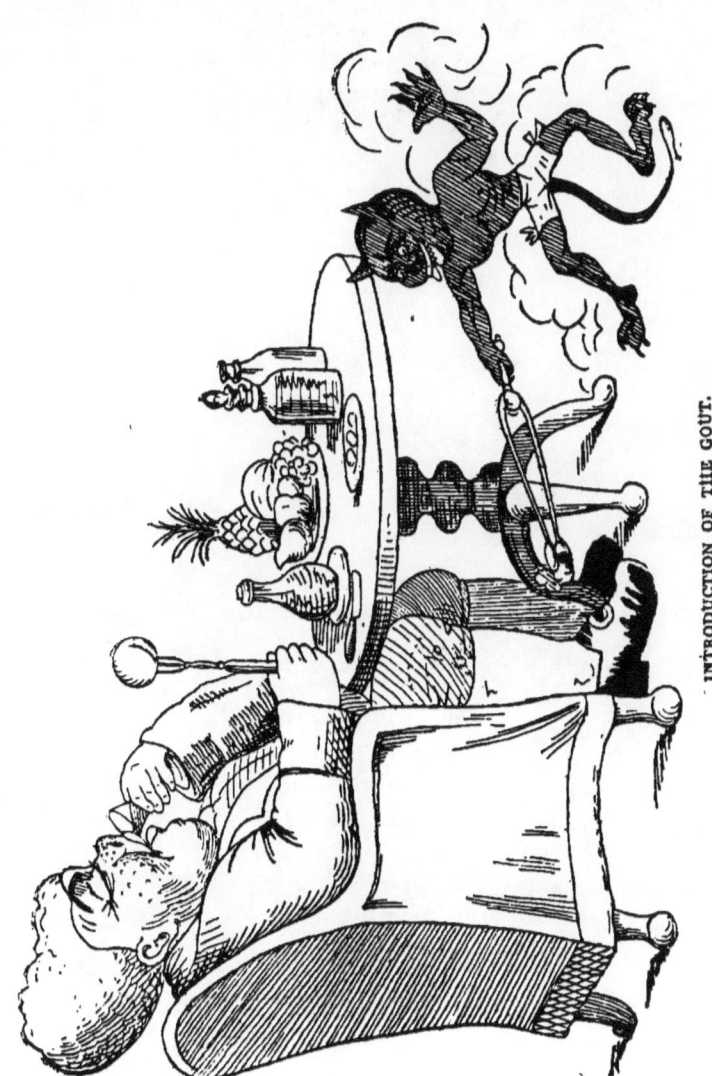

INTRODUCTION OF THE GOUT.

England, and sold as very full, rich, fruity, and tawny
Port. Port will not keep good in the cask for more
than two years without the addition of alcohol. The
Oporto merchants use a pure spirit distilled from the
wine itself. The old Port which we prize so highly
and pay for so dearly is seldom unaffected by brandy
or other spirit.

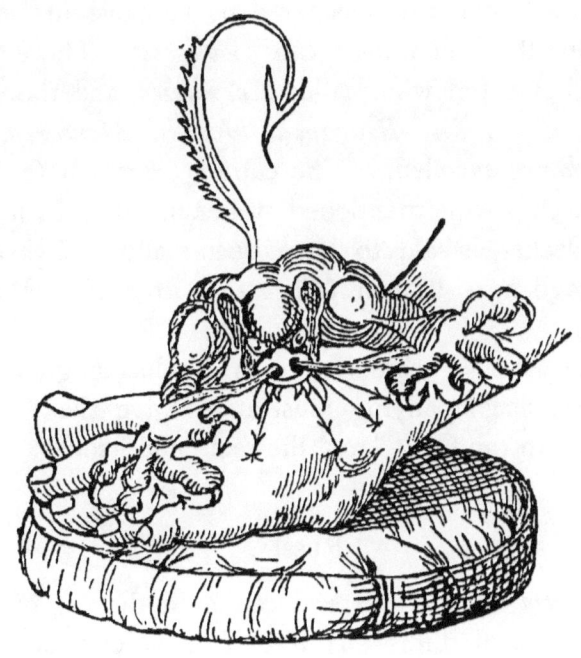

THE GOUT.

Some of the best wines are produced by Estrema
dura, such as *Bucellas, Collares, Lavradio, Chamusca,
Carcavellos, Barra a Barra*, and many others of which
not even the names are known in England. The
vines round Torres Vedras might, it has been said,
produce the finest wines in the world; if properly cul-

tivated. *Arinto* and *Estremadura* are comparatively new wines. The white wines of Tojal and the vintages of Palmella and Inglezinhos have only to be known to become popular. The province of Traz-os-Montes, in spite of its climate of *nove mezes de inverno, e tres de inferno*, produces excellent wines in the Piaz Vinhateiro. Those in the vicinity of the river Tua and the Sabor are considered by connoisseurs to resemble the celebrated *Clos Vougeot*. There is a remarkable red wine called *Cornifesto*, and the white wines of *Arêas, Bragança, Moraes, Moncorvo,* and *Nosedo* are excellent. The cup of *Charneco* (2 Hen. VI. ii. 3), a wine mentioned by Beaumont and Fletcher and Decker, is said to have been made at *Charneco*, a village near Lisbon (*European Magazine*, March, 1794).

Port-wine is accredited with producing gout, and the two accompanying illustrations give the "Introduction to the Gout," and the real fiend itself.

Russia.

Kahetia is a wine produced in a district of that name, east of Tiflis. It is of two descriptions, red and white, and is much esteemed throughout Transcaucasia. As it is kept in skins made tight with naphtha, it has generally a slight taste of leather and petroleum. *Gumbrinskoé* is a sweet wine grown in the Gumbri district of the Caucasus. *Donskoé Champanskoé*, the champagne of the Don, is said by Dr. Charnock to be a very good wine, and better than many sorts drunk in Britain. Russian wines generally, as those of many other countries, are largely diluted, and, like the majority of Greek wines, do not improve by keeping.

SICILY.

A thousand years before Christ, says Mr. Simmonds, districts of Sicily were famous for wine. The coins of Naxos (500 B.C.) bear the head of Bacchus on the obverse, on the reverse Pan, or a bunch of grapes. Of Sicilian wines, the light amber or brown wine of *Marsala* is best known. There is Ingham's L.P., and Woodhouse's; there is also the Old Brown. The Faro is perhaps the strongest wine of Sicily. The wine of Terre Forte is made near Etna, in some vineyards of Benedictine monks. Marsala, as we know it, is generally adulterated, or fortified, to use a more technical term. Even the "Virgin" has not escaped this common lot of wines. Much Marsala is indeed sold as Marsala, but much more is sold as Sherry. The wine of *Taormina* has the classic taste of pitch. Augusta produces a wine with a strong flavour of violets. This to some palates is the most agreeable wine drank in Sicily or elsewhere. The *Del Bòsco* of Catania, and the *Borgetto* have been both recommended by the subtle taste of Dr. Charnock. A dry wine called *Vin de Succo* is made about ten miles from Palermo. The wine of Syracuse somewhat resembles *Chablis*.

Spain.

As Spain succeeds France geographically, so it follows it in the excellence of its vinous productions. Throughout all ages this country has been distinguished for its wines. But the Spaniard's chief glory under heaven is in the preparation of white dry fortified wines such as sherries, and sweet wines such as *Malagas*. In the province of Andalusia is situated Xeres de la Frontera, and the convent of *Paxarete*, which produces a rich sweet sparkling drink. Here, too, are the vines of the *vino secco* and the *abocado*, and *Rota*,[1] which produces Andalusia's best red wines. Here are. *Ranico, Moguro*, or *Moguer*, a cheap light wine, *Negio*, and the capital *Seville*. Catalonia yields a large quantity of red wine shipped to England mostly as a drink for the general. The *Malaga* of Granada is well known. Sherry[2] wines are, or ought to be, the products of Cadiz, including Xeres de la Frontera, San Lucar de Barrameda,—where *Tintilla*, an excellent Muscadine red wine, is manufactured,—Trebujena, and Puerto de Santa Maria. The celebrated wine known as Manzanilla[3] is made in

---

[1] Rota wines are mostly coloured, or *Tintos*, whence our English sacramental drink. They are all simmered—at their best in youth, and their worst in age.

[2] Supposed by some to be the old English Sack. The reader interested may consult Hakluyt, Nicols, Hewell's Dictionary, and Venner's *Via Recta*.

[3] The etymology is uncertain. Some derive it from the town near Seville, others from the Spanish word for an apple, and others again from that for a camomile flower.

San Lucar de Barrameda. *Val de Peñas*[1] wines are commonly red. After the perfection of age, this celebrated product of La Manche[2] is, in the opinion of Redding, equal to any red wine in the world. Much wine of Catalonia is now imported into England as Catalan Port. Borja produces a luscious white wine. The country about Tarragona on the road to Barcelona is almost wholly occupied with wine making. *Beni-Carlos, La Torre, Segorbe,* and *Murviedro,* are all fair wines of Valencia. Alicant produces an excellent red wine, *vino tinto,* strong and sweet; when old, this wine is called *Fondellol.* Vinaroz, Santo Domingo, and Perales, offer red wines of moderate excellence. The best wines of Aragon are *Cariñena* and the *Hospital,* from the vine which the French call *Grenache.* In Biscay, at Chacoli, a *vino brozno,* or austere wine, is produced in large quantity. The best is made at Vittoria, and called *Pedro Ximenes.*[3] Fuençaral, near Madrid, offers a good wine seldom exported. The most famous wine-growing district of Granada is that of Malaga, termed Axarquia. This produces *Malagas, Muscatels, Malvasies,* and *Tintos.* The red wines called *Tinto de Rota* and *Sacra* are unfermented with only enough spirit for preservation, and are commonly advertised in our wine circulars as "suitable for sacramental purposes." *Guindre* is flavoured with cherries from which it derives its name.

[1] *Valley of Rocks,* indicating the soil on which it is grown.
[2] It is frequently damaged by the carelessness of the *vinatero,* or wine-seller, to such an extent that the proverb *Pregonar vino y vender vinagre* becomes, like wisdom, justified of her children.
[3] So called from the grape common in most parts of Spain.

Into this wine, as into some others, the Spaniards are wont to put roasted pears, under the conceit that thereby it is much improved in taste and rendered more wholesome. Hence arose the proverb *El vino de las peras dalo a quien bien quiéras*. Malaga Xeres is often known in England as the pale, gold, dry sherry,[1] as the wines of Alicant, Benicarlos, and Valencia are sold as a rich and fruity Port. The so-called *Amontillado* Sherry is very often the outcome of accident. Out of a hundred butts of sherry from the same vineyard, some, says a great authority, will be *Amontillado*, without the manufacturers being able to account for it. At Cordova, a dry wine called *Montilla* is commonly drunk.

SWITZERLAND.

Swiss wines are commonly consumed only in Switzerland. The best is produced in the Grisons, called *Chiavenna*, aromatic and white from the red grape. A white *Malvasia* of good quality is made in the Valais. It is luscious, as is *Chiavenna*. The Valais also furnishes red wines, made at La Marque and Coquempin in the district of Martigny. Schaffhausen gives plenty of red wine. The *wine of blood*[2] is manufactured at Basle. These wines are also known as those of the *Hospital* and *St. Jaques*. The red

---

[1] The fine old Amoroso, of which a small stock is still remaining.

[2] So called from the battle of Birs, in the reign of Louis XI., in which 1,600 Swiss opposed 30,000 French, and only sixteen of the former survived. The fallen succumbed, we are told, less to the power of the foe than to the fatigue of the fighting.

wines of Erlach, in Berne, are of a good quality. The red wine of Neufchâtel is equal to a third-class Burgundy. St. Gall produces tolerable wines. In the Valteline, the red wines are both good and durable, much resembling the aromatic wine of Southern France. These wines are remarkably luscious, and will, it is said, keep for a century. The largest amount of wine is produced by the Canton of Vaud. The wines of *Cully* and *Désalés*, near Lausanne, much resemble the dry wines of the Rhine.

APPLES FOR CIDER.

CIDER.

THE original meaning of the word *cider*[1] appears to have been strong drink. It was used to designate a liquor made of the juice of any fruit pressed, and an example of the word in this use is to be found in Wycliffe's Bible, in the speech of the angel to Zacharias (Luke i. 15), in allusion to his promised progeny: *He schal not drynke wyn and syder.* The next meaning is that of a liquor made from the juice of apples expressed and fermented.

[1] It is supposed by the erudite divine, Adam Clarke, to be probably borrowed from the Hebrew word שֵׁכָר, Greek σίκερα, which, according to St. Jerome (*Epist. ad Nepotianum de vita Clericorum, et in Isai. xxvii.* 1), means any intoxicating liquor, whether of honey, corn, apples, dates, or other fruits.

"A flask of *cider* from his father's vats,
Prime, which I knew."
                    TENNYSON : *Audley Court.*

We have little information about cider either from the Greeks or the Latins. It would seem that it was not known to them, if we may trust Ainsworth, who translates cider by *succus e pomis expressus*, and Byzantius, who gives μηλίτης (οἶνος) εἶδ. ποτοῦ as the equivalent for *cidre*.[1] Gerard, in his *Historie of Plants*, published in 1597, says that he saw in the pastures and hedgerows about the grounds of a "worshipful gentleman," dwelling two miles from Hereford, called M. Roger Bodnome, so many trees of all sorts that the servants drunk for the most part no other drink but that which is made from apples. The quantity, says Gerard, was such that by the report of the gentleman himself, the parson "hath for tithe many hogsheads of Syder." This reference to the servants and the parson drinking it, but not to the "gentleman," seems to show that the liquor was not then held in much esteem.

Bacon placed cider after wine, and we have followed in our arrangement of the present volume his august example. This great philosopher speaks of cider and perry as "notable beverages on sea-voyages." The cider of his day did not, he says, sour by crossing the line, and was good against sea-sickness. He also speaks of cider, a "wonderful pleasing and refreshing drink," in his *New Atlantis*.

[1] In a treatise of the Talmud, *Abodah Zarah*, fol. 40, col 2, cider is called "wine of apples."

John Evelyn's *French Gardener* gives much information on this subject, and his *Pomona* is, says Stopes, the first monograph on the manufacture of cider in England.

Cider is made in many parts of Barbary, and in Canada. In all the States, apples are abundant, particularly in New York and New England, and cider is a common drink of the inhabitants. And it is as excellent as it is common. That of New Jersey is generally considered the best. It is curious that the least juicy apples afford the best liquor. Cider of a superior quality is abundant in Cork, Waterford, and other counties of Ireland, where it was introduced, we are told, in the reign of Elizabeth. It was first made at Affane, in the county of Waterford.[1] Worledge's *Vinetum Britannicum*, 1676, and his *Most Easy Method for Making the Best Cider*, 1687, have been considered at full length by Mr. Stopes. Worledge's press is an improvement upon one shown in Evelyn's *Pomona*.

Cider appears in Russia under the name of *Kvas*. There is *Yàblochni kvas*, made of apples; *Grùshevoi kvas*, of pears, a perry; and *Malinovoi kvas*, of raspberries. George Turberville, secretary to the English Embassy to Moscow in the year 1568, mentions *kvas* in a description of the Russians of his time as :—

" Folk fit to be of Bacchus' train, so quaffing is their kind ;
Drink is their whole desire, the pot is all their pride.

Walker : *Hist. Essay on Gardening*, p. 166. *Anthologia Hibernica*, i. 194.

The soberest head doth once a day stand needful of a guide.
If he to banquet bid his friends, he will not shrink
On them at dinner to bestow a dozen kinds of drink,
Such liquor as they have, and as the country gives;
But chiefly two, one called *kwas*, whereby the Mousike lives,
Small ware and waterlike, but somewhat tart in taste;
The rest is mead, of honey made, wherewith their lips they baste."

Stopes is of opinion that the finest cider is made, not in the west, as has been commonly asserted, but in the east of England. This authority seems particularly to favour the Ribston pippins of Norfolk.

"Worcester," says Macaulay, in his *History of England*, ch. iii., " is the queen of the cider land; but Devon and Somerset, Gloucester and Norfolk, might dispute the title. To make good cider the apples should be quite ripe, as the amount of sugar in ripe apples is 11·0; in unripe apples, 4·9; in over-ripe apples, 7·95. The fermentation should proceed slowly. Brande says that the strongest cider contains, in 100 volumes, 9·87 of alcohol of 92 per cent; the weakest, 5·21. By distillation, cider produces a good spirit; but it is seldom converted to that purpose in consequence of its acidity, which, however, is greatly remedied by rectification.

Much cider is distilled in Normandy, and sent to this country under the name of *arrack*, or some other foreign spirit, according to its flavour. To the Normans the invention of this liquor has been attributed. They are also said to have received it from the Moors. Whitaker (*Hist. Manchester*, i. 321) says this drink was introduced into this country by the Romans; and

Simmonds (p. 25) that it was first used in England about 1284.

Cider has been immortalised by Phillips in a classical poem, in imitation of Virgil's Georgics, which, according to Johnson, "need not shun the presence of the original." Milton's nephew thought that cider—

> "far surmounts
> Gallic or Latin grapes."

Perry.

Perry is prepared from pears, as cider from apples It is capable of being used in the adulteration of champagne.[1] The harsher, redder, and more tawny pears produce the best drink. Perry is less popular than cider, but some consider it superior.[2]

[1] The extra dry old lauded or pale cremant, or the extra reserve Cuvée, 1884 vintage.

[2] For further information see Crocker, Marshall, Knight, and especially Stopes.

AN OLD CIDER MILL.

BRANDY.

The Invention of Brandy—Early Alchemists—Aqua Vitæ —Distillation—The Still-room—Ladies Drinking—Nantes and Charente—Johnson's Idea of Brandy—The Charente District—Manufacture of Brandy—The Cognac Firms.

WHO invented Brandy ? is a question that cannot be authoritatively answered offhand ; but the good people of some parts of Germany hold that it was the Devil. And their legend is, at all events, circumstantial.

Every one who is at all acquainted with old legends is fully aware that the Father of Evil is extremely simple, and has allowed himself, many times, to be outwitted by man. Once, especially, he was so guileless as to put trust in a Steinbach man, who cajoled him into entering an old beech tree, and there he was imprisoned until the tree was cut down. His first step, on regaining his freedom, was to revisit his own particular dominion, which, to his horror, he found empty !

This, naturally, would not do, and he set about repeopling hell without delay. He thought the quickest plan would be to start a distillery; so he hurried off at once to Nordhausen, where his manufacture of Brandy (his own invention) became so famous that people from all parts came to him to learn the new art, and to become distillers. From that time his Satanic Majesty has never had to complain of paucity of subjects.

It seems fairly established that the famous chemist Geber, who lived in the 7th or 8th century, was acquainted with distillation, and we know that it was practised by the Arabian and Saracenic alchemists, but have no knowledge whether they made any practical use of the *alcohol* they produced. They, at all events, gave us the word by which we now know the *spirit*, or ethereal part, of wine.

Alcohol, distilled from wine, is first reliably mentioned by a celebrated French alchemist and physician, Arnaud de Villeneuve, who died in 1313, who gave it the name of *aqua vitæ*, or water of life,[1] and regarded it as a valuable adjunct in physic, and as a boon to humanity. Raymond Lully, the famous alchemist, who is said to have been his pupil, declared it to be " an emanation from the Deity," and on its introduction it was supposed to be the elixir of life, capable of rejuvenating those who partook of it, and, as such, was only purchasable at an extremely high price.

We may see, by a book[1] written 200 years after the death of Arnaud de Villeneuve, the esteem in which Aqua Vitæ was held even after so great a lapse of time.

[1] The French name, *Eau de Vie*, having the same meaning.

"Aqua Vite is comonly called the mastresse of al medycynes, for it easeth the dysseases comynge of colde. It gyueth also yonge corage in a person, and cawseth hym to haue a good memorye and remembraunce. It puryfyeth the fyue wittes of melancolye and of all unclenes whan it is dronke by reason and measure. That is to understande fyue or syx droppes in the mornynge fastyng with a sponefull of wyne, usynge the same in the maner aforsayde the euyl humours can not hurte the body, for it withdryueth them oute of the vaynes.

¶ It conforteth the harte, and causeth a body to be mery.

¶ It heleth all olde and newe sores on the hede comynge of colde, whan the hede is enoynted therwyth and a lytell of the same water holden in the mouthe, and dronke of the same.

¶ It cawseth a good colour in a parson whan it is dronke and the hede enoynted the iwyththe space of xx dayes; it heleth Alopicia, or whan it is dronke fastyng with a lytell tryacle. It causeth the here well to growe, and kylleth the lyce and flees.

¶ It cureth the Reuma of the hede, whan the temples and the fore hede therwith be rubbed.

¶ It cureth Litargiam,[2] and all yll humours of the hede.

¶ It heleth the coloure in the face, and all maner of pymples. It heleth the fystule when it is put therein with the Iuce of Celendyne.

¶ Cotton wet in the same and a lytell wronge out agayn and so put in the cares at nyght goynge to bedde, and a lytell dronke thereof, is good against all defnes.

¶ It easeth the payn in the teethe, when it is a longe tyme holden in the mouthe, it causoth a swete brethe, and heleth the rottyng tethe.

¶ It heleth the canker in the mouthe, in the teethe, in the lyppes, and in the tongue, whan it is longe time holden in the mouthe.

¶ It cawseth the heuy togue to become light and wel spekyng.

[1] "The Vertuose boke of Distyllacyon of the Waters of all maner of Herbes, with the fygures of the styllatoryes, Fyrst made and compyled by the thyrte yeres study and labour of the most conynge and famous master of phisyke, Master Iherom bruynswyke. And now newly Translated out of Duyche into Englysshe," etc. Lond., 1572.

[2] Lethargy.

¶ It heleth the shorte brethe whan it is dro'ne with water wheras the liges be soden in, and banisheth al flemmes.

¶ It causeth good dygestynge and appetyte for to eat, and taketh away all bolkynge.[1]

¶ It dryveth the wyndes out of the body, and is good agaynst the evyll stomake.

¶ It caseth the fayntenes of the harte, the payn of the mylte, the yelowe Jaundis, the dropsy, the yll lymmes, the geute, in the handys and in the fete, the payne in the brestes whan they be swollen, and heleth al diseases in the bladder, and breaketh the stone.

¶ It withdryveth venym that hath been taken in meat or in drynke, whā a lytell tryacle is put therto.

¶ It heleth the Canckes[2] and all dyseases coming of colde.

¶ It heleth the brenkyng of the body, and of al membres whan it is rubbed therwith by the fyre biii dayes contynnynge.

¶ It is good to be dronke agaynst the sodeyn dede.

¶ It heleth all scabbes of the body, and all colde swellynges, enoynted or washed therwith, and also a lytell therof dronke.

¶ It heleth all shronke sinewes, and causeth them to become softe and right.

¶ It heleth the febres tertiana and quartana, when it is dronke an houre before, or the febres becometh on a body.

¶ It heleth the venymous bytes, and also of a madde dogge, whan they be wasshed therwith.

¶ It heleth all stynkyng woundes whan they be wasshed therwith."

From use in medicine, Aqua Vitæ soon came into domestic use, and here it given one of Iherom Bruynswyke's "Styllatoryes," which he says was the "comon fornays" which was "well beknowen amonge the potters, made of erthe leded or glased, and it may be removed from the one place to the other."

It was in a still of this sort that the old housewives of the sixteenth and succeeding centuries used to concoct their strong and cordial waters—a practice

[1] Belching.   [2] Pleurisy.

which has given, and left to, our own times, the name of "Still-room," as the housekeeper's own particular domain. They experimented on almost every herb that grew, and some of their concoctions must have been exceedingly nasty. Yet some of their recipes read as if they were comforting, and they were not deficient in variety.

Heywood, in his *Philocothonista, or The Drunkard, Opened, Dissected, and Anatomized*, 1635, p. 48, mentions some of them. " To add to these chiefe and multiplicitie of wines before named, yet there be Stills and Limbecks going, swetting out *Aqua Vitæ* and strong waters deriving their names from *Cynamon, Lemmons, Balme, Angelica, Aniseed, Stomach Water, Hunni*, etc. And to fill up the number, we have plenty of *Vsque-ba'ha*."

The old housewives' books of the latter end of the sixteenth century, until much later, are still in existence, and from them we may learn many drinks of our forefathers, how to make *Ipocras* (*very good*, especially when taken in a " Loving Cup "), to clarify *Whey*, to make *Buttered Beer, Sirrop of Roses or Violets, Rosa Solis, a Caudle for an old Man*, or to distil *Spirits of Spices, Spirits of Wine tasting of what Vegetable you please, Balme Water, Rosemary Water, Sinamon Water, Aqua Rubea*, Spirits of Hony, Rose Water, Vinegar, very many scents, and a distillation called *Aqua Composita*, which entered into many receipts. There are many formulæ for this, but Bruynswyke gives the following :—

"𝔄𝔔𝔘𝔄 𝔙𝔍𝔗𝔈 ℭ𝔒𝔐𝔓𝔒𝔖𝔍𝔗𝔄.

"𝔗𝔥𝔢 same 𝔴𝔞𝔱𝔢𝔯 𝔦𝔰 𝔪𝔞𝔡𝔢 some time of 𝔴𝔶𝔫𝔢 𝔴𝔦𝔱𝔥 𝔰𝔭𝔶𝔠𝔢𝔰 𝔬𝔫𝔢𝔩𝔶, 𝔰𝔬𝔪𝔢𝔱𝔶𝔪𝔢 𝔴𝔦𝔱𝔥 𝔴𝔶𝔫𝔢 𝔞𝔫𝔡 𝔯𝔬𝔱𝔢𝔰 𝔬𝔣 𝔱𝔥𝔢 𝔥𝔢𝔯𝔟𝔢𝔰, 𝔰𝔞𝔪𝔢𝔱𝔶𝔪𝔢 𝔴𝔦𝔱𝔥 𝔱𝔥𝔢 𝔥𝔢𝔯𝔟𝔢𝔰, 𝔰𝔬𝔪𝔢 𝔱𝔶𝔪𝔢 𝔴𝔦𝔱𝔥𝔱𝔥𝔢 𝔯𝔬𝔱𝔢𝔰 𝔞𝔫𝔡 𝔥𝔢𝔯𝔟𝔢𝔰 𝔱𝔬𝔤𝔶𝔡𝔢𝔯, 𝔣𝔬𝔯 𝔞𝔱 𝔞𝔩𝔩 𝔱𝔶𝔪𝔢𝔰 𝔱𝔥𝔢𝔯𝔢𝔱𝔬 𝔪𝔲𝔰𝔱 𝔟𝔢 𝔰𝔱𝔯𝔞𝔫𝔤𝔢 𝔴𝔶𝔫𝔢.

"Take a gallon of strong Gascoigne wine, and Sage, Mints, Red Roses, Time, Pellitorie, Rosemarie, Wild Thime, Camomil, Lavender, of eche an handfull. These herbes shal be stamped all togyder in a Morter, and then putte it in a clene bessell and do herto a pynte of Rose Water, and a quart of romney,[1] and then stoppe it close and let it stand so iii or iiii dayes. Whan ye have so done, put all this togyder in a styllatory and dystyll water of the same; than take your dystylled water, and pore it upon the herbes agayne into the styllatory, and strewe upon it these powders followynge.

¶ Fyrst cloves and cynamon, of eche an halfe ounce, Oryous[2] an ounce, and a few Maces, nutmeggs halfe an ounce, a lytell saffran, muscus, spica nardi, ambre, and some put campher in it, bycawse the materyals be so hote. Stere[3] all the same well to‑ gyder and dystylle it clene of, tyll it come fat lyke oyle, than set awaye your water, and let it be wel kepte. After that make a stronge fyre, and dystyll oyle of it, and receyve it in a fyole,[4] this oyle smelleth above all oyles, and he that letteth one droppe fall on his hande, it will perce through. It is wonderfull good, excellynge many other soberaygne oyles to dyvers dysseases."

Although the Still-room was serviceable for medicinal purposes, yet, as we have seen, there were many comforting drinks made, including *Vsquebath, or Irish aqua vitæ* (a recipe for which we will give in its proper place), and doubtless this contributed much towards the tippling habit of some ladies in the 17th and 18th centuries. We hear somewhat of this in the reign of good Queen Anne (who, by the bye, was irreverently termed " Brandy-faced Nan "), when they used to make, and drink, *Ratifia of Apricocks, Fenouillette of Rhé, Millefleurs, Orangiat, Burgamot*, *Pesicot*, and *Citron Water*, etc., etc., numerous allusions to which are made in the pages of " The Spectator," and other literature of the times. Edward Ward, who had

[1] A Spanish Wine.   [2] ? Orrice.   [3] Stir.   [4] Phial.

no objection to call a spade, a spade, thus plainly speaks out.[1]

"It would make a Man smile to behold her Figure in a front Box, where her twinkling Eyes, by her Afternoon's Drams of Ratifee and cold Tea, sparkle more than her Pendants. . . . Her closet is always as well stor'd with Juleps, Restoratives, and Strong Waters, as an Apothecary's Shop, or a Distiller's Laboratory; and is, herself, so notable a Housewife in the Art of preparing them, that she has a larger Collection of Chemical Receipts than a Dutch Mountebank. . . . As soon as she rises, she must have a Salutary Dram to keep her Stomach from the Cholick; a Whet before she eats, to procure Appetite; after eating, a plentiful Dose for Concoction; and to be sure a Bottle of Brandy under her Bed side for fear of fainting in the Night."

There is no necessity to multiply instances of the feminine liking for brandy, for everyone finds numerous examples in his reading, from Juliet's nurse,[2] who, after Tybalt's death, says, "Give me some *aqua vitæ*," to old Lady Clermont, of whom Grantley Berkeley tells the following story[3] :—

"Prominent among my earliest Brighton reminiscences are those of old Lady Clermont, who was a frequent guest at the Pavilion. Her physician had recommended a moderate use of stimulants, to supply that energy which was deficient in her system, and brandy had been suggested in a prescribed quantity,

---

[1] *Adam and Eve stript of their furbelows*, 1710 (?)
[2] Act III., s. 3. [3] *My Life and Recollections*, Vol. I., p. 50.

to be mixed with her tea. I remember well having my curiosity excited by this, to me, novel form of taking medicine, and holding on by the back of a chair to watch the *modus operandi*. Very much to my astonishment, the patient held a liqueur bottle over a cup of tea, and began to pour out its contents, with a peculiar purblind look, upon the *back* of a teaspoon. Presently, she seemed suddenly to become aware of what she was about, turned up the spoon the right way, and carefully measured, and added the quantity to which she had been restricted. The Tea, so strongly 'laced,' she now drank with great apparent gusto."

We derive our name of Brandy from the Dutch *brand-wijn*, or the German brannt-wein, that is, *burnt* or distilled *wine;* and in the 17th and 18th centuries it was generally spelt, and spoken of as brandy wine. But, also, in those centuries was it known by the name of " Nantz," from the town (Nantes, the capital of the Loire Inferieure) whence it came. But this name was changed early last century, when the trade left Nantes, and got into the Charente district, of which Cognac was the centre ; so what used to be "right good Nantz" of the old smuggling days, turned into the delicate, many-starred " Cognac " of our times.

It was an eminently respectable spirit. Whiskey was practically unknown out of Scotland and Ireland. Gin was the drink of the common people, and rum was considered only fit for sailors. Even Dr. Johnson, though so fond of his tea, was also fond of brandy, as Boswell chronicles of him, when in his 70th year :

"On Wednesday, April 7, I dined with him at Sir Joshua Reynolds's. Johnson harangued upon the qualities of different liquors; and spoke with great contempt of claret, as so weak, that 'a man would be drowned by it, before it made him drunk.' He was persuaded to drink one glass of it, that he might judge, not from recollection, which might be dim, but from immediate sensation. He shook his head, and said, 'Poor stuff! No, sir, claret is the liquor for boys; port for men; but he who aspires to be a hero' (smiling) 'must drink brandy. In the first place the flavour of brandy is the most grateful to the palate, and then brandy will do soonest for a man what drinking *can* do for him. There are, indeed, few who are able to drink brandy. That is a power rather to be wished for than attained.'"

And two years later on he gives another illustration of the doctor's liking for strong potations. "Mr. Eliot mentioned a curious liquor peculiar to his country, which the Cornish fishermen drink. They call it *Mahogany;* and it is made of two parts gin and one part treacle, well beaten together. I begged to have some of it made, which was done with proper skill by Mr. Eliot. I thought it very good liquor, and said it was a counterpart of what is called *Athol porridge*[1] in the Highlands of Scotland, which is a mixture of whiskey and honey. Johnson said 'That must be a better liquor than the Cornish, for both its component parts are better.' He also observed, '*Mahogany* must be a modern name; for it is not long since the wood called mahogany was known in this country. I

[1] Now called Athol brose.

mentioned his scale of liquors : Claret for boys—port for men—brandy for heroes. 'Then,' said Mr. Burke, 'let me have claret; I love to be a boy; to have the careless gaiety of boyish days,' Johnson : ' I should drink claret too, if it would give me that ; but it does not ; it neither makes boys men, nor men boys. You'll be drowned in it before it has any effect upon you.' "

But it was the spirit always drunk by gentlemen until well on in this century, as we see by Mr. Pickwick, whose constant resource in all cases of difficulty, was a glass of brandy. Pale brandy was not so much drank as brown, which is now only taken, when very old, as a liqueur, although a brown brandy of very dubious quality is to be met with in some country public houses. Brandy, like every other spirit, developes its ethers with age, gets mellower, and of exquisite flavour; and its popularity would undoubtedly be revived if the drinker were only sure he could get such brandy as the many starred brands of Hennessy and Martell, instead of that awful substitute so often given—British brandy, made of raw potato spirit.

The soil of the Charente slope is particularly adapted to the growth of the vine, although, as in all vine-growing countries some districts, and even small patches of land, produce finer wine than others. The grapes are white, not much larger than good-sized currants, and the vines seldom bear fruit until four or five years from their planting, and are most vigorous at the age of from ten to thirty. Many bear well up to fifty and seventy, and some are fruitful at one hundred years or more.

As a rule, the large firms do not distil the brandy they sell, but leave that operation to the small farmers round about, and then blend their products; as, to produce the quantity they sell, enormous distilling space would be necessary, wine only producing one-eighth or one-tenth of alcohol to its bulk. The farmer's distillery is very primitive; merely a simple boiler with a head or receiver, and a worm surrounded with cold water. There are generally two of these stills at work, and when once the farmer commences making his brandy, he keeps on day and night, bivouacking near the stills, until he has converted all his wine into crude spirit, as colourless as water, which he carts off, just as it is, to the brandy factory for sale. There it is tasted, measured, and put into new casks of oak, hooped round with chestnut wood. These casks are branded with the date, together with the quality and place of growth of the wine from which the brandy was distilled, and they remain some time in stock before their contents are blended in the proportions which the firm deem suitable.

This new spirit is housed on a floor over large vats, which are filled from selected casks, the spirit being filtered through flannel discs on its way. This mixes the various growths pretty well, but the spirit is run into other vats, being forced through filters of a peculiar kind of paper, almost like paste-board. When it gets to the second series of vats, it is kept well stirred, to prevent the heavier spirit sinking to the bottom. It is then drawn off into casks, which are bunged up, and stored for several years that the brandy may mature, and that the fusel oil may develope into the ethyls, which give such flavour and fragrance to the brandy.

Perhaps the oldest house in the Cognac district is Hennessy's, but it would be invidious to say that their brandy was superior either to Martell's, Otard and Dupuy's, the Société Vignicole, Courvoisier, or many other firms. That must be left to individual taste. But from these firms we can rely on having pure unadulterated brandies, the pure product of the vine, without any admixture of grain or beet spirit. At one time, adulteration was rife among the farmers, but in 1857 and 1858 several of them were prosecuted, and they are now credited with having abjured their evil ways.

J. A.

GIN.

Massinger's *Duke of Milan*—Pope's *Epilogue to Satires*—The *Dunciad*—William III.—Lord Hervey—Sir R. Walpole—The Fall of Madame Geneva—Hogarth's Gin Lane—Schiedam Adulteration—Gin Sling—Captain Dudley Bradstreet—Tom and Jerry Hawthorn.

GIN is an alcoholic drink distilled from malt or from unmalted barley or other grain, and afterwards rectified and flavoured. The word is French, *genièvre*, juniper, corrupted into *Geneva*, and subsequently into its present form. It is to the berries of the juniper that the best Hollands owes its flavour.

Perhaps one of the earliest allusions to gin is in Massinger's *Duke of Milan* (1623), Act I., scene i., when Graccho, a creature of Mariana, says to the courtier Julio, of a chance drunkard,

"Bid him sleep;
'Tis a sign he has ta'en his liquor, and if you meet
An officer preaching of sobriety,
Unless he read it in Geneva print,
Lay him by the heels."

In this extract the word is played upon, Geneva suggesting both the habit of spirit-drinking and Calvinistic doctrine.

When Pope wrote, the corrupted word "Gin" had become common. In the *Epilogue to the Satires*, I. 130.

> "Vice thus abused, demands a nation's care ;
> This calls the Church to deprecate our sin,
> And hurls the thunder of our laws on gin."

Pope has added a note to this passage, to the effect that gin had almost destroyed the lowest rank of the people before it was restrained by Parliament in 1736.

Another early allusion to Geneva is to be found in *Carmina Quadragesimalia*, Oxford, 1723, vol. i., p. 7, in a copy of verses contributed by Salusbury Cade, elected from Westminster to Ch. Ch. in 1714

The thesis of which Salusbury Cade maintained the affirmative, is whether life consists in heat, or in the original *An vita consistat in calore ?*

> "Dum tremula hyberno Dipsas superimminet igni
>   Et dextra cyathum sustinet, ore tubum,
> Alternis vicibus fumos hauritque, bibitque
>   Quam dat arundo sitim grata Geneva levat.
> Languenti hic ingens stomacho est fultura, nec alvus
>   Nunc Hypochondriacis flatibus ægra tumet.
> Liberior fluit in tepido nunc corpore sanguis,
>   Hinc nova vis membris et novus inde calor.
> Si quando audieris vetulam hanc periisse : Genevæ
>   Dicas ampullam non renovasse suam."

Which being Englished, is

> Dipsas, who shivers by her wintry fire,
> While her pipe's smoke ascends in spire on spire,

Alternate puffs and drinks—Geneva lays
That thirst the weed is wont in her to raise.
With this her belly propped, its pain expels ;
Intestine wind no more her stomach swells ;
A freer blood runs leaping through her frame,
New heat, new strength recalls the ancient game.
And should you hear she's dead, the cause you'll know
Was that Geneva in her jug ran low."

In the *Dunciad*, which Pope wrote in 1726 (book iii., l. 143), we read,—

" A second see, by meeker manners known,
And modest as the maid that sips alone ;
From the strong fate of drams if thou get free,
Another D'Urfey, Ward ! shall sing in thee !
Thee shall each ale-house, thee each gill-house [1] mourn,
And answering gin-shops sourer sighs return."

An early allusion to Geneva is in a poem by Alexander Blunt, Distiller, 8vo, 1729, price 6*d.*, called "Geneva," addressed to the Right Honourable Sir R—— W——. It commences,

"Thy virtues, O Geneva! yet unsung
By ancient or by modern bard, the muse
In verse sublime shall celebrate. And thou
O W—— statesman most profound! vouchsafe
To lend a gracious ear ; for fame reports
That thou with zeal assiduous dost attempt
Superior to *Canary* or *Champaigne*
Geneva salutiferous to enhance ;
To rescue it from hand of porter vile,
And basket woman, and to the bouffet

---

[1] Of the word gill-house a recent editor of Pope observes that it is doubtful whether it is to be understood as a house where gill, or beer impregnated with ground-ivy, was sold, or whether as an inferior tavern, where beer was sold by the measure known as a gill.

Of lady delicate and courtier grand
Exalt it ; well from thee may it assume
The glorious modern name of *royal* BOB!"

Though "Brandy cognac, Jamaica Rum, and costly Arrack" are alluded to, there is no mention of Hollands in the poem, which is a defence of *Geneva* against *ale*.

In this poem a statement is contained that Geneva was introduced by William III., and that he himself drank it.

"Great Nassau,
Immortal name! Britain's deliverer
From slavery, from wooden shoes and chains,
Dungeons and fire ; attendants on the sway
Of tyrants bigotted and zeal accurst,
Of holy butchers, prelates insolent,
Despotic and bloodthirsty! He who did
Expiring liberty revive (who wrought
Salvation wondrous! God-like hero! He
It was, who to compleat our happiness
With liberty, restored Geneva introduced.
O Britons. O my countrymen can you
To glorious William now commence ingrates
And spurn his ashes? Can you vilify
The sovereign cordial he has pointed out,
Which by your own misconduct only can
Prove detrimental? Martial William drank
Geneva, yet no age could ever boast
A braver prince than he. Within his breast
Glowed every royal virtue! Little sign,
O Genius of *malt liquor!* that Geneva
Debilitates the limbs and health impairs
And mind enervates. Men for learning famed
And skill in medicine prescribed it then
Frequent in recipe, nor did it want

Success to recommend its virtues vast
To late posterity."

In 1736 Lord Hervey, describing the state of England, says: The drunkenness of the common people was so universal by the retailing a liquor called Gin, with which they could get drunk for a groat, that the whole town of London and many towns in the country swarmed with drunken people from morning till night, and were more like a scene of a Bacchanal than the residence of a civil society.

Retailers exhibited placards in their windows, intimating that people might get drunk for the sum of 1*d.* and that clean straw would be provided for customers in the most comfortable of cellars.

On Feb. 20, 1736, in the ninth year of George II., a petition of the Justices of the Peace for Middlesex against the excessive use of spirituous liquors was presented to the House of Commons, setting forth- That the drinking of Geneva and other distilled spirituous liquors had greatly increased, especially among the people of inferior rank, that the constant and excessive use thereof had destroyed thousands of his Majesty's subjects, debauching their morals, etc., that the " pernicious liquor " was then sold not only by the distillers and Geneva shops, but many other persons of inferior trades, "by which means journeymen, apprentices and servants were drawn in to taste, and by degrees to like, approve, and immoderately to drink thereof," and that the petitioners therefore prayed that the House would take the premises into their serious consideration, etc. The House having resolved itself into a committee on Feb. 23, Sir Joseph Jekyll moved the following resolutions : (1) That the low price of spirituous liquors is the principal inducement to the excessive and pernicious use thereof. (2) That a discouragement should be given to their use by a duty. (3) That the vending, etc., of such liquors be restrained to persons keeping public brandy-shops, victualling houses, coffee houses, ale houses and inn-holders, and to such apothecaries and surgeons as should make use of the same by way of medicine only ; and, (4) That no person keeping a public brandy-shop, etc., should be permitted to vend, etc., such liquors, but by licence with duty payable thereon. These Resolutions were agreed on without debate.

On March 8, Mr. William Pulteney affixed a duty of 20*s.* per gallon on gin, on the grounds of ancient use and sanction, and of its reducing many thousands of families at once to a state of despair.

Sir Robert Walpole had no immediate concern in the laying of this tax on spirituous liquors, but suffered therefrom much unmerited obloquy. The bill was presented by Jekyll from a spirit of philanthropy, which led him to contemplate with horror the progress of vice that marked the popular attachment to this inflammatory poison. The populace showed their disapprobation of this Act in their usual fashion of riot and violence. We are told in Coxe's Walpole that numerous desperados continued the clandestine sale of gin in defiance of every restriction.

The duty of 20*s.* per gallon was repealed 16 Geo. II., c. 8. On the 28th of September, 1736, it was deemed necessary to send a detachment of sixty soldiers from Kensington to protect the house of Sir Joseph Jekyll, the Master of the Rolls, in Chancery Lane, from the violence threatened by the populace against this eminent lawyer. Two soldiers with their bayonets fixed were planted as sentinels at the little door next Chancery Lane, and the great doors were shut up, the rest of the soldiers kept garrison in the stables in the yard.

This agitation gave rise to many a ballad and broadside, such as the "Fall of Bob," or the Oracle of Gin," a tragedy; and "Desolation, or the Fall of Gin," a poem.

THE LAMENTABLE FALL OF MADAME GENEVA.—
29 *Sept.*, 1736.[1]

The Woman holds a song to ye tune, to ye Children in ye Wood.

"Good lack, good lack, and Well-a-day,
That Madame Gin should fall:
Superior Powers she must obey.
This Act will starve us all."

The Man has the second part to ye same tune.

"Th' Afflicted she has caus'd to sing,
The Cripple leap and dance;
All those who die for love of Gin
Go to Heaven in a Trance."

Underneath are these verses—

[1] There are two other prints connected with this event, all published at the same time. One is "The Funeral Procession of Madame Geneva, Sept. 29, 1736." The other is a Memorial, "To the Mortal Memory of Madame Geneva, who died Sept. 29, 1736. Her weeping Servants and loving Friends, consecrate this Tomb."

"The Scene appears, and Madame's Crew
In deep Despair, Exposed to view.
See Tinkers, Cobblers, and cold Watchmen,
With B——s and W——s as drunk as Dutchmen.
All mingling with the Common Throng,
Resort to hear her Passing Song.

"Whilst Mirth suppress'd by Parliament,
In Sober Sadness all lament,
Pursued by Jekyl's indignation,
She's brought to utter desolation.
With Oaths they storm their Monarch's name,
And curse their Hands that form'd the Scheme.

"All Billingsgate their Case Bemoan,
And Rag-fair Change in Mourning's hung;
Queen Gin, for whom they'd sacrifice
Their Shirts and Smocks, nay, both their Eyes.
Rather than She want Contribution,
They'd trudge the Streets without their shoes on."

The following verses on the Gin Act, in 1736, are supposed by John Nichols to be the production of Dr. Johnson.

"Pensilibus fusis cyatho comitata Supremo,
  Terribili fremitu stridula mæret anus.
O longum formosa vale mihi vita decusque,
  Fida comes mensæ fida comesque tori!
Eheu quam longo tecum consumerer ævo,
  Heu quam tristitiæ dulce lenimen eras.
Æternum direpta mihi, sed quid moror istis,
  Stat, fixum est, nequeunt jam revocare preces;
I, quoniam sic fata vocant, liceat mihi tantum,
  Vivere te viva te moriente mori."

A clever cento from the Latin poets, which may be thus represented in English :—

"> . . . Left with her last glass alone,
Thus loud laments her lot, the squeaking crone:
Farewell, my life and beauty, thou art sped,
Faithful companion of my board and bed.
My earthly term fain with thee would I live,
Who to my sorrowing heart can'st solace give.
Bereft of gin, alas! am I for aye!
The Act is passed. 'Tis all in vain to pray.
Go where the Fates may call, and know that I
Living, with thee would live, and dying, die!"

Hogarth's Gin Lane was advertised in 1751, with a note that, as its subject was calculated to reform some reigning vices peculiar to the lower class of people, in hopes to render them of more extensive use, the author had published them in the cheapest manner possible. "The cheapest manner possible" was one shilling which in those days was a fairly good price for a print. The following lame and defamatory verse was composed for the occasion by the Rev. James Townley:—

"GIN LANE.

Gin, cursed fiend, with fury fraught,
  Makes human race a prey;
It enters by a deadly drought,
  And steals our life away.
Virtue and Truth, driven to despair,
  Its rage compels to fly;
But cherishes, with hellish care,
  Theft, murder, perjury.
Damned cup, that on the vitals preys,
  That liquid fire contains;
Which madness to the heart conveys,
  And rolls it through the veins."

Hogarth tells us that in Gin Lane every circumstance of the horrid effects of gin drinking is brought to view *in terrorem.* Idleness, poverty, misery, and distress, which drives even to madness and death, are the only objects that are to be seen; and not a house in tolerable condition but the pawnbrokers and gin shop. The same moral is taught by Cruikshank, but not before his conversion to teetotalism.

Schiedam is the metropolis of gin, and its numerous distilleries are omnivorous, taking with equal relish cargoes of rye and buckwheat from Russia, and damaged rice or any cereal from other countries, and sometimes also potato spirit from Hamburg.

The distillery of De Kuypers is probably that of the greatest note, and that firm's black square bottles, packed in cases filled with hemp husks, are known all over the world. In Africa "square face" is king, but he frequently holds some counterfeit liquor, even sometimes the vilest of Cape Smoke.

Schiedam is the Mecca of the Dutchman, the birthplace of his beloved Schnapps. This drink is always acceptable, and fifty good reasons exist for drinking it.

The chief varieties of the aromatised popular spirit called gin are now known as Geneva, Hollands, and Schiedam. It is current in some parts of Africa as a species of coin.

Since, however, every distiller varies his materials and their proportions, the species of this beverage are practically unlimited. Generally, however, the distinction is clear between Hollands or Dutch and English gin. The former is commonly purer than the highly flavoured and too frequently adulterated British product.

The matters employed in the adulteration are very many. Corianders, crushed almond cake, angelica root powdered, liquorice, cardamoms, cassia, cinnamon, grains of paradise, and cayenne pepper, and many more substances take the place of the berries of the juniper tree. As these substances frequently produce a cloudy appearance, the liquid is subsequently refined by other adulterants, such as alum, sulphate of zinc, and acetate of lead.

The variety of gin dear to ancient beldams, which is known as Cordial, is more highly sweetened and aromatized than the ordinary quality.

The alcoholic strength of gin as commonly sold ranges from 22 to 48 degrees. The amount of sugar varies between 2 and 9 per cent.

Gin is a beneficial diuretic, but the compounds sold under that name are too often detrimental in their effects.

A popular drink called gin-sling takes its name from John Collins, formerly a celebrated waiter in Limmer's old house. The old lines on this drink ran as follows :—

> " My name is John Collins, head waiter at Limmer's,
>   Corner of Conduit Street, Hanover Square.
> My chief occupation is filling of brimmers
>   For all the young gentlemen frequenters there."

The poetry is very far from bad, and so was the liquor. It was a composition of gin, soda water, lemon, and sugar. John was abbreviated to gin and Collins to sling.

Gin has had many popular names, but why gin

should be called Old Tom by the publicans and lower orders of London has sometimes puzzled those who are inquisitive enough to consider the subject etymologically. The answer may, perhaps, be found in a curious book, called "The Life and Uncommon Adventures of Captain Dudley Bradstreet, Dublin, 1755." Captain Dudley, a government spy of the Count Fathom species, after declaring that the selling of Geneva in a less quantity than two gallons had been prohibited, says: "Most of the gaols were full, on account of this Act, and it occurred to me to venture upon the trade. I got an acquaintance to rent a house in Blue Anchor Alley, in St. Luke's parish, who privately conveyed his bargain to me: I then got it well secured, and laid out in a bed and other furniture five pounds, in provision and drink that would keep, about two pounds, and purchased in Moorfields the sign of a cat and had it nailed to a street window. I then caused a leaden pipe, the small end out about an inch, to be placed under the paw of the cat, the end that was within had a funnel to it.

"When my house was ready for business I inquired what distiller in London was most famous for good gin, and was assured by several that it was Mr. L——dale, in Holborn.[1] To him I went, and laid out thirteen pounds. . . . The cargo was sent to my house, at the back of which there was a way to go in or out. When the liquor was properly disposed, I got a person

---

[1] Whose premises were burnt down during the Lord George Gordon riots. Dickens immortalized Langdale in *Barnaby Rudge*. The distillery is still in existence at the same place.

to inform a few of the mob that gin would be sold by the cat at my window next day, provided they put the money in his mouth, from whence there was a hole which conveyed it to me." This, by the way, is a rare anticipation of our automatic sweetstuff, scent, and other machines. To continue : " At night I took possession of my den, and got up early next morning to be ready for custom. It was over three hours before anybody called, which made me almost despair of the project ; at last I heard the chink of money and a comfortable voice say, ' Puss, give me two pennyworth of gin !' I instantly put my mouth to the tube and bid them receive it from the pipe under her paw " — the cat seems to have changed its sex in this short interval of time—"and then measured and poured it into the funnel, from whence they soon received it. Before night I took six shillings, the next day about thirty shillings, and afterwards three or four pounds a day. From all parts of London people used to resort to me in such numbers that my neighbours could scarcely get in and out of their houses. After this manner I went on for a month, in which time I cleared upwards of two-and-twenty pounds.

So far Captain Bradstreet, " but," says the Editor of *Notes & Queries*, "the ghost of 'old Tom Hodges' will probably enter a protest against Captain Bradstreet's cat."

Another popular name for gin was used when Corinthian Tom and Jerry Hawthorn visited Bob Logic in the Fleet. Bob says, "Let us spend the day comfortably, and in the evening I will introduce you both to my friend the haberdasher. He is a good whistler,[1] and his shop always abounds with some prime articles that you will like to look at. . . ." A glass or two of wine made them as gay as larks, and a hint from Jerry to Logic about the whistler brought them into the shop of the latter in a twinkling.

Hawthorne, with great surprise, said, "Where are we? This is no haberdasher's. It's a ———"

"No nosing, Jerry," replied Logic, with a grin; "you're wrong, the man is a dealer in tape."

[1] A whistling shop was a sly grog-shop. No spirits were allowed in the Fleet prison, but of course they were introduced, and could be got at some places. The method of telling who could be trusted, was for the customers to whistle—hence the term.

WHISKEY.

Uisge-beatha—"My Stint"—Its Manufacture—Good and Bad—Early Mentions of Whiskey—Materials used in its Manufacture—St. Thorwald—Duncan Forbes and Ferrintosh—Duty on Whiskey—Silent Spirit—Artificial Maturing.

NO matter in what country, wherever it was known, alcohol has been hailed as the Water of Life, even in the Gaelic. *Uisge-beatha*, or, as we term it, whiskey, bears literally that interpretation. This is "the wine of the country," both in Ireland and Scotland, and the quantities drank, without any apparently hurtful effect, is astonishing to a southern Englishman. Northwards, on the border land, it is a question whether more whiskey is not drunk, *pro rata*, than in Scotland.

Still, even there, every one is not gifted, as was the Irishman spoken of by John Wilson Croker. He tells the story of a lawsuit, in which a life insurance company disputed a claim, on the ground that the death was caused by excessive drinking. One witness for the plaintiff was called, who deposed that, for the last eighteen years of his life, he had been in the nightly habit of imbibing *twenty-four tumblers of whiskey punch*. The cross-examining counsel wished to know whether he would swear to that, or whether he ever overstepped that limit. The witness replied that he was upon his oath, and would swear no farther; "for I never kept count beyond the two dozen, though there is no saying how many beyond I might drink to make myself comfortable; but *that's my stint.*"

Good whiskey should be made solely from the finest barley malt, and is so made by the largest and best distillers; but the smaller ones, and those who are in a hurry to get rich by any means, use all kinds of refuse grain, and produce a spirit which, if drank new, is neither more nor less than rank poison. The fusel oil, which is present in all distillations from grain, requires time to resolve itself into those delicate ethers, which, while enhancing the flavour and bouquet of the spirit, are harmless. Good whiskey, properly matured, mixed with a sufficient quantity of water, and used in moderation, is a good and a wholesome drink, acting also in lieu of food.

When this life-giving liquor was discovered is uncertain. Edward Campion, in his *History of Ireland*, 1633, speaking of a famine which happened in 1316, says that it was caused by the soldiers eating flesh and drinking *aqua vitæ* in Lent; and, in another place, he states that a knight, called Savage, who lived in 1350, having prepared an army against the Irish, allowed to every soldier, before he buckled with the enemy, a mighty draught of *aqua vitæ*, wine, or old ale.

Walter Harris, in his *Hibernica*, 1757, says that in the reign of Henry VIII. it was decreed that there be but one maker of *aqua vitæ* in every borough town, upon pain of 6s. 8d.; and that no *wheaten malt* go to any Irishman's country, upon pain of forfeiture of the same in value, except only bread, ale, or *aqua vitæ*.

In a little book, *Delightes for Ladies*, etc., 1602, is the following recipe for *Usquebath, or Irish Aqua Vitæ*:—

"To every gallon of good Aqua Composita, put two ounces of chosen liquerice, bruised and cut into small peeces, but first clensed from all his filth, and two ounces of Annis seeds that are cleane and bruised. Let them macerate five or six daies in a wodden Vessel, stopping the same close, and then draw off as much as will runne cleere, dissolving in that cleare Aqua Vitæ five or six spoonfuls of the best Malassoes you can get; Spanish cute, if you can get it, is thought better than Malassoes; then put this into another vessell; and after three or foure daies (the more the better), when the liquor hath fined itself, you may use the same; some add Dates and Raisons of the Sun to this receipt: those groundes which remaine, you may redistill, and make more Aqua Composita of them, and of that Aqua Composita you may make more Usquebath."

The distillation of whiskey in Ireland, on a large scale, is of comparatively modern date, the *poteen* having been manufactured in illicit stills, in inaccessible and unhandy places. Now, Roe's distillery turns out over two million gallons a year, and Jameson's more than a million and a half. The whiskey made by these firms, that of Sir John Power & Sons, and some others, is distilled from pure malt; but there are many distilleries that send out a spirit made from molasses, beet-root, potatoes, and other things, which cannot possibly be called whiskey, which has brought Irish whiskey somewhat into disrepute, to the great advantage of the Scotch distillers. Again, unmalted grain is used, which gives a practically tasteless spirit, which is almost entirely deficient in the grateful ethers, and is only so much raw alcohol and water, a very different article to that which occasioned the following verses :—

"Oh, Whiskey Punch, I love you much, for you're the very thing,
To level all distinctions 'twixt a beggar and a king.
You lift me up so aisy, and so softly let me down,
That the devil a hair I care what I wear, a caubeen or a crown.

"While you're a-coorsin' through my veins I feel mighty pleasant,
That I cannot just exactly tell whether I'm a prince or peasant;
Maybe I'm one, maybe the other, but that gives me small trouble,
By the Powers! I believe I'm both on 'em, for I think I'm seein' double."

Scotch whiskey is the same as Irish, and should be similarly made from pure malted barley. No one knows when it was first made; but, until the time of the Pretender, it was hardly known in the Lowlands, being a drink strictly of the Highlanders. There is a tradition of a certain St. Thorwald, whose name may be sought for in vain in the pages of Alban Butler, who had a cell in the side of a hill looking upon the Esk. He is said to have possessed a wonderful elixir, famous for curing all diseases, and, consequently, he was resorted to by pilgrims both far and near. Could it be that he had a whiskey still? I know not; but to this day a spring on the site of his hermitage helps to supply the Langholm distillery.

Perhaps the earliest historical account of Scotch whiskey is the grant, in 1690, to Duncan Forbes of Culloden, in consideration of his services to William III., of the privilege of distilling whiskey, duty free, in the barony of Ferrintosh. Naturally, a number of distilleries were erected there, and Ferrintosh became the generic term for whiskey. In 1785 this grant was annulled on payment of £20,000 to the representatives of Duncan Forbes, a proceeding which Robert Burns thus wrote about, in his "Scotch Drink":—

> "Thee, Ferrintosh! O sadly lost!
> Scotland laments from coast to coast!
> Now colic-grips an' barkin' hoast
>   May kill us a';
> For loyal Forbes' *chartered boast*
>   Is ta'en awa'."

The Highland risings made the Lowlanders more familiar with this spirit; but it was a long time before the drink became general, and a far longer before it was generally introduced into England. "Bonnie Prince Charlie" got too fond of it, and his affection for strong drinks was life-long. George IV., on his visit to Scotland, thought the best way to popularise himself on his arrival was to call for, and drink, a glass of whiskey; and even our good Queen has tasted "Athol-brose."

The manufacture of whiskey was encouraged for several reasons: first, that it gave employment; secondly, that it used up large quantities of grain, to the benefit of the farmer; and thirdly, it was hoped that it would, in many cases, supersede the French brandy, which was most extensively smuggled. But Government imposed so high a duty, that illicit stills sprang up everywhere, and contraband whiskey was universally drank, the smugglers openly bringing their wares down south, and in such force as to defy the Excise, and frequently the military. A wise step was then taken, and in 1823 the excise duty was lowered from 6s. 2d. to 2s. 4¾d. per imperial gallon, a proceeding which, in a year, doubled the output of exciseable spirits; but, by degrees, fiscal exigencies have raised it to 10s. per proof gallon. Now, the quantity of homemade spirits on which duty was paid for the year ending 31st March, 1890, is as follows:—

England.	Scotland.	Ireland.
Galls.	*Galls.*	*Galls.*
12,636,060	9,463,012	7,521,998

or in all, 29,621,070 gallons, yielding a revenue of £14,810,522.

It would be invidious to particularize any of the large Scotch distilleries, which mostly owe their fame to the excellence of their malt and the extreme purity of their water, together with the fact that peat is extensively used as fuel, even to the drying of the malt; but "Glenlivet" has a name as world-wide as "Ferrintosh." Do we not read in the *Bon Gualtier Ballads* that—

"Fhairhson had a son
　　Who married Noah's daughter,
　And nearly spoiled ta flood,
　　By trinking up ta water;
　Which he would have done,
　　I at least pelieve it,
　Had ta mixture peen
　　Only half Glenlivet"?

It was such a famous place that, according to the *Ordnance Gazetteer of Scotland*, there were as many as 200 illicit stills there, in brisk work, at the beginning of the present century.

"Small still" whiskey is undoubtedly the best, for only good materials can be used, as the distillation carries over the flavour of the malt. Hear what Dr. Thudicum says [1]:—

"The product of the patent still derives its name from the fact that it is mere alcohol and water, having no distinctive qualities, telling no tales to nose or palate of the source from which it was obtained, and hence, in the almost poetic spirit of the trade, it is commonly called 'silent spirit.' The owner of a patent still, instead of being confined, like a whiskey distiller, to the use of the best materials, is able to make his spirit from any, even spoiled and waste, materials, and with little reference to any other quality than cheapness. The worst of the spirit thus produced is fit only for methylation, preparatory for being used for trade purposes, exclusive of consumption as a beverage. When intended for a beverage, it must be rectified and flavoured. It thus serves as a basis

[1] *Alcoholic Drinks*, 1884, p. 67.

for the implanting of artificial flavours, which may be those of sham whiskey, sham brandy, or sham rum. . . .

"The presence of grain ethers is the condition of the genuineness of whiskey. Silent spirit, on the other hand, undergoes no change by keeping, and must be flavoured to become drinkable. For that purpose it is either made smoky, to become like Scotch, or it is mixed with Irish pot whiskey, to become like Irish whiskey."

There is yet another and a newer way of altering whiskey, which was shown in the Brewers' Exhibition at Islington, October, 1890, and described in an advertisement in a morning paper as "A Transformation Scene; no Pantomime." This new process of maturing spirits is by subjecting them to the action of compressed air confined in a close chamber. Nothing but atmospheric air is used, which is filtered through pure water before being compressed. The air chamber shown was a cylindrical vessel, which, in practice, would be some twelve feet high or more. It is supplied with a finely perforated floor, at a convenient distance below the top, and it has, besides, one or two lower floors of metallic gauze. The cylinder is charged with the liquor to be treated, and the compressed air is then let into it. The taps having been closed on the completion of this operation, a rotary pump keeps the liquor in continuous circulation as it passes through the floors in the form of a fine shower. As soon as it reaches the gauze floor it breaks up into spray; and, in this minute state of sub-division, it is acted on by the condensed air. This air, rising through a pipe, collects at the top of the cylinder, and in that way it is prevented from interfering with the steady flow of the shower. A slight circulation of the air is at the same time promoted. On the process being completed, the liquor is run into casks, and the air which remains in the vessel is allowed to escape, the quantity of alcohol in combination with it not being worth saving.

The object of this process is to bring about the oxidation of the essential oils contained in the whiskey or other spirit, and to promote their conversion into ethers. It is claimed that this transformation does take place, and that the spirit is changed from a new spirit, and has all the character, mellowness, and flavour of that matured by time. This change is said to be effected in twenty-four hours, and that the spirit has, in that period, put on a maturity of ten years.

J. A.

WOODEN CUAGH OR QUAIGH.
(*Brit. Mus.*)

RUM.

Derivation of Name—Whence Procured—Its Manufacture—Its Price—Trade Rum.

THE etymon of the name of this spirit is somewhat dubious. Some have it that it was formerly spelt (as it now is in French) *Rhum*, and that it is derived from *rheum*, or ρεῦμα, a flowing, on account of its manufacture from the juice of the sugar cane. Others say that, as rum has the strongest odour of any distilled spirit, it is a corruption of the word *aroma*.

Rum is made from the refuse of sugar, and can, of course, be produced wherever sugar is grown. This is notably the case in the West Indies, and the best rum comes thence. The finest, and that commanding the highest price in the market, is from Jamaica; Martinique and Guadaloupe perhaps come next; and Santa Cruz has a very good name. British Guiana, the Brazils, Natal, Queensland, and New South Wales all produce it.

It is made from molasses and the skimmings of the boiling sugar. Molasses is the syrup remaining after the separation of all the saccharine matter which will crystallize, and is a dense, viscous liquid, varying from light yellow to nearly black, according to the source from which it is obtained; but its distillation will not produce rum. Sugar or molasses, if distilled, will produce alcohol, but it will have no character of rum. This peculiar odour is imparted to it by the addition, in distillation, of "skimmings," which are the matters separated from the sugar in clarifying and evaporation; that is to say, the scum of the precipitators, clarifiers and evaporators is mixed with the rinsing of the boiling pans, and is thus called. They contain all the necessaries of fermentation, and when mixed with molasses and "dunder," which is the fermented wash left from distillation, are distilled into rum.

The odour of rum is very volatile; so much so, that it should be casked immediately after distillation. The raw spirit is extremely injurious; but it improves so much by age that, at a sale in Carlisle in 1865, rum, known to be 140 years old, sold at three guineas a bottle. Like all alcohol, rum, when distilled, is white, the colour being given to it, as it used to be in brown brandy, by caramel (burnt sugar). Much of the rum sold in England is made from "silent" spirit, flavoured with butyric ether; and it is this stuff which is sold as "trade rum" for export to Africa. Some years since an action was brought by an African merchant against the vendor of "trade rum" for damages caused by it to his trade. All went merrily till the negroes drank the rum, when it suddenly ceased, owing to its colouring their excreta red, probably owing to the colouring matter.

In the old days of punch drinking, rum was the great ingredient in that beverage, but its use has gradually died out, except among sailors, it still being served out in the navy, on account of its supposed warming qualities. Rum and milk, taken before breakfast, is also a beverage used very extensively.

J. A.

LIQUEURS.

I.

Derivation of Term—Eichhoff—Gregory of Tours—Liqueur Wines—Herb Wines—Scot's *Ivanhoe*—Hydromel—Murrey—Delille—Montaigne—Monastical Liqueurs—Arnold de Villeneuve—Catherine de Medicis—Elixir Ratafia.

THE word *liqueur* has been traced by Eichhoff to a Sanskrit root, viz., *laks* or *lauc*, to see, appear. It is now commonly understood of a drink obtained by distillation, a beverage of which alcohol is the base.

To the ancients liqueurs appear to have been unknown. The art of distillation on which they depend was not apparently discovered till the middle ages. Fermented wines, of which some description will be found in another part of this book, occupied their place at dinner and dessert. Old Falernian when mixed with honey probably bore some near resemblance to what is now understood by liqueur. But this drink was found to have such disastrous effects by way of intoxication that it was forbidden to women to drink of it.

Our ancestors, perhaps in imitation of the ancients, composed a sort of liqueur with the must of wine, in which they had infused berries of the *lentiscus*, or a portion of its tender wood. The artificial wines made either with this *lentiscus*, or with other aromatic herbs, called by Gregory of Tours *vina odoramentis immixta*, were the only approaches to the modern liqueurs, even some time after the discovery of the process of distillation.

Among these liqueur wines must be mentioned that species of cooked wine which was the result of a portion of must reduced to half or a third of its original bulk by boiling. The capitularies of Charlemagne speak of this drink as *vinum coctum*, and the southern provinces called it *Sabe*, from the Latin *sapa*, which with the Romans had the same signification. Both Galen and Hippocrates refer to a Greek composition called *Siræum* or *Hepsema*, which, says Pliny, we call *sapa*. The fashion in which this wine was cooked is shown in the *Pitture antiche d'Ercolano*, t. I., tab. 35.

Those artificial wines which consisted solely of infusions of aromatic or medicinal plants, such as absinthe, aloes, anise, rosemary, hyssop, and so on, were called *herb wines*, and were frequently employed as remedies and preventives. With a herb wine, the wine of a honied absinthe, it was that Fredegonda poisoned him who reproached her with the murder of the Pretextate. The most famous of these wines were those into which entered, besides honey, the spices and aromatic confections of Asia, to which were given the name of pigments. The highly spiced and "most odoriferous" wine sweetened with honey is one of those drinks which Cedric bids Oswald, in *Ivanhoe*,[1] to place upon the board for the refreshment of the Knight Templar. It is mentioned in company with the oldest wine, the best mead, the mightiest ale, the richest *morat*,[2] and the most sparkling cider.

The poets of the thirteenth century speak of this decoction with transport. They regarded it in the light of an exquisite delicacy. As no gentleman's library is complete without the presence of some particular work of which a bookseller is anxious to dispose, so no feast at which pigment was not present was held to be complete by the medieval *gourmet*. Indeed this drink seems to have been all too sweet, and was, in consequence of its inebriating property, like the honied Falernian, partially prohibited. The Council of Aix-la-Chapelle in 817 decreed that on festival days only might this voluptuous cup be introduced into conventual repasts.

Hydromel and hippocras were allied to this category of fermented and almost alcoholic drinks, but they were not liqueurs. Finally certain liqueurs were composed entirely of juices of fruits and held the rank and title of wines. Such were cherry, gooseberry, strawberry wine, and others. Another liqueur wine often cited by the thirteenth-century poets is *Murrey*, a thin drink coloured or otherwise affected by mulberries.

The word liqueur appears to have had a considerable latitude of signification. We talk now of

[1] Scott's *Ivanhoe*, cap. iii.
[2] *Morat* is a composition of honey and mulberries, from which latter its name is derived.

coffee and liqueur, but according to the French poet Delille, who lived at a time very near our own, coffee itself was included under the latter category—

"Cest toi, divin café, dont l'aimable liqueur
Sans altérer la tête épanouit le cœur":

which presents us with a view of coffee akin to that held by Cowper of tea, when he talks in his *Task* (Book IV.) of

"the cups
That cheer but not inebriate."

Liqueurs, indeed, properly so called were not known till long after the distillation of wine had been recognised, probably about the fourteenth century. Many years elapsed before these preparations escaped from the domination of the alchemists. Those religious who employed distillation for the confection of balsams and panaceas seem to have been the first to discover them to the world. Montaigne, in the strange account he has written of his travel in Italy, speaks of the Jesuits of Vicenza—the *Jesuates* as he calls them—who had a liquor shop in their fair monastery, in which were sold phials of scent for a crown. The good fathers appear to have busied themselves in the intervals of their religious exercises with distilling waters of different herbs and flowers for the public use, as well for medicine as for sensual delight. Speaking of Verona, Montaigne says he saw also a religious of monks who call themselves *Jesuates* of St. Jérosme. They are dressed in white under a smoked robe with little white caps. They are not priests, neither do they say mass, nor preach,[1] and they are for the most part ignorant. But they make a boast to be excellent distillers of *eau de naffé*[2] and other waters, both in Verona and elsewhere.

Monastical liqueurs are worthy of a paragraph to themselves. So long as monks have existed, they seem to have manifested a taste for the concoction of these drinks. We can scarcely pass the shop window of a liqueur-seller without having our attention attracted by what the French call a *Kyrielle* or litany of flasks of diverse forms, decorated with tickets bearing such titles as the following:—*Liqueur des Chartreux, Liqueur des Benedictins, Liqueur des Carmes, Liqueur des Trappistes, Liqueur des Pères de Garaison, Liqueur du P. Kermann*, and so on. A large volume might well be composed on these liqueurs alone. About their supposed virtues,—aperient, digestive, antiapoplectic, antispasmodic, anticholeric, tonic, etc., that book might be well supposed likely to stretch out as far as the list of Banquo's issue to the diseased imagination of Macbeth.

The search for the philosopher's stone and the powder of projection was by no means wholly fruitless. It strengthened the hands of chemistry. It was also the cradle of liqueurs. In the early part of the middle ages the learned inhabitants of the convents

---

[1] According to their first institution the Jesuits were not priests. This was conceded to them afterwards by Paul V. Their primitive principal occupation was the assistance of the sick and the distillation of salutiferous waters, whence they were known as "*padri dell' acquavite*," or Fathers of brandies.

[2] A liqueur made with the flower of citron.

devoted their leisure time, of which they appear to have had no lack, to the so-called *magnum opus*. The *magnum opus*, the quintessence, the elixir of long life, were three different denominations of one and the same thing. Monkish intellectual toil was chiefly connected at that time with the study of essences, spirits, alcohols, and distillations. The plants which they sought with the greatest eagerness were rosemary, arnica, elder, camomile, sweet trefoil, rose, borage, balm mint, snake weed, iris, etc.

In the thirteenth century, Arnold de Villeneuve, a celebrated physician, possessed with this devil of a *magnum opus*, formulated the question of the quintessence or elixir of long life in these terms, which became afterwards a dogma for all his monastic successors. "This is the secret, viz., to find substances so homogenous to our nature that they can increase it without inflaming it, continue it without diminishing it . . . as our life continually loses somewhat, until at last all is lost." The outcome of the long and patient labours of the monkish alchemists was certain elixirs and liqueurs, of which the secret composition was transmitted from generation to generation in convents and monasteries. Such liqueurs were in their origin simply a pharmaceutic product. It is only within the last few years comparatively that they have been converted into delicacies after dinner. Our age bears the hall mark of positivism. The monks labour no longer for the sole glory of God and comfort of the sick. Their object at the present day is to effect, it is affirmed, a ready and productive sale.

L

It may be so; happily it is not our business to determine. It is certain that a vast development has taken place in the manufacture of the majority of the monkish liqueurs. The *Chartreux* of *L'Isère* now realize annual benefices of considerable value, of which a portion is said to be contributed to the continually diminishing Papal exchequer, under the title of Peter's pence. Of this medicinal liqueur the active and benevolent element is gathered from herbs scattered on the Alpine mountains cold, or on the slopes of the Pyrenees, or in the sombre forests of the north (see the Prospectus), or in the shops of the apothecaries. But they all assuredly depend upon cognac for their element of life. *Benedictine*, with its four cabalistic letters, A M D G,[1] is made by the monks of Fécamp, at the famous Carthusian monastery of *La Grande Chartreuse*, near Grenoble. The elixir of long life, *de Sept-Fonds*, is made in a convent of the Trappists of l'Allier, and *Trappistine* is the work of the good fathers of the abbey of *La Grâce-Dieu* (Doubs). It is, however, affirmed that only Chartreuse, coloured yellow or green at will, and Trappistine, are the works of religious hands, while all other liqueurs are made by the laics. The methods of fabrication employed in the convents are now well known.[2] Benedictine is the only liqueur which has escaped analysis.

Absinthe is not strictly a liqueur. It substitutes bitter for sweet. This strong spirituous liquor, so prejudicial to French health and morality, is, however,

[1] *Ad majorem Dei gloriam.*
[2] Roret's "*Manuel du distillateur-liquoriste.*"

commonly called a liqueur. Its base is an alcoholate, composed of anise, coriander, and fennel. It is flavoured with wormwood, a species of *artemisia*, and other plants containing *absinthin*. It is said to be commonly coloured with indigo and sulphate of copper. It is prepared chiefly in Switzerland, but much of it is made at Bordeaux.

Arnold de Villeneuve, in his medical treatise, written in Latin, *On the preservation of youth and the retardation of age*, has a sermon upon Golden water. "I have not," he says, "read the properties of this water in books of distinguished authority, but it is to be presumed that, if it exists, it is so sublime a work that they have concealed the method of its preparation, and have even refused to mention its name. Of gold, however, they have spoken, and set it among cordial medicines. They have praised it for the comforting of the heart and for the palliation of leprosy. It is possible that since we every day find things diversified by alteration of substance, acquiring the operations of those other things into which they have been transformed, so out of wine may be made a water of life very different from wine both in colour and in substance, in effect and in operation. And the doubt here is, not about the fact, but how it is brought about. That the bodies of all metals may be reduced into water by the ingenuity of mankind, experience allows us not to question; but the operation and nature of those things by which this end is obtained it is no easy matter to discover."

This golden water was originally nothing else than

eau de vie in which had been macerated certain herbs and aromatic spices to give it taste and colour; afterwards minute portions of metallic gold were added. The ingredients mentioned by Arnold de Villeneuve are rosemary flowers, from which, he says, the water obtains its golden colour, cinnamon, grains of paradise, cloves, cubebs, liquorice, and the like.

In the mind of the middle ages, gold was held to be a remedy for every ill. Many people applied themselves to the task of dissolving this metal and rendering it potable. It was put into drinks, baths, victuals, pills, and the pharmacopeia of the time abounds in elixirs of gold, tinctures of gold, drops of gold, and so on. To please the public eye, those pieces of the precious metal were cast into the composition which we now know as *Eau de vie de Dantzig*.

Catherine de Medicis brought into France all the voluptuous discoveries and superfluities of Italy, and helped to augment considerably the number of new liqueurs and to popularize their usage. Henry II. was especially fond of the *anisette* of Marie Brizard of Bordeaux. Sully, in 1604, examining the objects of luxury in France, found *Populo* and *Rossolio* to have the chief share in the public estimation and expenditure. Of them *Populo* is mentioned in the Letters of Gui-Patin.[1] It was composed of spirits of wine, water, sugar, musk, amber, essence of anise, and essence of cinnamon.

Rossolis, our *Rossolio*, or *Rossoli*, said to be derived,

[1] *Gui-Patin Lettres*, ii. 425.

in consequence of its extreme excellence, from the dew of the sun, *ros solis*, was made of burnt brandy, sugar, and the juice of sweet fruits, such as cherries or mulberries. Louis XIV. was much attached to this particular liqueur. That prepared for him was said to differ a little from the ordinary compound. A receipt is given of the king's drink.

Equal quantities of *eau de vie* and Spanish wine, in which were infused anise, coriander, fennel, citron, angelica, and sugar-candy dissolved in camomile water, and boiled to a thick syrup, were a distinctive feature in this royal liqueur.

Owing to oblivion or ignorance of the *anisette* of Henri II. this monarchical recognition of *rossolio* has led to the supposition that liqueurs were invented to invigorate the senile decrepitude of Louis XIV., but it has been shown that they existed long before his time. George IV. is said to have been attached to liqueurs in much the same way as Louis XIV., who may have supposed that they in some measure improved his health or arrested his decay.

The liqueur industry is chiefly continental, and the liqueurs are very numerous. Holland is famous for its *Curaçoa* and Russia for its *Kummel*, and almost every large district of France has its own speciality of liqueur. Bordeaux[1] is remarkable for its *Anisette*,

[1] One of the most important liqueur manufactories is that of Marie Brizard and Roger of Bordeaux. In 1755 Marie Brizard, in the Quartier S. Pierre, a lady of much devotion and charity, devoted a large portion of her time, in imitation of the monks, to the concoction of medicinal cordials. Of these, her *Anisette*, so called from its chief ingredient, soon attained a wide reputation. Roger married

Dijon for its *Cassis*, Marseilles for its *Absinthe*, Grenoble for its *Ratafias*, and Paris and Lyons are each noted for many different kinds.

The English have attained as yet no high rank as liqueur manufacturers. The prosaic nature of the Trade Returns includes all liqueurs of foreign origin under the heading of "*Sweetened or mixed Spirits.*" It makes no distinction between Eaux and Crèmes or between Ratafias and Elixirs. We have been told that elixirs are yellow and aromatized, and eaux or crèmes white, while ratafias are substantially infusions of fruit. Originally this may have been so. It is not the case at present.

Both *Elixir* and *Ratafia* are interesting from an etymological standpoint. The latter word has excited considerable discussion. Menage, writing it as it was commonly written in his time, *ratafiat*, says it is a term derived from the East Indies. Leibnitz, on the contrary, holds it to be a corruption of *rectifié* applied to alcohol. Another etymology is *rata fiat*. Parties were supposed to enter into a contract, and after drinking the liqueur to say, " Let it be ratified."

Elixir[1] is an Arabic word derived from the Greek, by which the alchemists denoted their powder of projection or philosopher's stone.

---

the niece of this lady, and the firm is now known under their joint names. They manufacture many other liqueurs, but are still chiefly famous for the old medicinal cordial.

[1] الاكسير, *alacsir*, from Gr. ξηρόν, dry.

LIQUEURS.

II.

Liqueur Maker's Guide. GERMAN LIQUEURS: Eau d'Amour—Eau Divine. DANTZIG LIQUEURS: Eau Miraculeuse—Eau Aerienne. FRENCH LIQUEURS: Vespetro — Scubac — Absinthe — Maraschino, etc. The Verger—Vermath, etc.

To a humble and unpretending volume, little known by the world, to the *Cordial and Liqueur Makers' Guide, and Publicans' Instructor*, we are indebted for a large part of the information in the present chapter. This excellent and possibly unique volume of modern date contains some two hundred receipts for the manufacture of the most favourite drinks in their greatest perfection; in addition to a variety of miscellaneous matter of much practical utility to the publicans' profession, though of no immediate interest probably to the readers of the present book. For instance, we are taught therein the mysteries of *Spirit Beading*, or, in exoteric language, the putting a head on weak spirits, and the *fining* of sherry, port, gin, ale, and porter. Most of the receipts, we are assured, have never before appeared in print. They are the result of an experience of some thirty years. A warning is given in the preface about the common and extensive adulteration of liqueurs with essential oils, turpentine, and spirits of wine.

In the first chapter of the *Cordial and Liqueur Makers' Guide*, we find receipts for those familiar beverages which are most common in our respectable public firms— public house is what Bentham would call an emotional term—such as *Peppermint, Cloves, Rum Shrub, Aniseed, Caraway, Noyeau, Raspberry, Gingerette, Orange Bitters, Wormwood Bitters, Lemonade, Capillaire, Cherry Brandy, Cinnamon, Lovage, and Usquebaugh*—of these the receipt for *Lovage* may be taken as a sole representative.

This aromatic drink, which is comparatively rare, is perhaps not generally known to be prepared from a plant indigenous to Liguria, a country of Cisalpine Gaul—from which country its name is through sundry philological decadences derived.[1] After reading this, the student of human nature and mercantile morality will be fully prepared to learn that the plant indigenous to Liguria enters in no way into its composition.

Mix, says the receipt, five drams of oil of nutmegs, five drams of oil of cassia, and three drams of oil of caraway in a quart of strong spirits of wine. Shake it well, and put it into a ten gallon cask with two gallons more of spirits of wine. Dissolve twenty pounds of lump sugar in hot water, add this to the spirit with a quarter of a pint of colouring, and fill up the cask with water. Fine it down with two ounces of alum dissolved in boiling water, and put into the goods[1] hot;

[1] Here is the etymological process for the linguistic student:

afterwards add one ounce of salts of tartar, and stir the whole well together.

The receipts which follow of German, Dantzig, and French liqueurs postulate a preliminary grinding of all dry substances, such as cloves or cinnamon; the cutting into the smallest pieces of leaves, flowers, peels; and the reducing to a paste, by means of a marble mortar, of almonds and fruit kernels with a small quantity of spirits to prevent them *oiling*.[1] These ingredients should be allowed to soak in the spirit for a month with diurnal shakings in a warm place. Then the spirit must be poured off and the water added after the quantity in the receipt. After standing a few days, pour off, press out all the liquid, mix with the spirit, add sugar and colouring matter, and filter through a flannel bag. In the matter of gold and silver leaf, an attempt to break it when dry would reduce one half to dust, and so spoil the appearance of the liqueur. It must be spread on a plate which has a little thin syrup on it. The leaf must also be covered with the syrup, and then torn by means of two forks into small pieces about the size of a canary seed. The leaf should not be added until the liqueur is in the bottle. The reader will observe the common use of capillaire.[2]

Ligusticum; Lat., *levisticum;* Fr., *luvesche, leveshe, livèche*; O. Eng. *livish, lovage.* The Italian has the form *libistico,* and the Portuguese *levistico.*

[1] A technical term.

[2] So called because said to be prepared from the maidenhair fern, *Adiantum capillus Veneris;* "but," says Pereira (*Materia Medica*), "the liqueur sold in the shops under this name is nothing but clarified syrup flavoured with orange-flower water."

German Liqueurs.

Eau de Sultane Zoraide.

Lemon peel, 8 ounces; orange peel, 8 ounces; figs, 8 ounces; dates, 4 ounces; jessamine flowers, 4 ounces; cinnamon, 3 ounces; spirits of wine, 60 o.p., 19 quarts; orange-flower water, 2 quarts; pure water, 12 quarts; capillaire, 8 quarts. *Colour,*[1] *rose.*

Eau Nuptiale.

Parsley seed, 6 ounces; carrot seed, 5 ounces; aniseed, orris root, 2 ounces each; mace, 1½ ounces; spirit, 60 o.p., 19 quarts; rose water, 7 pints; water, 11 quarts; capillaire, 9 quarts. *Colour, yellow.*

Eau d'Amour.

Bitter almonds, lemon peel, 12 ounces each; cinnamon, 6 ounces; mace, 1 ounce; cloves, 1½ ounces; lavender flowers, 8 ounces; spirits of wine, 60 o.p., 19 quarts; Muscat wine, 8 quarts; oil of amber, 36 drops; water 7 quarts; capillaire, 7 quarts. *Colour, rose.*

Eau de Yalpa.

Marjoram, cinnamon, 3 ounces each; fennel seed, thyme, sweet basil, bitter almonds, figs, balm, 2 ounces each; carrot seed, sage, 1 ounce each; cardamom,

---

[1] These colours by which *soi-disant* connoisseurs profess to determine the excellence of the liqueur, are in most cases merely adscititious. Rules are given for their manufacture. Rose, for instance, is the outcome of cochineal or sanders wood steeped for a fortnight in spirits of wine. Blue, of indigo and sulphuric acid. Yellow, of saffron. Pink, of cudbear, a corruption of the name of the chemist, Dr. *Cuthbert* Gordon, who first employed this lichen; and green, of blue and yellow mixed.

cloves, ½ ounce each; spirits of wine, 60 o.p., 19 quarts; essence of vanilla, 50 drops; essence of amber, 50 drams; water, 14 quarts; capillaire 8 quarts. *Colour, scarlet.*

Eau Divine.

Lemon peel, 1½ pounds; coriander, 4 ounces; mace, cardamom, 1 ounce each; spirits of wine, 60 o.p., 19 quarts; oil of bergamot, 1½ drams; oil of Neroly,[1] 2 drams; water, 14 quarts; capillaire, 8 quarts.

Eau de Pucelle.

Juniper berries, 1½ pounds; fennel seed, 4 ounces; angelica seed, cinnamon, 3 ounces each; cloves, 1 ounce; spirits of wine, 60 o.p., 19 quarts; water, 13 quarts; capillaire, 10 quarts. *Colour, yellow.*

Other German liqueurs, according to our authority, are *Eau de Zelia, de Rebecca, de Fantaisie, the ruby Eau des Epicuriens, the Elixir Monfron, the Eau Divine, the Eau d'Orient de Napoleon, de Didon, du Dauphin, de Santé, Royale, Américaine, de Paix, de J. Saint-Aure, de Mille-Fleurs, d'Argent, de Montpellier, d'Ardelle, de Turin, de Tubinge, du Sorcier-Comte, de Vertu, de Chypre, de Jacques, Romantique, Crême Voizot, Aqua Bianca,* and many others.

DANTZIG LIQUEURS.
Eau Miraculeuse.

Orange peel, lemon peel, 1 pound each; cinnamon, ginger, 6 ounces each; rosemary leaves, 2 ounces;

---

[1] A pharmaceutical term for volatile oil of orange flowers. Said to be derived from an Italian princess, Néroli, who invented it.

galanga,[1] mace, cloves, 1 ounce each; orris root, 1½ ounces; spirits of wine, 60 o.p., 19 quarts; capillaire, 8 quarts; water, 14 quarts. *Colour, red.*

Eau Aerienne.[2]

Figs, 12 ounces; cumin, 5 ounces; leaves of rosemary, fennel seed, 4 ounces each; cinnamon, 5 ounces; sage, sassafras, 2 ounces each; lavender flowers, camomile flowers, orris root, 4 ounces each; spirits of wine, 60 o.p., 19 quarts; capillaire, 8 quarts; water, 14 quarts.

Other Dantzig liqueurs mentioned are the *Eau de vie de Dantzig, Eau Forcifère, Christophelet, Eau Carminative, de Musettier, de Girofle, Persicot, Amer d'Angleterre,* and *Eau des Favorites,* the ruby gold sprinkled *Eau de Lisette,* the yellow *Krambambuli,*[3] the *Eau de Baal,* and the *Liqueur des Évèques.*

FRENCH LIQUEURS.
Vespetro.[4]

Angelica seed, 3 ounces; coriander seed, 2 ounces; fennel seed, aniseed, ½ ounce each; lemons sliced,

---

[1] From Arabic خلنج *Khulanj,* "a tree from which wooden bowls are made," Richardson. A dried rhizome brought from China, an aromatic stimulant of the nature of ginger. The drug is mostly produced by *Alpinia officinarum.*

[2] Also called Luft-Wasser.

[3] Only an Italian, we are told, can make this liqueur. The composition is a dark secret, but, we are also told, it originated in Austria, and is a mixture of tea, wine and milk in unknown quantities.

[4] Said, on account of its carminative properties, to be derived from the three words *vesse, pet,* and *rot,* which it is not incumbent upon us to translate.

oranges sliced, 6 ounces each; spirits of wine, 60 o.p., 12 quarts; water, 9½ pints; capillaire, 3 pints.

Eau de Scubac.[1]

Lemon peel, 6 ounces; coriander, 4 ounces; aniseed, juniper berries, cinnamon, 2 ounces each; angelica root, 1½ ounces; saffron, 1 ounce; spirits of wine, 60 o.p., 10 quarts; orange-flower water, 2 quarts; capillaire, 4 quarts; water, 8 quarts.

Elixir de Garus.[2]

Myrrh, aloes, 2 drams each; cloves, nutmegs, 3 drams each; saffron, 1 ounce; cinnamon, 5 drams; spirits of wine, p., 5 quarts; sugar, 6 pounds.

Amiable[3] Vainqueur.

Spirits of wine, p., 25 quarts; essential oil of citron, 1 ounce; of neroli, of angelica, ½ ounce each; tincture of vanilla, 1 dram; sugar 12 pounds; water, 4 quarts.

Guignolet[4] d'Angers.

Spirits of wine, p., 12 quarts; cherries with the stones, raspberries, gooseberries, red currants, 1 pound each; oil of cinnamon, of cloves, 10 drops each; sugar, 7 pounds; water, 2 quarts.

Huile des Jeunes Mariés.

Aniseed, fennel seed, 2 ounces each; angelica seed, cumin seed, caraway seed, 1 ounce each; coriander, 3

---

[1] Merely a corruption of *Usquebaugh*.

[2] So called from the inventor. Said to be useful in stomachic affections.

[3] *Sic*, aimable (?)

[4] So called because made with *guignes*, Sp. *guindas*; dark red, very sweet cherries, smaller than the *bigarreaux*. The *Guignolet d'Angers* is especially famous.

ounces; spirits of wine, p., 4 quarts; distilled water, 3 quarts; sugar, 10 pounds. *Colour, yellow.*

Other French liqueurs worthy of notice are *Eau Archiepiscopale, des Financiers, de Noyeau, de Phalsbourg, de Jasmin, des chevaliers de Saint Louis, des Pacificateurs de la Grèce, Souvenir d'un Brave, Goûte Nationale, Coquette Flatteuse, Ratafias* of different kinds, such as *Absinthe, Angelique, Celery, Quatre Graines,*[1] *Cerises, Noyeau* and *Carve,*[2] *Amour sans Fin, Gaîté Française, Plaisir des Dames, Citronelle, Elixir Columbat, Eau des Chevaliers de la Legion d'Honneur, Eau des Amis, Crême de Macaron,* and *Eau de Pologne,* the crimson *Alkermes,* the emerald *Huile des Venus,* the *Elixir des Anges,* the pale straw-coloured *Eau de vie d'Andaye,*[3] the crimson *Nectar des Dieux,* and *Missilimakinac.*

The most important, or rather the most popular in this country, of the very numerous alcoholic preparations which are flavoured, or perfumed, or sweetened, or more commonly treated in all these three ways to be agreeable to the taste are, placing them as they suggest themselves :—

Kümmel, or *Kimmel,* as it is sometimes incorrectly written, from the German name of the herb *cumin,* is made with sweetened spirit, generally brandy, flavoured with coriander and caraway seeds. It is

[1] This is composed of fennel, celery, coriander, and angelica.

[2] Sometimes written *Karoy. Carum carve,* L., from the Greek κάρον, an ombelliferous plant of which the root by culture becomes edible. The fruit is analogous to that of anise.

[3] Also written more correctly *d'Hendaye*; white, yellow, and green, according to its alcoholic strength.

chiefly produced at Riga, and is much esteemed in Java and the Eastern Archipelago generally.

Maraschino is distilled from bruised cherries. The fruit and seed are crushed together. It is commonly prepared in Italy and Dalmatia from a delicately flavoured variety called *Marazques* or *Marascas*, a small, black, wild cherry, so named, it is said, from its bitterness. Zara, in Dalmatia, is the principal place of production of *Maraschino*.

Cassis[1] (or *Cacis*) is a sort of ratafia made with the fruit of the cassis, the vulgar French name of a species of gooseberry with black berries.

Noyau, or *Crême de Noyau*, derived from the French word for a kernel, is commonly prepared from white brandy, bitter almonds or amygdalin, sugar candy, mace, and nutmeg. Its distinctive flavour comes from the amygdalin, or the kernels of peaches, plums, cherries, apricots, and other fruit. In Dominica the bark of the noyau tree (*Cerasus occidentalis*) is used, and in France the leaves of a small convolvulus-like tropical plant called *Ipomœa dissectis*. It is coloured white and pink.

Ratafias are called by du Verger *liqueurs de conversation*, and *eau clairettes* and *hypoteques*, an old term of which Menage expresses himself unable to find the derivation as applied to a liqueur. The Master Distiller considers them preferable to spirituous liqueurs. Procope, the ancient Master of Paris, includes under this term liqueurs, or syrups, as we

[1] *Cassis* would appear to be the name of a *ville* (*Bouches-du-Rhone*) which has a commerce of wine and fruit.

should say, of cherries, strawberries, gooseberries, apricots, peaches, and other fruits. He it was who first proposed the pressure of the fruits, without infusing them entire. Some years afterwards, Breard, one of the chiefs of the fruitery of Louis XIV., gave these liqueurs the name of *Hypoteques* to distinguish them. The products both of Procope and Breard were of the highest excellence. "'I,' says du Verger, 'have always considered Procope's Ratafias as finer and more delicate, those of Breard softer and more flowing; but,' he adds, 'as tastes differ, both their Ratafias have their approvers and their critics. It is difficult to equal them in cold countries, either in taste or in smell.'" They are called *Liqueurs of conversation*, because, according to this authority, in talking after meals, you may drink of them three or four times as much as of other liqueurs without fear of any inconvenience. Nay, they nourish and fortify the stomach, and in addition to being pleasant to the palate, are good friends of the liver.

The first *Ratafia* was called *Eau de Cerises*, or cherry water. The kernels should be added to the juice of the fruit with cinnamon and mace in small quantities. This renders the composition beneficent, strengthens the brain, and banishes the vapours.

The *Eau clairette de framboises* is also composed of cherries, though a few strawberries are added to give the dominant flavour. It should, therefore, says the Master Distiller, be rather called *Eau clairette framboisée.*

L'eau clairette de groseilles has a specific virtue against biliousness.

L'eau clairette de grenade is the most agreeable of *Ratafias*, but has an astringent property.

L'eau clairette de coings is still more estimable than the preceding, and imparts a new activity to the limbs.

Eau clairette de Chamberri should be made of the ripest black grapes, a small quantity of spirit of wine, a little sugar, and other ingredients. In addition to giving an appetite, it rejoices the heart. The longer it is kept, as in the case with all *Ratafias*, the better.

The white *Ratafias*, or *Hypoteques*, should be mixed with cinnamon, mace, cloves, and coriander. Under these circumstances they render the blood balsamic. The best fruits for white *Ratafias* are oranges, peaches, and apricots.

Curaçoa derives its name from the group of small islands in the West Indies, situated near the north shore of Venezuela, in the Caribbean Sea. The liqueur is made in these islands by the Dutch. It is also made at Amsterdam from orange peel imported from the Curaçoas. The bitter orange used is the *Citrus bigaradia*.

It is commonly obtained by digesting orange peel in sweetened spirits, and flavouring with cinnamon, cloves, or mace. The spirits employed are usually reduced to nearly 56 under proof, and each gallon contains about $3\frac{1}{2}$ pounds of sugar. *Curaçoa* varies in colour. The darker is produced by powdered Brazil wood, mellowed by caramel.

Parfait Amour is a liqueur composed of several ingredients, such as citron, clove, muscat, and others.

Kirsch, Kirschwasser, or *Kirschenwasser*, or cherry water, is the genuine drink of the Black Forest. The head-quarters of this liqueur, as Griesbach and Petersthal in the Reuch valley, are rich in cherry trees of the Machaleb variety. H. W. Wolff, in his *Rambles*, rises into an almost poetic description of its virtues. " It is," he says, referring to the Black Foresters, " their general stimulant and comforter, their consoler in grief, their promoter of conviviality, their safety valve in trouble or excitement." After this, little can be added without the danger, or rather the certainty, of *bathos*. When genuine—for alas, it shares the common fate of drinks, adulteration—it is said to be ardent and slightly poisonous. In other words, it contains "that excellent stomachic, hydrocyanic acid." Of late the Black Foresters have rivalled the Servians in a spirit distilled from wild plums. Stollberg thinks *Kirschenwasser* in no way inferior to the spirit made from corn at Dantzic,[1] and others hold it equal to the Dalmatian *Maraschino*. The liqueur is also made in Germany, France, and elsewhere.

Pomeranzen, or *Pomeranzen-Wasser*, somewhat resembling our orangeade, is principally drunk in Northern Germany.

Raspail was originally, as many other liqueurs, medicinal, and was so called from the name of its inventor. Mariani has made an *Elixir à la coca du Pérou*. This, like *Raspail*, is an agreeable tonic.

Vermuth[2] is composed of white wine, angelica, absinthe, and other aromatic herbs.

[1] *Stolberg's Travels*, i., 146.
[2] Germ. *Wermuth*, absinthe or wormwood, plant of genus

Many sweet wines approach very nearly liqueurs. Of these are in Austria some sweet wines of Transylvania and Dalmatia. In Spain, the *Tinto d'Alicante*, and the white *Muscats* of Malaga. In France, *Hermitage, Grenache, Colmar*, and the *Muscats* of Rivesaltes and of Roquevaire. In Cyprus, *La Commanderie*. In Italy, the *Muscats* of Vesuvius, Orvieto and Montefiascone, the holy wine of Castiglione, the white wines of Albano, and the aromatic wine of Chiavenna. In Greece, the *Malmseys* of Santorin and the Ionian Isles. In Russia, the wines of *Koos* and *Sudach* in the Crimea; and in Mexico, those of *Passo del Nocte, Paras, San Luiz de la Paz*, and *Zelaya*.

In the *Widdowes Treasure*, London, 1595, are receipts for *Sirrop of Roses* or *Violets*, and two receipts for *Rosa Solis*, and in the *Good Housewife's Jewele*, London, 1596, are receipts for distilling of *Rosemary water, Imperiall water, Sinamon water*, and the *Water of Life*.

Artemisia—perhaps originally connected with *warm*, on account of the warmth it produces in the stomach. This bitter, though commonly quoted under liqueurs, should be classed with *Quinine Wine, Angostura, Khoosh*, etc., *Juglandine*, made in France from the walnut, *Malakoff* made in Silesia, the *Shaddock* and *Quassia* bitters of the West Indies, and the *Schapps* bitter of Switzerland.

AMERICAN DRINKS.

Cobblers—Cocktails—Flips, etc.—Punch—Varieties—A Bar Tender—Anstey's *Pleader's Guide*—A Yard of Flannel—Bottled Velvet—Rumfustian, etc.

THE great authority, probably the greatest authority, on this interesting subject is a gentleman who, with the true modesty of genius, allows himself to be known only by the pseudonym of *Jerry Thomas*. Formerly a bar-tender at the Metropolitan Hotel, New York, and the Planter's House, St. Louis, he is said to have travelled over Europe and America in "search of all that is recondite in this branch of the spirit art." His very name, says one of his admirers, is synonymous in the lexicon of mixed drinks with all that is rare and original.

Among the chief American drinks are, being alphabetically arranged, *cobblers, cocktails, cups, flips, juleps, mulls, nectars, neguses, noggs, punches*—of which there are at least three score—*sangarees, shrubs, slings, smashes*, and *toddies*.[1]

[1] The dictionary explanations of these terms are commonly unsatisfactory. The experience of the bar-tender is more than the learning of the lexicographer. *Cobbler*, indeed, is well explained as compounded of wine, sugar, lemon, and sucked up through a

The *cobbler* is an American invention, though now common in other countries. It requires small skill in its composition, but should be arranged to please the eye. Of this drink the straw is the leading characteristic.

The *cocktail* is a comparatively modern discovery. In this drink *Bogart's Bitters* occupies invariably a prominent place. The *Crusta* is an improvement on the *cocktail*, and is said to have been invented by Santina, a celebrated Spanish caterer. Its *differentia* is a small quantity of lemon juice and a little lump of ice. The paring of a lemon must also line the glass, from which feature it probably derives its name.

Flip has been immortalised by Dibdin as the favourite beverage of sailors, though it has been asserted that they seldom drink it; a somewhat hazardous statement, unless limited to the times in which there is none to be had. The essential feature in *a flip* is repeated pouring between two vessels, supposed to

straw; but of *cocktail* we only learn that it is a compounded drink much used in America. The etymologies given are generally satisfactory. *Julep* is from كُلاب rose water. *Mull* from *mulled*, erroneously taken as a past participle. According to Wedgwood, *mulled* is a form of *mould*, and *mulled* ale is funeral ale, *potatio funerosa*. *Nogg* is from *noggin*, signifying a pot, and then the strong beer which it contains. *Negus* is commonly known to have been the invention of Col. Francis Negus in the reign of Anne. *Punch* is of course from the Hindustani پانج signifying 5, from its five original ingredients, to wit, *aqua vitæ, rose water, sugar, arrack*, and *citron juice*. A very unsatisfactory derivation of *Sangaree* is from the Spanish *sangria*, the incision of a vein. *Shrub* is clearly the Arabic شرب or syrup. *Smash*, explained curtly as iced brandy and water. *Slang.* is probably from the smashing of the ice; while *sling* seems evidently to be from the German *schlingen*, to swallow.

produce smoothness in the drink. The Slang Dictionary holds *flip* to be synonymous with *Flannel*, the old term for gin and beer drunk hot with nutmeg, sugar, etc., a play on the old name *lamb's wool*. The anecdote of Goldsmith drinking *flannel* in a nighthouse with George Parker, Ned Shuter, and the demure, grave-looking gentleman, is well known.

MINT JULEP.

The *julep* is especially popular in the Southern States, and is said to have been introduced into England by Captain Marryatt. That romance-writing seaman in his work on *America*, says: "I must descant a little upon the *mint julep*, as it is, with the thermometer at 100°, one of the most delightful and insinuating potations that ever was invented, and may be drunk with equal satisfaction when the thermometer is as low as 70°. There are many varieties, such as those composed of *Claret, Madeira*, etc., but the ingredients of the real *mint julep* are as follows. I learned how to make them, and succeeded pretty well." Then follows the receipt :—

"Put into a tumbler about a dozen sprigs of the tender shoots of mint, upon them put a spoonful of white sugar, and equal proportions of peach and common brandy so as to fill it up one-third, or perhaps a little less. Then take rasped or pounded ice and fill up the tumbler. Epicures rub the lips of the tumbler with a piece of fresh pine apple, and the tumbler itself is very often incrusted outside with stalactites of ice. As the ice melts, you drink."

"I once," says the marine author of this receipt, of which the reader has *ipsissima verba*, "I once overheard two ladies talking in the next room to me, and one of them said, 'Well, if I have a weakness for any one thing, it is for a *mint julep!*'"

This weakness of the American lady was, in the opinion of the Metropolitan Hotel barman in New York, very amiable, and proved, not only her good taste, but her good sense.

In *mulls*, which may be made of any kind of wine, the essential feature is the boiling. Sugar and spice, of which the nursery song tells us little girls are manufactured, are also invariably used in *mulls*. We give a rhymed receipt for mulled wine, not for the sake of the poetry, which is indifferent, but for that of the cookery, which is not bad.

> "First, my dear madam, you must take
> Nine eggs, which carefully you'll break,

> Into a bowl you'll drop the white,
> The yolks into another by it."

Here the poet was evidently hard pressed for a rhyme.

> "Let Betsy beat the whites with switch,
> Till they appear quite frothed and rich;
> Another hand the yolks must beat
> With sugar, which will make them sweet."

An ordinary effect of sugar. Poet probably hard pressed as before.

> "Three or four spoonfuls maybe 'll do,
> Though some perhaps would take but two.
> Into a skillet next you'll pour
> A bottle of good wine, or more;
> Put half a pint of water, too,
> Or it may prove too strong for you."

This is personal, nay more, it might to some good people be offensive, as indicating deficiency of cerebral power or endurance.

> "And while the eggs by two are beating,
> The wine and water may be heating;
> But when it comes to boiling heat,
> The yolks and whites together beat
> With half a pint of water more,
> Mixing them well, then gently pour
> Into the skillet with the wine,
> And stir it briskly all the time."

Poet again hard pressed.

> "Then pour it off into a pitcher,
> Grate nutmeg in to make it richer,
> Then drink it hot, for he's a fool
> Who lets such precious liquor cool."

Of *nectar* we have no information worth the reader's acceptance. It appears to be applied indifferently to any dulcet drink.

Negus may be made of any sweet wine, but is commonly composed of port. "It is," says Jerry Thomas, "a most refreshing and elegant beverage, particularly for those who do not take punch or grog after supper."

Egg-nogg, of which other *noggs* seem to be the lineal descendants, though a beverage of American origin, has "a popularity that is cosmopolitan. In the South of the United States it is almost indispensable at Christmas time, and at the North it is a favourite at all seasons." In Scotland the beverage is called "*auld man's milk*." The presence of the egg constitutes the *differentia* in this drink. Every well-ordered bar has a tin egg-nogg "*shaker*," which is a great aid in mixing. The historian will be glad to learn that it was General Harrison's favourite beverage, and the consumptive and debilitated person that it is full of nourishment.

Punch[1] is remarkable for its variety. It is con-

---

[1] The verdict of Francois Guislier du Verger, the master-distiller in the art of chemistry at Paris, in his *Traité des Liqueurs*, in 1728, is altogether unfavourable to what he calls *Le Ponge*. "It is," he says, "an English liqueur, and a man must be English to drink it; for I think it cannot be to the taste of any other nation in the world. It upsets the stomach, provokes the bile, and violently affects the head. How, indeed, can it be otherwise, seeing that it is composed of white wine, Eau de vie, citrons, a little sugar, and bread crumbs." And then follows the observation: "If water were put instead of Eau de vie, with an equal quantity of wine, a citron, and four ounces of sugar, a liqueur suitable to every one would be the result, a liqueur which would do as much good as the other does harm."

sidered necessary by the adept to rub the sugar on the rind of the citron or lemon, to extract properly what the experienced drinker calls "the ambrosial essence." The extraction of the ambrosial essence, and the making the mixture sweet and strong, using tea instead of water, and thoroughly amalgamating all the

"A CROWN BOWL OF PUNCH."

compounds, so that the taste of neither the bitter, the sweet, the spirit, nor the element shall be perceptible one over the other, is the grand secret of making *punch*. And to this, as to other learning, there is no royal road. It must, alas! be laboriously acquired by practice. Many are the mysteries of its concoction. For instance, it is essential in making *hot punch* that

that you put in the spirits before the water; in *cold punch* the other way. The precise portions of spirit and water, or even of the acidity and sweetness, can have no general rule. To attempt offering one would only mislead. A certain inspiration must animate the artist. It has been asserted that no two persons make this drink alike. This remark is admirable, and might probably be applied not only to punch, but to every drink that has yet been composed.

It has been said that of *punches* there are at least threescore. Here follow a few of the many varieties: *Brandy, Sherry, Gin, Whiskey, Port, Sauterne, Claret, Missisippi, Vanilla, Pine Apple, Orgeat, Curaçoa, Roman, Glasgow, Milk,* and *Regent's*, brewed by George IV.; *St. Charles', Louisiana, Sugar House, La Patria, Spread Eagle, Imperial, Rochester,* and *Rocky Mountain; Non-Such, Philadelphia, Fish-House, Canadian, Tip-Top, Bimbo, Nuremburgh, Ruby, Royal, Century Club, Duke of Norfolk, Uncle Toby,* and *Gothic*.

People have immortalised themselves by the invention of *punches* to which a grateful country has attached their names. Of these famous ones are General Ford, for many years commanding engineer at Dover; Dr. Shelton Mackenzie, of Glasgow; D'Orsay; and M. Grassot, the eminent French comedian of he Palais Royal, who communicated his receipt to Mr. Howard Paul, the equally eminent entertainer, when performing in Paris.

Last, though not least, the military have thus distinguished themselves by the *National Guard,* the

7th Regiment Punch, the *69th Regiment* Punch, the *32nd Regiment* or *Victoria* Punch, and the *Light Guard* Punch.

The *sangaree*, originally a West Indian drink, is as unsatisfactory in its explanation as in its etymology. It seems, indeed, to be little more than spirit and water, with sugar and nutmeg to taste. It very nearly approaches, if it is not identical with, *toddy*.[1]

Shrubs[2] are unsatisfactory, like *sangarees*. They seem to have no distinctive or differentiating feature. The most common kinds are *Rum*, *Brandy*, *Cherry*, and *Currant*.

Slings are very closely related to *toddies*. Their difference is, indeed, infinitesimal, so far as we are able to learn.[3]

---

[1] Such at least is the signification of *sangaree* as far as American drinks are concerned. But *Sang-gris* is said by Bescherelle to be a mixture of tea in wine amongst the sailors of the North. Perhaps the name is taken from the colour. It recalls David Garrick's "Why, the tea is as red as blood." In the West Indies it is made of Madeira, water, lime juice, and sugar. Spices are sometimes added. Pinckard's "West Indies," i. 469.

[2] *Shrub* is called *santa* in Jamaica. It is made in the West Indies with rum, syrup, and orange-peel.

[3] The Slang Dictionary, however, defines *Sling* as a drink peculiar to Americans, generally composed of gin, soda-water, ice, and slices of lemon. At some houses (understand public) in London *gin slings* may be obtained. Francatelli has an exquisite note on *Gin Sling*, which he directs to be sucked through a straw. "I fear that very genteel persons will be exceedingly shocked at my words; but when I tell them that the very act of imbibition through a straw prevents the gluttonous absorption of large and baneful quantities of drink, they will, I make no doubt, accept the vulgar precept for the sake of its protection against sudden inebriety."

Of the *smash*, even Jerry Thomas speaks slightingly. He says, " This beverage is simply a *julep* on a small plan." It, however, can boast of three species —*gin*, *brandy*, and *whiskey*, and for all a small barglass must be used. It is usual, though not apparently essential, to lay two small pieces of orange on the top, and to ornament with the berries of the season.

Toddy is the Hindustani *tári tádi*, or juice of the palmyra and cocoa-nut. *Tar* is the Hindustani word for a palm. It is the name given by Europeans to the sweet liquors produced by puncturing the spathes or stems of certain palms. In the West Indies *toddy* is obtained from the trunk of the *Attalea cohune*, a native of the Isthmus of Panama. In South-Eastern Asia the palms from which it is collected are the *gomuti*, *cocoa-nut*, *palmyra*, *date*, and the *kittul* (*Caryota urens*). When newly drawn the liquor is clear, and in taste resembles malt. In a very short time it becomes turbid, whitish, and sub-acid, quickly running into the various stages of fermentation, and acquiring an intoxicating quality.

In our use of the word, *toddy* seems to mean nothing more than spirit and water sweetened, with the occasional addition of lemon peel. *Whiskey toddy* is the common and favourite species, though there are also *apple*, *gin*, and *brandy toddies*. *Toddy* differs from grog in being always made with boiling water, but this distinction is not universally maintained, nor, indeed, used by the best authors. *Whiskey* is probably the " vulgar " kind alluded to by Anstey in his *Pleader's Guide*, Lect. 7.

"First count's for that with divers jugs,
To wit, twelve pots, twelve cups, twelve mugs,
Of certain vulgar drink called *toddy*,
Said Gull did sluice said Gudgeon's body."

The names of American drinks form an amusing study. Passing over the well known sleepers, sifters, flosters, knickerbockers, ching-chings, Alabama fog-cutters and thunderbolt cocktails, the lightening smashes and eye-openers of Connecticut, the corpse revivers, the Mother Shiptons and the Maiden's Prayers, we propose to give a list of some of the most remarkable titles, with receipts added, to satisfy the appetite of any who care to compound them.

A Yard of Flannel.

A yard of flannel, otherwise called *egg flip.*—Boil a quart of ale in a tinned saucepan. Beat up yolks of four with the whites of two eggs. Add four table-spoonfuls of brown sugar and a *soupçon* of nutmeg. Pour on this by degrees the hot ale, taking care to prevent mixture from curdling. Pour back and forward repeatedly, raising the hand as high as possible. This produces the frothing and smoothness essential to the goodness of the drink. It is called *a yard of flannel* from its fleecy appearance.

White Tiger's Milk
(à la Thomas Dunn English, Esq.).

Half a gill apple jack, ½ gill peach brandy, ½ teaspoonful aromatic tincture,[1] white of an egg well

---

[1] Aromatic tincture: Ginger, cinnamon, orange peel, each 1 oz.; valerian, ½ oz.; alcohol, 2 quarts. Macerate for fourteen days and filter through unsized paper.

beaten. Sweeten with white sugar to taste. Pour the mixture into 1 quart of milk, stir well, and sprinkle with nutmeg. This receipt will make a quart of the compound.

Bottled Velvet

(à la Sir John Bayley).

A bottle of Moselle, ½ a pint of sherry, small quantity of lemon peel, 2 tablespoonfuls of sugar. Well mix, add a sprig of verbena, strain, and ice.

Stone Fence.

One wine glass of whiskey (Bourbon), 2 small lumps of ice. Use large bar-glass, and fill up with sweet cider.

Sleeper.

To a gill of old rum add 1 ounce of sugar, 2 yolks of eggs, and the juice of half a lemon. Boil ½ a pint of water with 6 cloves, 6 coriander seeds, and a bit of cinnamon. Whisk all together, and strain into a tumbler.

Rumfustian.

Whisk yolks of a dozen eggs, and put into a quart of beer and a pint of gin. Put a bottle of sherry into a saucepan, with a stick of cinnamon, a grated nutmeg, a dozen lumps of sugar, and the thin rind of a lemon. When the wine boils, pour it on gin and beer, and drink hot.

Bimbo Punch.

Steep in 1 quart cognac brandy 6 lemons, cut in thin slices, for six hours. Then remove lemon without squeezing. Dissolve 1 pound loaf sugar in 1 quart boiling water, and add this hot solution to the cognac. Let it cool.

Bishop.

Stick an orange full of cloves, and roast it. When brown, cut it in quarters, and pour over it 1 quart of hot port. Add sugar to taste, and let mixture simmer for half an hour.

Archbishop.

The same as *Bishop*, with substitution of best claret for port.

Cardinal.

The same as *Archbishop*, with substitution of champagne for claret.

Pope.

The same as *Cardinal*, with substitution of Burgundy for champagne.

Locomotive.

Put 2 yolks of eggs into a goblet with 1 oz. of honey, a little essence of cloves, and a liqueur glass of Curaçoa; add 1 pint of high Burgundy made hot, whisk together, and serve hot in glasses.

Pousse l'Amour.

Fill a small wineglass half full of maraschino, then put in yolk of 1 egg; in this pour vanilla cordial, and dash the surface with cognac.

Blue Blazer

(use two large silver-plated mugs with handles).

One wine glass Scotch whiskey, 1 ditto boiling water. Mix whiskey and water in one mug; ignite, and, while blazing, pour from one mug to the other. Sweeten to taste, and serve in a bar tumbler, with a piece of lemon peel. *Blue Blazer* is really nothing more than ordinary whiskey and water.

Black Stripe.

Into a small bar-glass pour 1 wine glass of Santa Cruz rum and 1 tablespoonful of molasses; cool with shaved ice, or fill up with boiling water, according to season. Grate nutmeg on top. This is ordinary rum and water.

The following appeared in *Moonshine*, and may fitly conclude our chapter on American drinks, for which the verdant English youth has paid to the cunning dispenser so many nimble ninepences :—

" Thou art thirsty, Amaryllis; say to what dost thou incline?
    Wilt thou toy with amber bubbles at the *Fons Burtonis*
        brink?
    Shall I crown the crystal goblet with the flashing *Rhenish*
        wine?
    Or it may be thou would'st wish for an *American long*
        drink?
    Shall I brew a *Flash of Lightning* or a *Bourbon Whiskey-*
        skin?
    Or a *Saratoga Brace-up?* Sweetest, you have but to
        say.
    Nay, perhaps a *Bottle Cocktail* would your kind approval
        win?
    Or a *Santa Cruz Rum Daisy* will be something in your
        way?
    I can recommend a *Morning-Glory Cocktail* to your taste,
    And a *Corker* or a *Nerver* there are few who will de-
        spise;

Tom and Jerry offers pleasures it were folly rank to waste ;
　In a *Nectar* for the dog-days sweet Elysian rapture lies.
Be not silent, Amaryllis, name your poison, whatsoe'er
　You've a mind for, be it *Thunder, Locomotive,* or *Egg Nogg.*
I have all ingredients handy, and I reckon I'm all there
　When the question's on the *tapis* as to what shall be the grog."

AN AMERICAN BAR-TENDER.

BEERS.

Definition — Different Modes of Manufacture — Antiquity — Osiris, the Inventor — Adam's Ale — Egyptian — Scandinavian — Adulterations. AFRICA: Pitto, Ballo, Bouza. AMERICA: Persimon, Chica, Vinho de Batatas. BAVARIA: Schenk and Lager. BELGIUM: Lambic, Faro. BORNEO: Ava or Cava. CHINA: Samtchoo.

THE dictionary definition, or rather description, of Beer is "an alcoholic liquor made from any farinaceous grain, but generally from barley." This barley clause is, of course, not true in all countries, nor is beer always made from a farinaceous grain. For the rest, the description is all that could be desired. After the barley is malted and grained, its fermentable substance is extracted by hot water. To this extract or infusion hops, or some other plant of an agreeable bitterness, are added, and it is afterwards boiled for some time, both to concentrate it and to obtain all the useful matters from the hops. The liquor is subsequently allowed to ferment in vats. The time allowed for fermentation depends upon the quality and kind of beer. After it has become clear it is stored for drink.

This ordinary popular description of beer will be

probably sufficient to satisfy the general reader. But we must add to it a second explanation of beer, which is applied to a fermented extract, not from any farinaceous grain, but from the roots and other parts of various plants, as ginger, spruce-sap, beet, molasses, and many more. The scientific inquirer may learn the mysteries of malting and brewing, which are very nearly distinct trades, in the many treatises on beer-making which have adorned the literature of this and other countries. In these he may read as much as he wills of the *steeping* of the barley, its extension, its absorption of water, and the time occupied in this process; of the *couching* and *sweating*, as it is called, a result of the partial germination of the grain; of the *flooring*, or spreading out like hay over a field; of the *kiln-drying*, or the introduction of the half-germinated grain into a kiln with a perforated floor, with the necessary and variable amount of heat beneath it. And if all this is not enough, he may continue to read at full length of *cornings* or *cummings*, of *pale* and *amber-coloured malt*, of *grinding the malt*, of *washing the malt thus ground*, of *boiling the worts with hops*, of *cooling the worts*, of *fermenting the worts*, and, finally, of *clearing and storing*.

Beer is probably a word of German, as ale, signifying the same thing, is of Scandinavian, origin. But the source of the German word is a moot question of comparative philology. Those interested in this matter may find abundant information in a note inserted by M. A. Schleicher in the *Zeitschrift* of Kuhn. We are led thereby to a Gothic form, *pius*, which in its turn conducts us to the Lithuanian *pyvas*. *Pyvas* or *pivas*—since etymology is a science *dans laquelle les consonants font peu de chose, et les voyelles rien de tout* —may be easily attached to the secondary root *piv* found in the Sanskrit *pivâmi*. In Indo-European tongues, and in accordance with the dictum of Voltaire, p, b, v, are interchangeable as labials. And so we come to the conclusion that *pivas*, or its descendant *beer*, means nothing else but *drink;* or, in other words, that this particular form of drink is *the* drink *par excellence*. And so we might rest content, were it not for the uneasy scruples of a certain M. Pictet, who has introduced a Slavic origin. But of etymology this taste will suffice.

Twenty centuries before the Christian era, Osiris, according to some authors, invented beer,[1] and according to others it has been at all times a drink of the Hebrews. We have, indeed, heard of Adam's ale, but that term has been generally applied to a species of drink which would hardly come under our present category. It is perhaps more probable that the beverage of Osiris and the early Hebrews was a simple infusion of barley without more. Pliny, however, Theophrastus, and Tacitus, speak of beer as known from very early times to the people of the North, who were prevented by their situation from the cultivation of wine.[2]

[1] Those who wish to investigate the antiquity of beer may find ample matter to supply their desire in a work commonly attributed to Archdeacon Rolleston, entitled, "Οινος Κριθινος, *a dissertation concerning the origin and antiquity of barley wine*." Oxford, 1750.

[2] Much has been written on the comparative merits of wine and

The ancient beer of Egypt is compared by Diodorus Siculus to wine on account of its strength and flavour. This Egyptian beer is indeed spoken of by Herodotus as *barley wine*, a title which still survives in some of the windows of our public-houses. At present beer is the habitual drink of the English, German, Dutch, and Scandinavian races. A drink, better called *barley water* than *beer*, appears to have been the favourite beverage of the Danes and Anglo-Saxons, our ancestors in the remote past. Before Christianity had enlightened and corrected their views about the delights of a future state, these benighted folk supposed that the chief felicity enjoyed by the good—in those days synonymous with the brave—after their death and transplantation into Odin's paradise, would be to drink in large goblets large quantities of ale. Perpetual intoxication thus entered largely into their conception of celestial joy.

Beer as we understand it—modified, that is, by the introduction of the hop—was probably little known in England before the beginning of the sixteenth century. The varieties of beer at the present time are

beer. Perhaps as good a remark as any on this subject was made by a modern tradesman who, wishing to sell both, explained that, while strongly advocating the introduction of wine, he did not at all intend to depreciate the merits of our national beverage, beer. Where, he continued, plenty of out-door exercise is taken, and little intellectual effort is demanded, good beer is perhaps the most wholesome of all drinks ; and therefore he advised the " labouring man," who could not probably afford to buy wine, to drink beer, while others, who might be supposed able to afford wine, were warned that they could not drink beer with impunity.

numerous. Some of them will be considered later on in detail. There are, however, only three principal types of fabrication,—the Belgian, Bavarian, and English. The beers of England, as of France, and for the most part of Germany, become sour by the contact of air. This defect is absent from Bavarian beers.

So favourite a drink has, of course, been largely adulterated. Taste, colour, and smell are frequently due to unscrupulous falsifications. Bitterness is produced by strychnine, aloes, nux vomica, gentian, quassia, centaury, pyrethrum, absinthe, and many other ingredients. Colour is obtained by liquorice, chicory, and caramel; and flavour by other additions, which perhaps it is better not to particularize. Water, of course, is added to beer, as to most drinks, to enlarge the quantity and therefore the price. Potatoes are frequently a substitute for grain. Potash is introduced to give the much-desired "*head*," chalk to diminish acidity, and chloride of sodium, or common salt, for the sake of what is called a *piquant* flavour. It were well if these little eccentricities of the beer vendors had here their confine; but the sacred hunger for gold has added, alas! to these, virulent and narcotic poisons,[1] such as belladonna and opium, henbane and picric or carbazotic acid. In the city of London this kind of adulteration was formerly, it was fondly imagined, to some extent prevented by some ancient

---

[1] The world has little altered since the time of Martial (i. 19).

"*scelus est jugulare Falernum,*
Et dare Campano toxica sæva mero."

guardians, known as *ale-conners*, who had the right of entering all public-houses and tasting their ales.

Only the most important beers of different countries are given in the following list, arranged alphabetically for convenience of reference :—

AFRICA.

Captain Clapperton (*Expedition to Africa*, i., 133, 187) found at Wow-wow, the metropolis of Borghoo, a kind of ale bearing the name of *pitto*, obtained from the same grain as that used for the same purpose in Dahomey, and by a process nearly similar to the brewing of beer in England from malt, only that no hops were added, a defect which prevented it keeping for any length of time. The people of the countries from the Gambia to the Senegal use a kind of beer called *ballo*. At a village called *Wezo* there is a beer called *otèe*, a sort of ale made from millet, of a very enlivening nature. Another sort of beer, called *gear*, is found at Ragada. At *Whidah* an excellent beer is made from two sorts of maize. The Jews at Taffilet use beer of their own brewing. Isaacs (*Travels in Africa*, ii. 319) says that the Zoola nation, between Delagoa Bay and the Bay of Natal, has a description of beer, with which the natives are wont to get drunk. This beer is made from a seed called *loopoco*, something in size and colour like rape. It has powerful fermenting properties, and forms a beverage of a light brown hue, potent and stimulating. In Sofala a beer is made from rice and millet; also in Abyssinia is to be found a drink of many names—*tallah*, or *selleh*, or *donqua*, or *sona*—commonly brewed from wheat, millet or barley, mixed with a bitter herb called *geso*. According to Bruce, Abyssinian beer of an inferior kind is made from *tocusso*. This is really a variety of *bouza*, which is also made from *teff*, the *poa abyssinica* of botanists.

America.

Persimon beer, from the fruit of the date plum (*Diospyros Virginiana*), is drunk in North America. In South America, long before the Spanish conquest, the Indians prepared and drank a beer obtained from Indian corn, called *chica* or maize beer. The process followed in making *chica* is very similar to that of beer brewing in Britain. The maize is moistened with water, allowed partially to germinate and dried in the sun. The maize malt so prepared is bruised, treated with warm water, and allowed to ferment. The liquor is yellow, and has an acid taste something like cider. It is in common demand on the west coast. In the valleys of the Sierra the maize malt is subjected to human mastication, not invariably by the young and beautiful girls, but by old ladies and gentlemen who still retain, by the indulgence of nature, the requisite dental arrangement. The saliva mixed with the chewed morsel is supposed to produce a more excellent *chica*. Indeed, the result is so choice that this kind is commonly called Peruvian nectar. *Chica* can also be made from barley, rice, peas, grapes, pine-apples, and manioc. The Brazilians have a beer called *Vinho de Batatas*, from the Batata[1] root. *Sora*, a Peruvian beer, was formerly forbidden by the Incas because of its extremely intoxicating nature.

Austria.

The most famous beer is perhaps the Pilsener, or white beer, from Pilsen in Bohemia, the favourite drink in Vienna. Gratzer is brewed from wheat malt.

Bavaria.

The peculiar flavour of the Bavarian ale is perhaps a result of the very free use of pitch or resinous matters to protect the wood of the fermenting tun, but it seems more probable that it is due to the commixture of pine tops. *Schenk* beer is draught beer, in contradistinction to *Lager*, or store beer. The one is drunk in summer, the othe rin winter. *Bock beer*[2] and *Salvator*, dark heavy kinds of stout, are both well known. *Kaiserslautern* is the name of a famous brewage in Rhenish Bavaria.

Belgium.

White beers, the result of a mixture of oats and wheat, called *Walgbaert* and *Happe*, were made in Brussels in the fifteenth century. *Roetbier* and *Zwartbier* were, as their names tell us, red and black beers. *Cuyte* was at one time a favourite and aristocratic

---

[1] This is the sweet potato, introduced into Europe before the common potato.

[2] For an interesting account of this, vid., Dr. Charnock's *Verba Nominalia*.

drink. It has since fallen from its high estate. There are some forty kinds of beer, at least, now manufactured in Brussels. The white beer of Louvain in South Brabant is the most esteemed; but an Englishman has described it as having the flavour of pitch, soapsuds and vinegar. The winter brew is termed *Faro*, the summer *Lambic*. The *Faro* is by some said to be prepared from the strong *Lambic* and a small beer called *Mars*. All Belgium beers, according to the opinion of some experts, have a certain stamp of vinosity. In addition to the *Lambic* and *Faro*, which are distinguished in this particular, may be mentioned the *Uitzet* of Flanders, the *Arge* of Antwerp, and *Fortes-Saisons* of the Walloons. The white sparkling beers of Louvain are the best of summer beers, they are succeeded by those of *Hougaerde* and *Diest*. The brown beers of *Malines* and the *Saison* of *Liege* possess good reports. Latterly the *Grisettes* of *Gembloux*, the beer of *Dinant*, the *blonde* of *Buiche*, and the ale of *Oppuers* have been creditably mentioned.

BORNEO.

The aborigines[1] of Borneo, if we are to believe Commodore Roggewein,[2] are the " basest, most cruel and perfidious people in the world." They are " honest, industrious, strongly affectionate and self-denying," if we are to credit the account of the Italian missionary, Antonio Ventimiglia. When such diversity of opinion is manifested about the people,

[1] *Beajus*, which in Malay signifies a wild man.
[2] Roggewein's *Voyage Round the World*.

some discordance might naturally be supposed to exhibit itself in the matter of their potations. But this is not thus. The great drink of the Beajus is allowed on all hands to be the *ava* or *cava*, prepared from the *piper methysticum*, or intoxicating pepper plant. This is a shrub with thick roots, long heart-shaped leaves, and a clump or spike of berries. The root is chewed only—it is satisfactory to learn—by young girls with good teeth and dainty mouths.[1] Water or cocoa-nut milk is poured on the masticated pulp, fermentation ensues, and the *Beajus* drink and become drunken. The mass of chewed matter is kneaded with considerable dexterity by practised professionals. " Every tongue is mute," says Mariner—one of the crew of a vessel seized by the natives in the commencement of this century,—" while this operation is going on ; every eye is upon them, watching every motion of their arms as they describe the various curvilinear turns essential to success." *Ava* is also drunk in Otaheite, in the Feejee islands, and those of the Marquesas and of the South Seas.

CHINA.

Tar-asun, extracted from barley or wheat, is the beer of China. It is sweet, and commonly drunk warm, before distillation. The mixed liquor from which it is prepared is called *tchoo*, or wine; after that, *sam* or *san*

[1] According to Kotzebue, old woman chew, as in the South American *chica*—let us hope this cannot be correct—and little girls spit on it to thin the paste. Kotzebue's *New Voyage Round the World*, vol. ii., p. 170.

is prefixed, to show its hot nature. *Samtchoo*—the word is spelt in many ways—may, says Barrow (*Travels*, p. 304), be considered the basis of the best *arrack*, itself a mere rectification of the above spirit with the addition of molasses and the juice of the cocoa-nut tree. *Bell's Travels*, ii. 9.

ENGLAND.

Love of the English for Beer—A National Drink—Private Brewing—A French View of English Society—Sir John Barleycorn—The " Black Jack " and " Leather Bottel "—" Toby Philpot "—Burton-on-Trent—Bottled Beer—Brewers—The Village Alehouse—Various Beers.

" Back and syde goo bare, goo bare,
Both hande and foote goo colde ;
But, Bellie, God send the good ale inowghe
Whether hyt be newe or old."

" Brynge us home good ale, syr, brynge us home good ale,
And for our der lady's love, brynge us som good ale.
Brynge us home no beff, syr, for that is full of bonys,
But brynge us home goode ale y-nough, for that my love alone ys ;
Brynge us home no wetyn brede, for y^t be ful of branne,
Nothyr of no ry brede, for y^t is of ye same ;
Brynge us home no porke, syr, for y^t is verie fatt,
Nothyr no barly brede, for neythir love I that ;
Brynge us home no muton, for that is tough and lene,
Neyther no trypys, for thei be seldyn clene ;
Brynge us home no veel, syr, that do I not desyr,
But brynge us home good· ale y-nough to drynke by ye fyer ;
Brynge us home no syder, nor no palde [1] wyne,
For, and y^u do, thow shalt have Criste's curse and mine."

[1] From the old French *Pallir*, to become vapid, lose spirit. Washy stuff.

The foregoing verses epitomise the praise of good beer. The first is from one of the earliest known drinking songs in the English language—the last is an old Wassail song—the Wassail bowl, which was of hot spiced ale, with roasted apples bobbing therein, —a kindly way of welcome on New Year's Eve, of Saxon derivation as its name "Wes-hal," *be of health*, or *your health*, testifies.

That the Anglo-Saxon took kindly to his beer, we have already seen; and that that feeling exists at the present day is undoubted, for what says the refrain of a comparatively modern drinking song?

> "I loves a drop of good beer—I does—
> I'se partickler fond of my beer—I is—
> And —— their eyes,
> If ever they tries
> To rob a poor man of his beer."

Its popularity has never waned—and it has reached to such a height that the brewing trade seems to be instituted for the propagation of Peers of the realm— a fact which Dr. Johnson even could not have foreseen, although, at the sale of Thrale's brewery, he did say that they had not met together to sell boilers and vats, but "the potentiality of growing rich beyond the dream of avarice."

It was the national drink—for tea and coffee were not introduced into England until the middle of the seventeenth century—and it is only of very modern times that the "free breakfast table" fad of statesmanship has made those beverages so popular, by bringing them within the means of the very poorest.

Beer was, perforce, drank morning, noon and night by those, and they were the vast majority, who could not afford wine—and, as a rule, after the Norman Conquest, when the Anglo-Saxons copied the soberer

customs of their conquerors, the English were not drunkards as a nation; in fact, although almost all their jests hinge on drinking, there is in most of them an underlying moral, which in print are as telling as in this illustration, which, in deference to nasty Mrs. Grundy, has been slightly toned down. Here is very cleverly satirised for reprobation the phases of men under the influence of drink. How it transforms them into beasts, some like lions, others like asses and calves, sensual as hogs, greedy as goats, stupid as gulls.

Every man brewed his own beer up to the seventeenth century, when we find Pepys speaking of Cobb's strong ales at Margate; and in the reign of Queen Elizabeth the public brewing had begun at Burton, for an inquiry was made by Walsingham to Sir Ralph Sadler, the governor of Tutbury Castle, as to "What place neere Tutbury, beere may be provided for her Majesty's use?" and the answer was that it might be obtained at Burton, three miles off. Good Queen Bass would, indeed, have fared badly without her beer, for her breakfast beverages were always beer and wine.

Yet every one was fairly sober. They were weaned on alcoholic liquors, and, consequently, enjoyed them as foods, as they undoubtedly are, if properly used. It is very well to "see our sen as others see us," but it is almost impossible to agree with Estienne Perlin, who published his *Description des Royaulmes d'Angleterre et d'Escosse*, at Paris in 1558, in which he says that the English "sont fort grands yvrongnes." His description is, we feel, as untrustworthy as his English. "Car si un Anglois vous veult traicter, vous dira en son langage, *vis dring a quarta rim vim gasquim, vim hespaignol, vim malvoysi*, c'est a dire veulx tu venir boire une quarte de vin du gascoigne, une autre

O

d'espaigne, & une autre de malvoisie, en beuvant & en mengeant vous diront plus de cent fois *drind iou*, c'est a dire je m'en vois boyre a toy, & vous leur responderes en leur langage *iplaigiu*, qui est a dire, je vous plege. Si vous les remarcies vous leurs dires en leurs langages, *god tanque artelay*, c'est a dire, je vous remercie de bon cœur. Eulx estans yvres, vous jureront le sang et le mort que vous beures tout ce que vous tenes dedans vostre tace, & vous diront ainsi, *bigod sol drind iou agoud oin.*" It is much to be feared that the worthy Frenchman, if his description is to be at all relied on, mixed with rather a fast lot.

Ale was looked upon as a kindly creature, and our ancestors of the seventeenth century had several ballads in praise of the "little Barleycorn" and the indictment, as well as the "Bloody Murther," of Sir John Barleycorn. From this latter the peasant poet, Burns, plagiarised right royally. There was also a very curious Chap book published in the early part of the eighteenth century, entitled,

"The whole TRIAL and INDICTMENT of
Sir JOHN BARLEY-CORN—*Knt*.

A Person of Noble Birth and Extraction, and well known by Rich and Poor throughout the Kingdom of *Great Britain*: Being accused of several Misdemeanours, by him committed against His Majesty's Liege People; by killing some, wounding others, and bringing Thousands to Beggary, and ruins many a poor Family.

Here you have the Substance of the Evidence given in against him on his Trial, with the Names of the Judges, Jury, and Witnesses. Also the Comical Defence Sir *John* makes for himself, and the Character given him by some of his Neighbours, namely, *Hew-*

son the Cobbler, an honest friend of Sir John's, who is entomb'd as a *Memorandum*, at the *Two Brewers* in *East Smithfield*.

Taken in Short Hand by Thomas Tosspott, *Foreman of the Jury*."

One of the witnesses, hight Mistress *Full-Pot*, the

hostess, called in his defence, thus winds up her evidence,—

"Nay, I beseech you, give me leave to speak to you; if you put him to Death, all *England* is undone, for there is not such another in the Land that can do as he can do, and hath done; for he can make a Cripple to go, he can make a Coward to fight with a valiant Soldier, nay, he can make a good Soldier feel neither Hunger or Cold. Besides, for Valour in himself, there are few that can encounter with him, for he can pull down the strongest Man in the World, and lay him fast asleep."

Of course, the jury found a verdict of *Not Guilty*.

Beer has a large literature of its own, principally metrical, but this has pretty well been collected in two books—*The Curiosities of Ale and Beer*, by John Bickerdyke; and *In Praise of Ale*, by W. T. Marchant—either of which would be a valuable addition to any one's library. Yet in neither of them have I met with Ned Ward's *Dialogue between Claret and Darby Ale*," published 1691, in which each of the drinks speak for themselves; and, of course, the arguments of ale are all potent over his antagonist. Space will only allow of a very short extract.

"*Darby*.—I'm glad to know you, High and Mighty *Sir;*
　　　　Think you your pompous empty Name could stir
　　　　My Choler? No, your Title makes me fear
　　　　As much as if you'd been *Six Shilling Beer*.
Claret.—Thou *Son of Earth*, thou dull insipid thing,
　　　　To level me, who am of Liquors *King*,

With lean *Small Beer*, but that thou art not worth
My Anger, else I'de frown thee into Earth.
Darby.—I neither fear your Frown, nor court your Smile;
But, if I'm not mistaken all this while,
By other names than Claret you are known—
Claret.—You do not hear me, Sir, the Fact disown,
Some call me *Barcelona*, some *Navar*,
Some *Syracuse*, but at the Vintner's Bar
My name's *Red Port*. But call me what they will,
Claret I am, and will be Claret still," etc., etc.

Not content with praising the liquor ale, our ancestors fell to eulogising the vessels used for its

consumption, and the "Black Jack" and "Leather Bottel" both came in for their meed of praise. I give sketches of a fine example of each, which I have drawn from the national collection in the British Museum.

The Black Jack is a jug or pitcher, made of leather, which was sometimes ornamented with a silver rim and a silver plate with the owner's name or coat of arms engraved thereon. Here is a short lyric, "In praise of the Black Jack."[1]

[1] See second part of *Westaminster Drollery*, 1672.

"Be your liquor small, or as thick as mudd,
The cheating bottle cryes, good, good, good,
Whereat the master begins to storme,
Cause he said more than he could performe.
  And I wish that his heires may never want Sack,
  That first devis'd the bonny black Jack.

No Tankerd, Flaggon, Bottle nor Jugg
Are half so good, or so well can hold Tugg,
For when they are broke, or full of cracks,
Then they must fly to the brave black Jacks.
  And I wish, etc.

When the Bottle and Jack stands together, O fie on't,
The Bottle looks just like a dwarfe to a Gyant;
Then had we not reason Jacks to chuse
For this'l make Boots, when the Bottle mends shoes.
  And I wish, etc.

And as for the bottle you never can fill it
Without a Tunnell, but you must spill it,
'Tis as hard to get in, as it is to get out,
'Tis not so with a Jack, for it runs like a Spout.
  And I wish, etc.

And when we have drank out all our store,
The Jack goes for Barme to brew us some more;
And when our Stomacks with hunger have bled,
Then it marches for more to make us some bread.
  And I wish, etc.

I now will cease to speak of the Jack,
But hope his assistance I never shall lack,
And I hope that now every honest man,
Instead of Jack will y'clip him John.
  And I wish, etc."

But the composer of "A Song in praise of the Leather Bottel" could rise to the magnitude of his subject in a far superior manner than the preceding poet, the refrain of his song being of a higher type.

"And I wish in Heaven his Soul may dwell,
That first devised the Leather Bottel."

The uses of the Bottel were so manifest, and its material so superior to any other, that it occupied a higher position. It was better than wood, for it would not run, and was unbreakable. When a man and his wife fell out, as will occasionally happen even in the best matrimonial existence, the bottel could be thrown at each other, without great injury either to human, or the bottel. It held no temptation to steal,

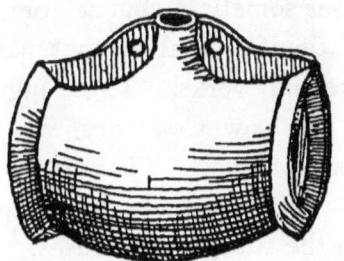 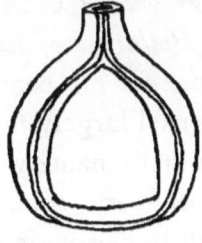

as if it were of silver; nor could it be broken, as if it were of glass—because, as the song justly says,—

"Then what do you say to these Glasses fine?
Yes, they shall have no Praise of mine;
For when a Company there are sat,
For to be merry, as we are met;
Then, if you chance to touch the Brim,
Down falls your Liquor, and all therein;
If your Table Cloath be never so fine,
There lies your Beer, your Ale or Wine;
It may be for a small Abuse,
A young Man may his Service lose;
But had it been in a Leather Bottel,
And the Stopple in, then all had been well."

The rhymester recapitulates the gratitude of all classes for this extremely handy and unbreakable convenience, and winds up thus, somewhat sadly—

"Then when the Bottel doth grow old,
And will good Liquor no longer hold,
Out of its side you may take a Clout,
Will mend your Shooes when they'r worn out;
Else take it, and hang it upon a Pin,
It will serve to put many Trifles in,
As Hinges, Awls, and Candle-ends,
For young Beginners must have such things.
Then I wish, etc."

The next most popular English drinking vessel was the *greybeard*, or as it was sometimes, but seldom, called the *Bellarmine*, from the Cardinal of that name so famous for his controversial works. These jugs were imported largely from the Low Countries, where the Cardinal's name was a reproach. These greybeards are of very common occurrence, being frequently found in excavating on the sites of old houses.

Two centuries after the greybeard, came the brown Staffordshire *Toby Philpot*, an enormously stout old gentleman, whose arms and hands encircle his enormous paunch, and his three-cornered hat forms a most convenient lip, whence the ale can be poured. It owes its origin to a once very popular drinking song, entitled "The Brown Jug," which is an imitation from the Latin of Hieronymus Amaltheus, by Francis Fawkes, M.A., published in 1761, which is the date of the accompanying illustration.

"Dear Tom, this brown jug, which now foams with mild ale,
Out of which I now drink to sweet Nan of the Vale,

Was once Toby Philpot, a thirsty old soul,
As e'er cracked a bottle, or fathom'd a bowl;
In bousing about, 'twas his pride to excel,
And amongst jolly topers he bore off the bell.

It chanced as in dog-days he sat at his ease,
In his flower-woven arbour, as gay as you please,
With his friend and a pipe, puffing sorrow away,
And with honest Old Stingo sat soaking his clay,
His breath-doors of life on a sudden were shut,
And he died full big as a Dorchester Butt.

His body, when long in the ground it had lain,
And time into clay had dissolved it again,
A potter found out, in its covert so snug,
And with part of Fat Toby he form'd this brown jug;
Now sacred to friendship, to mirth, and mild ale—
So here's to my lovely sweet Nan of the Vale."

Burton-on-Trent may be termed the Metropolis of English Beer, and there, veritably, "Beer is King." This pre-eminence is attributed to the quality of the water, which seems peculiarly fitted for brewing purposes, and the fact that the large brewers there located use none but the finest malt and hops procurable. There is an old saying, that wherever an Englishman has trodden, and where has he not? there may be found an empty beer bottle. And, truly, he does carry the taste for his natural beverage wherever he goes, and the export trade is enormous, every ship wanting freight, filling up with bottled beer, as a safe thing. Fuller, in his *Worthies of England* (ed. 1662, p. 115), gives his account of the origin of bottled beer. Speaking of Alexander Nowell, who was made Dean of St. Paul's as soon as Queen Elizabeth came to the throne, he mentions his fondness for fishing, and says, "Without offence it may be remembred, that leaving a *Bottle* of *Ale* (when fishing) in the *Grasse*; he found it some dayes after, no *Bottle*, but a *Gun*, such the sound at the opening therof. And this is believed (Casualty is *Mother* of more *Inventions* than *Industry*) the original of *bottled-ale* in *England*."

The London brewer had to be content, before Sir Hugh Myddleton brought the New River to the Metropolis, with the water obtained from the Thames, for Artesian wells were not, and other well water must, from the crowded state of the City, have been highly charged with organic matter. But their trade was so important that they were incorporated into a Gild, and the Brewer's Company is now in existence, having their Hall in Addle Street, Wood Street. The City still maintains the importance of beer as a beverage by keeping an Ale Conner, whose duty is to taste ales, and see that the price charged is not excessive. Their oath of office may be found in the *Liber Albus*, published at the instance of the Government.

The names of our great English brewers are too well known among the English people to need recapitulation—and space is too scarce to describe their premises. The London draymen have always been noted as a race of tall stalwart men, and brewers generally have taken a pride in getting the largest and strongest horses for their work. These two draymen are of the time of George I., and the weight they are carrying contrasts favourably with the satire of a huge dray horse dragging a four and a half gallon

UNIV. OF
CALIFORNIA

VILLAGE INN.

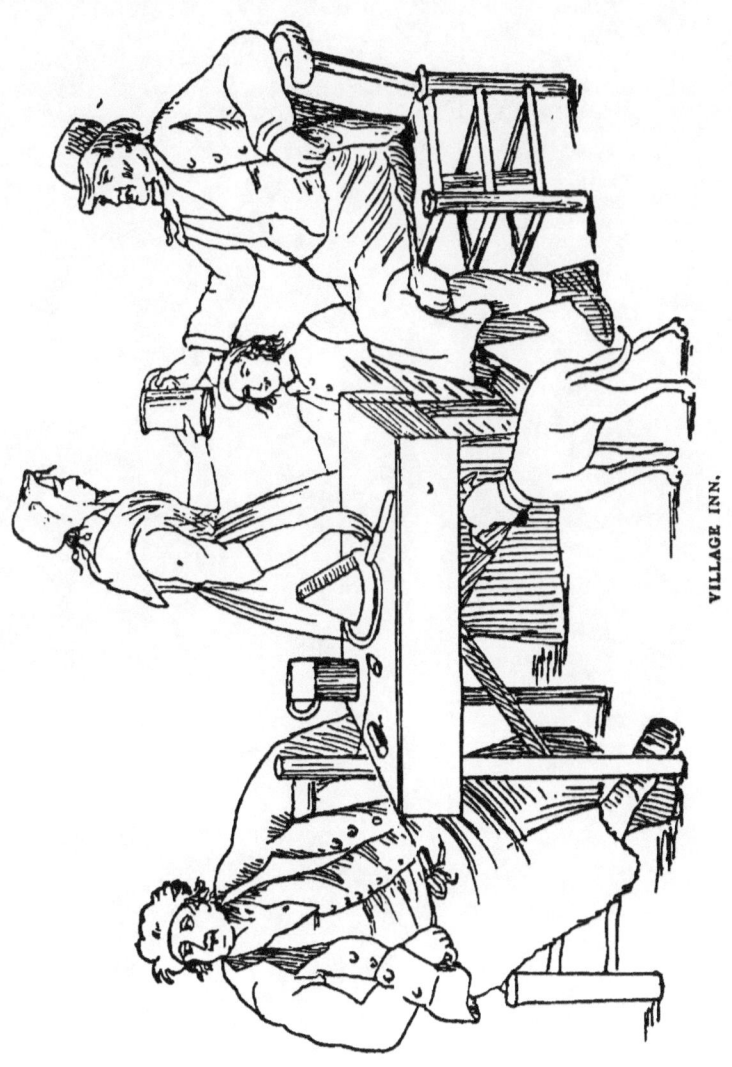

VILLAGE INN.

cask. On one notable occasion brewers' draymen have gone beyond their last. When General Haynau visited Barclay's Brewery, they rose in indignation against him and chased him from the place, because it

was alleged that the General had caused a lady to be flogged!

The Village Ale-house is, or was, the village club, and certainly is a welcome place of rest for the wayfarer. They are always clean, and frequently quaint, although now-a-days it would be hard to find, as Rowlandson did, a turnspit dog on duty.

The names of ales are legion; but some are worthy of a passing notice on account of their strength, such as some of the College Ales, those brewed at the birth of an heir—to be drank at his coming of age,

Ten Guinea Ale etc., and there are any quantity of pseudo beers—*i.e.* those not made from malt and hops, China Ale, Radish Ale, ale made from beet or mangel wurzel, and heather beer, which latter is of so great antiquity that its method of manufacture is said to have been lost with the extirpation of the Picts, although some say it was brewed by the Danes. It is probable that the flowers and tops of the heath were used as a substitute for hops, as, previous to the introduction of the latter plant, broom, wormwood and other bitter herbs were used.

J. A.

After Rowlandson.

FRANCE: Cerevisia; Double Bière; Adulteration. GERMANY: Mum; Beer Factories; Faust. INDIA: Pachwai, Piworree. JAPAN: Saki; Kæmpfer. RUSSIA: Kvas; Vodki; Pivo. SWEDEN: Spruce. TARTARY: Baksoum.

FRANCE.

In France beer was originally known as *cervoise* from the Low Latin *cerevisia*. There are two sorts, white and red; the latter has more hops. When much grain enters into the composition it is called *double bière*. Its qualities vary here as elsewhere, according to the grain employed in its manufacture, the malt, and the fermentation. It has been commonly adulterated with *ledum palustre* or wild rosemary, a strong narcotic. Allusions to beer are comparatively infrequent in French works. The details of its manufacture, which present no remarkable points of variation, may be found in any French work on brewing.

GERMANY.

Of the many beers of this country, perhaps the most deserving of notice here is the *Mum* of Brunswick, well known and appreciated for its excellence. The process observed in its manufacture has been, it is said, always kept a mystery,[1] and to prevent discovery, the men who brewed it were hired for life. The origin of the word *Mum* is obscure. The German *Mumme*, a strong ale producing silence[2] from intoxication; the Danish word for a mask, because it

[1] General Monk's receipt is given in the *Harleian Miscellany*, i., 524. London, 1744.
[2] "Mum's the word," etc.

exhibits the parties drinking it with a new face; and *Christian Mummer* of Brunswick, the supposed inventor of the drink, have been by turns suggested. The varied kinds of *Schenk*, or winter beer, and *Lager*, or summer beer, are fairly well known. The Leipzig Goose and the Berlin white beer are refreshing drinks in summer. An excellent description of *Bierbrauerei* apparatus is given in Brockhaus' *Conversations Lexikon*, Band iii. The most important beer factories are in Munich,[1] Erlangen, Zirndorf, Nürnberg, and Vienna.

German beer is far less potent than that of England, but want of strength is made up by the quantity taken. From the time of Goethe, and long before, Germans were great consumers of beer, and the scene in his "Faust," of students in Auerbach's Cellar, was typical of his time. Now-a-days there is no degeneracy in the German beer drinker, and a Viennese "Saufender Renommist" will drink his thirty half-pints of *Märzen* at a sitting. German beers are now readily attainable at any German restaurant in London.

India.

The Hill-tribes of India commonly consume *Pachwai*, prepared from rice and other grain in Bengal. In Nepaul a beer named *Phaur*, made from rice or wheat, is brewed much in the same manner as English ale, which it is said strongly to resemble. It is in considerable repute and, according to Hamilton,[2] wheat

[1] *Der Bierbrauer*, Prag. 1874.
[2] Hamilton's *Account of Nepaul*.

and barley are in Nepaul reared for the express purpose of making the beer and other drinks similar to it. In the West Indies the negroes make a fermented drink resembling beer from *cassava*, which in Barbadoes is termed *piworree*,[1] and in other places *ouycou*.

This plant, the *manioc* or *mandioc* of America, grows to the size of a small tree, and produces roots like our parsnips.[2] *Ouycou* is sometimes brewed very strong. It is considered nourishing and refreshing, as indeed most drinks which gratify the palate seem to be considered. Molasses and yams are used in its preparation. The liquor is red. *Piworree* or *paiwari* is also made by the Indians in Honduras, as in Brazil, from cassava. Cassava bread carbonised superficially is placed in hot water until fermentation arises. To promote this, feminine chewing is found efficacious. The taste, says Simmonds, is said to resemble that of ale, but is not "quite so agreeable—this may easily be believed." *Cela dépend*, as in the case of the *chica* of the sierras of South America.

JAPAN.

Kæmpfer, in his *History of Japan*, i., 121, tells us that in the manufacture of *Sacke* or *Saki*[3] a strong and wholesome beer produced from rice, the Japanese are not excelled by any other people. This beer, a very ancient drink, is white when fresh, but becomes brown,

[1] Pinckard's *Notes*, p. 429.
[2] Robertson's *History of America*, ii. 7.
[3] This is the beverage in general use. Titsingh's *Japan*. Some writers have connected it with our "*sack*."

After A. L. Mayer.

CALIFORNIA.

if it remains long in the cask. It is manufactured to the highest degree of excellence in Osacca, and thence exported to other countries. The beer's name is said to be derived from that of this city, being the genitive case of the word, with the initial letter omitted. It is wholesome and pleasant, but should be drunk moderately warm.[1] There are many varieties of *saki*, distinguished by different names.

Russia.

Quass, or *Kvas*, a word signifying *sour*, an ancient Scythian beverage, is the ordinary household beer of Russia. A variety of it called *Kisslyschtschy* is variably described as exceedingly pleasant, and as an abominable small beer, something like sweet wort or treacle beer, almost as vile as the *Vodki* or Russian gin. These matters of course depend on individual taste. The Russian *pivo*, also in common use, is said to resemble German beer, but German beers are many and diverse.

Sweden.

Swedish beer is made at Stockholm. *Spruce* beer is much in use. This drink is said to have originated from a decoction of the tops of the spruce fir. In Norway and Denmark as well as in Sweden this liquor is made from boiling the leaves, rind and branches of pines. But the *Spruce* beer of Great Britain and Ireland—either white or brown, according as sugar or molasses is employed in the making—is

---

[1] When cold, it is said to produce *serki*, a species of fatal colic

an essence or fluid extract procured by boiling the shoots, tops, bark and cones of the Scotch fir (*pinus sylvestris*). *Spruce beer* is supposed to be of much medicinal value as an antiscorbutic. Samuel Morewood presents us with a gratifying reflection on this matter. While, he says, *Spruce* is beneficial to the health of man, it has not, by its " consequence depreciated his character, or lowered him in his moral dignity."

Tartary.

The beer to be met with in Tartary is for the most part of an indifferent quality. That brewed from barley and millet by the Turkestans, termed *baksoum*, more resembles water boiled with rice than beer. They, however, admire it, and affirm that it is an invaluable remedy for dysentery. The reader will have already perceived that it is a cosmopolitan practice to pamper the appetite under the pretence of preserving the health. *Baksoum* is acid in taste, of no scent, a feeble intoxicant, and cannot be kept for any length of time.

Non-Alcoholic Drinks.

TEA.

I.

Popularity of Tea as a Drink—Consumption in England, and comparative Use all over the World—Legend of its Origin—Date of its Use—Growth of the Plant—Different Kinds of Tea—Great Falling off in the Exports from China—Ceylon Tea—High Prices of—Statistics—Analysis of Tea.

OF all non-alcoholic beverages, Tea claims the pre-eminence, being drank by nearly, if not quite, half the population of the world, and common alike to all climes and all nations.

In China it is the national beverage, and it is used not only as an ordinary drink, but it is the chief factor in visits of ceremony, and in hospitality. Japan, too, is a large consumer, and its houses of entertainment are "Tea" houses. In the wilds of Thibet its use is universal, and so it is on the steppes of Tartary, where, however, it is made as nauseous and repulsive a drink as possible. In Russia, it is the traveller's comfort, and every post house is bound by law to have its *samovar* hot and boiling, ready for the wayfarer. In Australia, New Zealand, and Tasmania, the "billy" of tea is familiar, and forms the only drink of the shepherd, the stockman, and the digger. All the British colonies and possessions are devotees to the "cup which cheers, but not inebriates." Great Britain herself is a great tea drinker, whether it be the "five o'clock tea," which has developed into a cult, with vestments peculiar thereto; the poor seamstress, stitching for hard life, who takes it to keep herself awake for her task; or the labourer, who takes his tin bottle with him to the field. In fact, go where you will, in every civilized portion of the world (except Greece, where the consumption is merely nominal), and you will find drinkers of tea.

Great Britain is the centre of the tea trade of the world, and in 1889 she imported a total quantity of 222,147,661 lbs., the declared value of which was £9,987,967. Of this she took for her own consumption, and paid duty thereon, 185,628,491 lbs, which, at 6*d.* per lb. duty, produced a revenue of £4,640,704. Wisely or not, Mr. Goschen, in the Budget for 1890, reduced the duty to 4*d.* per lb.

In spite of this enormous quantity of tea drank in Great Britain, she does not rank as the largest consumer per head, which, leaving out China, Japan, Thibet, and Tartary, where statistics are unknown, is as follows :—[1]

[1] For this list we are indebted to the courtesy of Messrs. Gow, Wilson & Stanton, 13, Rood Lane, London, E.C.

Australian Colonies,
New Zealand,
Tasmania,
Great Britain,
Newfoundland,
Canada,
Bermuda,
United States,
Holland,
Cape Colony,
Natal,
Russia,
Denmark,
Uruguay,
Argentine Republic,
B. Honduras,
Barbadoes,
Trinidad,
Antigua,
British Guiana,
Persia,

Portugal,
Bahamas,
Switzerland,
Norway,
Germany,
Grenada,
Morocco,
St. Vincent,
Jamaica,
Belgium,
Sweden,
France,
Roumania,
Austria-Hungary,
Bulgaria,
Spain,
Turkey (no returns),
Italy   (ditto),
Greece (nominal),
Mauritius, 1888, 106,589 lbs.
Sierra Leone, 1888, 6,008 lbs.

The tea shrub grows wild in Assam, and in other parts between the limits of N. Latitude 15° to 40°, and this zone is most favourable to its growth in its cultivated form, although of late years Ceylon, which is nearer the equator, has made enormous strides in the production of tea. Up to the present time, however, China has furnished the largest quantity, and for centuries has enjoyed the monopoly of its production; a monopoly now broken down, and every day vanishing, mainly owing to the roguery of its manufacturers and the folly of its growers.

Of course, such a plant could have had no common origin, and no reader need be surprised at its story. The legend runs that Prince Darma, or Djarma, the third son of King Kosjusvo, went, very many centuries ago, from India to China, where he abode, and became celebrated for his piety. Like the *fakirs* of India, he showed his religious tendencies in a morbid manner—living only under heaven's canopy, fasting for weeks together, and eliminating sleep altogether from his daily wants. Tradition says that this state of things continued for years, until, one day, weary nature asserted her pre-eminence, and Darma slept. Imagine his holy horror on his awakening! Something of the same kind must have possessed Cranmer when he stretched forth his right hand in the flames of his funereal pyre, with the heart-wrung exclamation, "This hand hath offended." So with Darma; filled with pious horror, his first thought was, how to expiate his offence, and his peccant eyelids were, consequently, cut off and thrown upon the ground. Next day, returning to the spot where he had involuntarily sinned, he saw two shrubs, of a kind never before beheld in China. He tasted them, found them aromatic, and, moreover, possessing the quality of imparting wakefulness to their consumer. The discovery and miracle became noised abroad, and hence the popularity of tea in China.

But, apart from this legend, the Chinese themselves have no certain record of the introduction of tea into their country. They believe that it was in use in the third century, and in the latter end of the fourth century, Wangmung, a minister of the Tsin dynasty, made it fashionable and much increased its consumption. In all probability it was chewed at that time, for a decoction of it does not appear to have been drank until the time of the Suy dynasty, when the Emperor Wass-te, suffering from headache, was cured by drinking an infusion of tea leaves, by the advice of a Buddhist priest. In the early seventh century this manner of using the shrub was general, and it has maintained its popularity unto the present time, making itself friends wherever it is introduced.

The tea-plant somewhat resembles the Camellia Japonica, and Linnæus, imagining that the black and green teas came from different shrubs, named them *Thea bohea* and *Thea viridis*. Fortune has definitely settled that both green and black tea are made off the same plants, and it is now taken that there is but one tea-plant, the *Thea Sinensis*, of which, however, there are several varieties, induced by climate, soil, etc.

Tea-plants are grown from seeds, and are made bushy by pinching off the leading shoots. They are planted in rows, each plant being three or four feet distant from the other, and the leaves are stripped in the fourth of fifth year of its growth, and are plucked until the tenth or twelfth, when the plant is grubbed up. May and June are the general months of picking, which is done mostly by women; but the time varies according to the district.

The young and early leaves give the finest and most delicate teas, but the flavour very much depends upon the drying and roasting; but still some soils and climates have a great deal to do with the taste, the finest tea in China growing between the 27th and 31st parallels of latitude.

The Trade names of teas imported from China to England are: *Black*—Congou, Souchong, Ning Yong and Oolong, Flowery and Orange Pekoe. The latter, and Caper, being artificially scented, are, therefore, carefully eschewed by *cognoscenti*. *Green*—Twankay,

THEA SINENSIS.

Hyson Skin, Hyson, Young Hyson, Imperial, and Gunpowder. Black tea has the rougher taste, and produces the darkest infusion. Green tea, however, has the greater effect upon the nerves, and if taken strong, acts as a narcotic, producing, with some people, tremblings and headaches, and on small animals even causing paralysis. It is, therefore, generally mixed with black in small proportion, say ¼ lb. to 1 lb. black tea. There is also what is called *brick tea*, which is consumed in the North of China, Tartary, and Thibet, but which we never see in England. This choice tea is made from the stalks and refuse and decayed twigs, mixed with the serum of sheep and ox blood, which, when it is pressed into moulds, hardens it.

The Russians are said to get the finest tea that comes out of China—called Caravan Tea—which is made into large bales, covered with lead. This goes to Russia entirely overland, and to this fact some attribute its superior and delicate flavour.

The tea trade of China is rapidly going from her, and she has but herself, and the shortsighted knavery of her growers and manufacturers, to thank for it. According to a Tea Circular,[1] the following are the imports and deliveries of China tea from 1st to 30th June :—

1888.	1889.	1890.
6,697,000 lbs.	508,000 lbs.	452,000 lbs.

a truly fearful falling off. English people got tired of the flavourless stuff sent from China, and India and Ceylon having perfected the manufacture (which at first start of the industry of tea growing in those parts was not good), send us delicious tea, of a much higher market value than that of China.

Ceylon tea, especially, has enormously won the favour of the English tea-drinking community in a

[1] Messrs. William, James & Henry Thompson, 38, Mincing Lane, London.

very few years, as the following short statistics, taken from a Tea Circular,[1] will show,—

The total value of all the Ceylon tea in bond in 1880 was £5,024.
    Ditto   ditto   ditto   1888 „ £1,555,095.

The duty on above, at 6d. per lb., was respectively   £2,871.
                                                                                 £464,664.

showing that not only had the quantity imported enormously increased, but so had the quality, as shown by the enhanced market value. One instance, although an exceptional one, will show what Ceylon can produce in the way of tea. On 13th January, 1890, was sold at the London Commercial Tea Sale Rooms, a consignment of tea from the Gallebodde Estate, Ceylon, which experts described as the finest tea ever grown. This unique tea was of the brightest gold colour, resembling grains of gold. Its sale excited the keenest competition, and it was eventually knocked down for £4 7s. per lb., but it was resold a few days afterwards to a wholesale firm at the enormous price of £5 10s. per lb.

"Much excitement prevailed yesterday in the London Commercial Tea Sale Rooms, Mincing Lane, on the offering of a small lot of Ceylon tea, from the Gartmore Estate. This tea is composed almost entirely of small 'golden tips,' which are the extreme ends of the small succulent shoots of the plant. Competition was of a very keen description, the tea being ultimately knocked down to the Mazawattee Ceylon Tea Com-

[1] Messrs. Gow, Wilson & Stanton.

pany at the unprecedented price of £10 2s. 6d. per pound."—*Standard*, March 11th, 1891.

Another circular of the same firm of tea brokers gives a list of 132 tea gardens in Ceylon.[1]

Indian tea is fast helping to supersede China tea, and another Tea Circular[2] points out that, "Towards the 190 million lbs. probably required for home use during the coming year, India and Ceylon together will contribute fully 150 millions." It also gives the following :—

"LONDON STATISTICS FOR YEAR ENDING 31ST MAY."

		1888.	1889.	1890.
Import,	Indian ...	86,371,000	94,954,000	101,052,000
	Ceylon ...	14,705,000	26,390,000	34,246,000
	China ...	117,185,000	98,695,000	90,097,000
	Java ...	2,989,000	4,170,000	3,107,000
Total		221,250,000	224,209,000	228,502,000
Delivery,	Indian ...	85,619,000	91,368,000	101,168,000
	Ceylon ...	12,578,000	23,830,000	31,947,000
	China ...	116,870,000	105,668,000	87,652,900
	Java ...	3,133,100	3,862,000	3,280,000
		218,200,000	224,728,000	224,047,000

[1] In September, 1890, a small parcel of Flowering Pekoe fetched, at public sale, 36s. per lb., and this price has been largely exceeded on former occasions.

"A parcel of tea from the Oriental Bank Estates Company's Havilland Estate in Ceylon was sold at auction in Mincing Lane yesterday for £17 per lb., or over one guinea an ounce."—*Standard*, May 6th, 1891.

"A small lot of Golden Tip Ceylon tea from the Gartmore Estate was sold by auction in Mincing Lane yesterday to the Mazawattee Ceylon Tea Company at £25 10s. per lb."—*Standard*, May 8th 1891.

[2] Messrs. Wm. Jas. and Hy. Thompson.

Of which—
Home Consumpt. ... 183,000,000   185,250,000   187,940,000
Export   35,200,000   39,500,000   36,107,000

There are three active substances in tea, which we should do well to notice: Volatile Oil, Theine, and Tannin.

The volatile oil can be distilled by ordinary process, and it contains the aroma and flavour of tea in perfection. Its action on the human body is not thoroughly known, with the exception that it is injurious in a greater or less degree. The Chinese are well aware of the fact, and will rarely use tea until it is a year old, thus allowing some of it to evaporate, and it is probably owing to this oil that tea-tasters (who taste as much by smell as by palate) are subject to attacks of headache and giddiness.

Theine is the principle which gives to tea its power of lessening the waste of the tissues in the human body, and, when separated from the decoction, it forms an alkaloid having no smell, a slightly bitter taste, and is composed of colourless crystals. It is also an active agent in Maté or Paraguay tea, in coffee (when it is called caffeine, although identical in substance), in Guarana, which is used as coffee in Brazil, and in the Kola Nut of Africa.

The third product, tannin, gives roughness of flavour to the tea, and is particularly developed by allowing the infusion to stand a long time. It is harmless; at least, its combination in tea has never been found to be hurtful; Its presence is at once shown by dropping some tea on the clean blade of a knife, when it will produce a black stain—the tannin derived from oxgalls, and a solution of iron, forming the ink with which we write.

That Chinese tea has been, and is, largely adulterated, is an indisputable fact, and in those bygone days, when all our supply came from China, it had to be borne. Now, at all events, the Indian and Ceylon teas are pure, and can be taken without the slightest fear. The green teas used to be most adulterated, but the black teas could also tell their tale of fraud.

J. A.

TEA.

II.

Introduction of Tea into Europe—Early Authorities thereon—"Tay"—Its Introduction into England—Excise Duty thereon—Thomas Garway's Advertisement.

WHEN tea was first introduced into Europe is still an unsettled question, and the earliest mention that the writers can find (that is, to verify) is in a volume of Travels by Father Giovanni Pietro Maffei,[1] published 1588 (book vi., p. 109). Speaking of his travels in China, he says: "Quanquam è vitibus more nostro non exprimunt merum, uvas quodam condimenti genere in hyemem adservare, mos est; cœterum ex herba quadam expressus liquor admodum

[1] *Joannis Petri Maffeii Bergomatis, e Societate Jesu, Historiarum Indicarum*, etc. *Florentiæ*, 1588.

salutaris, nomine Chia, calidus hauritur, ut apud Japonios : Cujus maxime beneficio, pituitam, gravedinem, lippitudinem nesciunt; vitam bene longam, sine ullo ferme languore traducunt, oleis alicubi carent." "Although they do not extract wine from the vines as we do, but have a custom of preserving the grapes as a kind of condiment for the winter, they yet press out of a certain herb, a liquor which is very healthy which is called Chia, and they drink it hot, as do the Japanese. And the use of this causes them not to know the meaning of phlegm, heaviness of the head, or running of the eyes, but they live a long and happy life, without pain, or infirmity of any sort."

Another early mention of it is in a book by Giovanni Botero,[1] which was translated into English by Robert Peterson, "of Lincolne's Inne, Gent." He says (p. 75), "They haue also an herbe, out of which they presse a delicate iuyce, which serues them for drincke instead of wyne. It also preserues their health, and frees them from all those euills, that the immoderat vse of wyne doth breed vnto us."

Early in the seventeenth century tea was becoming known in Europe, mainly through the instrumentality of the Dutch East India Company, and we learn much about it in the writings of Father Alexandre de Rhodes, who, after thirty-five years' travel, gave the benefit of his experiences to the public. He left Rome in October, 1618, and thus writes about " De l'Vsage du Tay, qui

---

[1] *Delle Cause della grandezza delle Città*, etc., del Giovanni Botero. *Milano*, ed. 1596, p. 61.

est fort ordinaire en la Chine."[1] He says, "One of the things which, in my opinion, contributes most to the great health of this people, who often attain to extreme old age, is *Tay*, the use of which is very common throughout the East, and which is beginning to be known in France, by means of the Dutch, who bring it from China, and sell it at Paris at 30 francs the pound, which they have bought in that country for 8 or 10 sols, and yet I perceive that it is very old, and spoilt. Thus it is that we brave Frenchmen suffer strangers to enrich themselves in the East India trade, whence they might draw the fairest treasures of the world, if they had but the courage to undertake it as well as their neighbours, who have less means of being successful than they have.

"*Tay* is a leaf as large as that of our pomegranate, and it grows on shrubs similar to the myrtle: it does not exist elsewhere throughout the world, but in two provinces of China, where it grows. The chief is that of Nanquin, whence comes the best *Tay*, which they call *Chà;* the other is the province of Chin Chean. The gathering of this leaf in both these provinces is made with as much care as we exercise in our vintage, and its abundance is so great, that they have enough to supply the rest of China, Japan, Tonquin, Cochin China, and several other kingdoms, where the use of tea is so common, that those who drink it but three times a day are most moderate, many taking it ten or

---

[1] *Divers Voyages et Missions du P. Alexandre de Rhodes, en la Chine, & autres Royaumes de l'Orient*, etc. Paris, 1653, p. 49.

twelve times, or, in other words, at all hours of the day.

"When the leaf is gathered, it is well dried in an oven, after which it is put in tin boxes, which are tightly closed, because if the air gets to it it, is spoiled, and has no strength, the same as wine that is exposed to the air. I leave you to judge if Messieurs the Hollanders take care of that when they sell it in France. To know whether the *Tay* is good, you must see that it is very green, bitter, and so dry as to be easily broken with the fingers. If it passes these tests, it is good; otherwise, be assured it is not worth much.

"This is how the Chinese treat the *Tay* when they take it. Some water is boiled in a very clean pot, and when it boils it is taken off the fire, and this leaf is put therein, according to the quantity of water : that is to say, the weight of a crown of *Tay* to a large glass of water. They cover the pot well, and, when the leaves sink to the bottom of the water, then is the time to drink it, for then it is that the *Tay* has communicated its virtue to the water, and made it of a reddish colour. They drink it as hot as they can, for it is good for nothing if it gets cold. The same leaves which remain at the bottom of the pot will serve a second time, but then they boil them with the water.

"The Japanese take *Tay* differently, for they make it into powder, which they throw into boiling water, and swallow the whole. I know not whether this method of making it is more wholesome than the former; I always use it thus, and find that it is common among the Chinese. Both mix a little sugar with the *Tay* to correct the bitterness, which, however, does not seem disagreeable to me.

"There are three chief virtues in *Tay*. The first is to cure and prevent headache; for my part, when I had a headache, by taking *Tay*, I felt so comforted, that it seemed to draw all my pain away, for the principal force in *Tay* is to expel those gross vapours that mount to the head, and inconvenience us. If it is taken after supper, it generally hinders sleep; yet there are some in whom it causes sleep, because by only expelling the grossest vapours, it leaves those which induce sleep. For myself, I have experienced it often enough, when I have been obliged to sit up all night hearing the confessions of my native Christians, which frequently happened; I had only to take *Tay* at the hour when I should have been going to sleep, and I could go all night without wishing for sleep, and next morning I was as fresh as if I had had my usual slumber. I could do this once a week without being incommoded. Once I tried to continue this wakefulness for six consecutive nights, but on the sixth I was quite knocked up.

"*Tay* is not only good for the head; it has a marvellous effect in comforting the stomach, and aiding the digestion, so that it is ordinarily drank after dinner, but not generally after supper, if sleep is required. The third thing that *Tay* does is to purge the reins of gout and gravel, and it is, perhaps, the true reason why these maladies are unknown in these countries, as I have said before."

One thing is very certain. Tea would not have

been in use any length of time in France before it would be drank, as a novelty, in England, and by the year 1660 it had become in such general use that it was made a vehicle for taxation, as we see by the 12 Chas. II., c. 23 : "For every gallon of Chocolate, Sherbet, and Tea, made and sold, to be paid by the Makers thereof, Eightpence," and men were appointed to visit the coffee-houses twice daily to see the quantity brewed.

But this was so inconvenient, that in 1688, after giving this scheme a good trial, the Act was repealed by 1 Will. & Mary, c. 40, and the duties on coffee, chocolate, and tea (for this latter 1*s.* per lb.) were charged and collected at the Custom House, because " It hath been found by experience, that the collecting of the duty arising to your Majesties by virtue of several Acts of Parliament, by way of excise, upon the liquors of Coffee, Chocolate and Tea, is not only very troublesome and unequal upon the retailers of those liquors, but requireth such attendance of officers, as makes the neat receipt very inconsiderable."

In the British Museum is a broadside folio advertisement, supposed to be about A.D. 1600, of a tobacconist, one Thomas Garway, who kept a coffeehouse in Exchange Alley, known up till late years, when it has disappeared in the universal rage for improvements, as Garraway's Coffee House. It is as follows :—

"An Exact Description of the Growth, Quality, and Vertues of the Leaf TEA, by *Thomas Garway* in *Exchange Alley*, near the *Royal Exchange* in *London*, and Seller and Retailer of TEA and COFFEE.

"TEA is generally brought from *China*, and groweth there upon little Shrubs or Bushes, the Branches whereof are well garnished with white Flowers that are yellow within, of the bigness and fashion of sweet Brier, but smell unlike, bearing thin green leaves about the bigness of *Scordium*, *Mirtle*, or *Sumack*, and is judged to be a kind of *Sumack*: This Plant hath been reported to grow wild only, but doth not, for they plant it in their Gardens about four foot distance, and it groweth about four foot high, and of the Seeds they maintain and increase their Stock. Of all places in *China* this Plant groweth in greatest plenty in the Province of *Xemsi*, Latitude 36 degrees, bordering upon the West of the Province of *Honam*, and in the Province of *Namking*, near the City of *Lucheu*; there is likewise of the growth of *Sinam*, *Cochin China*, the Island *de Ladrones* and *Japan*, and is called *Cha*. Of this famous Leaf there are divers sorts (though all of one shape) some much better than the other, the upper Leaves excelling the other in fineness, a property almost in all Plants, which Leaves they gather every day, and drying them in the shade, or in Iron pans over a gentle fire till the humidity be exhausted, then put up close in Leaden pots, preserve them for their Drink *Tea*, which is used at Meals, and upon all Visits and Entertainments in private Families, and in the Palaces of Grandees. And it is averred by a Padre of *Macao*, native of *Japan*, that the best *Tea* ought not to be gathered but by Virgins who are destined to this work, and such *Quæ non dum Menstrua patiuntur; gemmæ quæ nascuntur in summitatæ arbuscula servantur Imperitoriē, ac præcipuis ejus Dynastis: quæ autem infra nascuntur, ad latera, populo conceduntur.* The said Leaf is of such known vertues, that those very Nations so famous for Antiquity, Knowledge, and Wisdom, do frequently sell it amongst themselves for twice its weight in Silver, and the high estimation of the Drink made therewith, hath occasioned an inquiry into the nature thereof among the most intelligent persons of all Nations that have travelled in those parts, who, after exact Tryal and Experience by all Wayes imaginable, have commended it to the use of their several Countries, for its Vertues and Operations, particularly as followeth, viz.:—

"*The Quality is moderately hot, proper for Winter or Summer.*

"*The Drink is declared to be most wholesome, preserving in perfect health untill extreme Old Age.*

"*The particular Vertues are these :—*

"It maketh the Body clean and lusty.

"It helpeth the Head-ach, giddiness and heaviness thereof.

"It removeth the Obstructions of the Spleen.

"It is very good against the Stone and Gravel, cleansing the Kidneys and Vriters, being drank with Virgin's Honey instead of Sugar.

"It taketh away the difficulty of breathing, opening Obstructions.

"It is good against Lipitude distillations, and cleareth the Sight.

"It removeth Lassitude, and cleanseth and purifieth adult Humors and a hot Liver.

"It is good against Crudities, strengthening the weakness of the Ventricle or Stomack, causing good Appetite and Digestion, and particularly for Men of a Corpulent Body, and such as are great eaters of Flesh.

"It vanquisheth heavy Dreams, easeth the Brain, and strengtheneth the Memory.

"It overcometh superfluous Sleep, and prevents Sleepiness in general, a draught of the Infusion being taken, so that, without trouble, whole nights may be spent in Study without hurt to the Body, in that it moderately heateth and bindeth the mouth of the Stomach.

"It prevents and cures Agues, Surfets and Feavers, by infusing a fit quantity of the Leaf, thereby provoking a most gentle Vomit and breathing of the Pores, and hath been given with wonderful success.

"It (being prepared and drank with Milk and Water) strengtheneth the inward parts, and prevents Consumptions, and powerfully asswageth the pains of the Bowels, or griping of the Guts, or Looseness.

"It is good for Colds, Dropsies, and Scurveys, if properly infused, purging the Blood by Sweat and Urine, and expelleth Infection.

"It drives away all pains in the Collick proceeding from Wind, and purgeth safely the Gall.

"And that the Vertues and Excellencies of this Leaf, and Drink, are many and great, it is evident and manifest by the high esteem and use of it (especially of late years) among the Physitians and Knowing men in *France, Italy, Holland,* and other parts of Christendom; and in *England* it hath been sold in the Leaf for six pounds, and some times for ten pounds the pound weight, and, in respect of its former scarceness and dearness, it hath been only used as a *Regalia* in high Treatments and Entertainments, and Presents made thereof to Princes and Grandees till the year 1657. The said *Thomas Garway* did purchase a quantity thereof, and first publickly sold the said *Tea* in Leaf and Drink, made according to the directions of the most knowing Merchants and Travellers into those Eastern Countries; And upon knowledge and experience of the said *Garway's* continued care and industry in obtaining the best *Tea*, and making Drink thereof, very many Noblemen, Physitians, Merchants and Gentlemen of Quality have ever since sent to him for the said Leaf, and daily resort to his House in *Exchange Alley* aforesaid, to drink the Drink thereof.

"And that Ignorance nor Envy have no ground or power to report or suggest that what is here asserted of the Vertues and Excellences of this pretious Leaf and Drink hath more of design than truth, for the justification of himself and satisfaction of others, he hath here innumerated several Authors, who, in their Learned Works, have expressly written and asserted the same, and much more, in honour of this noble Leaf and Drink, *viz., Bontius, Riccius, Jarricus, Almeyda, Horstius, Alvarez Semeda, Martinious* in his *China Atlas,* and *Alexander de Rhodes* in his Voyage and Missions, in a large discourse of the ordering of this Leaf, and the many Vertues of the Drink, printed at *Paris* 1653 part 10. Chap. 13.

"And to the end that all Persons of Eminency and Quality, Gentlemen and others who have occasion for *Tea* in Leaf, may be supplyed, These are to give notice that the said *Thomas Garway* hath *Tea* to sell from sixteen to fifty Shillings the pound.

"And whereas several Persons using *Coffee*, have been accustomed to buy the powder thereof by the pound, or in lesser, or greater quantities, which, if kept two dayes looseth much of its first Goodness. And, forasmuch as the Berries after drying may be kept, if need require for some Moneths; Therefore all persons living remote from *London*, and have occasion for the said powder, are advised to buy the said *Coffee* Berries ready dryed, which being in a Morter beaten, or in a Mill ground to powder, as they use it, will so often be brisk, fresh, and fragrant, and in its full vigour and strength as if new prepared, to the great satisfaction of the Drinkers thereof, as hath been experienced by many in this City. Which Commodity of the best sort, the said *Thomas Garway* hath alwayes ready dryed to be sold at reasonable Rates.

"Also such as will have *Coffee* in powder, or the Berries undryed, or *Chocolata*, may by the said *Thomas Garway* be supplied to their content: With such further Instructions and perfect Directions how to use *Tea, Coffee* and *Chocolata*, as is, or may be needful, and so as to be efficatious and operative, according to their several Vertues.

" Finis.

"Advertisement. That *Nicholas Brook*, living at the Sign of the *Frying-pan* in St. *Tulies* Street against the Church, is the only known man for the making of Mills for grinding of *Coffee* powder; which Mills are by him sold from 40 to 45 shillings the Mill."

J. A.

TEA.
III.

Pepys and Tea—First English Poem on Tea—Price of Tea temp Queen Anne—Scandal over the Tea Cup—Jonas Hanway and Dr. Johnson on Tea—Love of the latter for this Beverage —How to make Good Tea.

BY Garway's Advertisement we get at one fact, that the use of tea had not been brought into popular use before 1657: a fact which is borne out by that old *quid nunc* Pepys, who would surely have noticed it, as, indeed, he did as soon as it was brought under his ken. He mentions it in his diary under date 25th Sept., 1661, as being then a novelty, at all events to him. " I did send for a Cup of Tee, a China Drink of which I never drank before." And again, 28th June, 1667, "Home, and there find my wife making of Tee, a drink which Mr. Pelling the Pottichary tells her is good for her cold and defluxions." So that even then it was not a common drink with people well to do, as we know Pepys was. The old English custom of drinking beer at breakfast died very hard— nay, it is not yet dead—surviving in farm houses in many places in the country, notably in Somersetshire; and when tea became cheap enough to be drank by the middle classes, those beneath them in the social scale indulged in sage tea, and infusions of other home grown herbs.

As it increased in popularity, the poets got hold of it, and numerous were the laudatory verses in Latin respecting its virtues. But, as far as I can find, the earliest English poem about it was by Waller, as under :—

"OF TEA.

COMMENDED BY HER MAJESTY.[1]

"Venus her Myrtle, Phœbus has his bays;
Tea both excels, which she vouchsafes to praise.
The best of queens,[1] and best of herbs, we owe
To that bold nation [2] which the way did shew
To the fair region where the Sun does rise,
Whose rich productions we so justly prize.
The Muses' friend, Tea does our fancy aid,
Repress those vapours which the head invade,
And keeps that palace of the soul serene,
Fit on her birthday to salute the Queen."

As years went on, its popularity became greater, and it is satisfactory to find by the following extract from Lord Clarendon's diary, 10th Feb., 1688, that the tea imported was good, and that it was treated properly. "Le Père Couplet supped with me; he is a man of very good conversation. After supper we had tea, which he said was as good as any he had drank in China. The Chinese, who came over with him and Mr. Fraser, supped likewise with us."

With time, the consumption of tea increased, and its price was much lower; but still, taking the money

---

[1] Catharine of Braganza, wife of Charles II.
[2] Portugal.

value in the time of Queen Anne, in relation to our own it was excessively dear, and its value fluctuated much. Black tea varied in 1704 from 12s. to 16s. per pound; in 1706, 14s. to 16s.; in 1707, which seems to have been an exceptionally dear year, 16s., 20s., 22s., 24s., 30s., and 32s. In 1709 it was from 14s. to 28s.; and in 1710, 12s. to 28s. Green tea in 1705 was 13s. 6d.; in 1707, 20s., 22s., 26s.; in 1709, 10s. to 15s.; and in 1710, 10s. to 16s. The difference between new and old is given once; the new tea is 14s., and the old 12s. and 10s.

The margins in price are not only accounted for by difference in age, but it was well known that old leaves were re-dried and used in the cheaper sorts; indeed, there is a very curious advertisement in the advertising portion of the *Tatler*, Aug. 26th, 1710: " Bohea Tea, made of the same Materials that Foreign Bohea is made of, 16s. a Pound. Sold by R. Fary only, at the Bell in Grace Church Street, Druggist. Note. The Natural Pecko Tea will remain, after Infusion, of a light grey colour. All other Bohea Tea, tho' there be White in it will Change Colour, and is artificial."

Tea was now "in Society," and was made the medium of pleasant little *réunions*. The accompanying illustration gives a Tea-party, temp. Queen Anne, by which it appears that the cups had no handles at that time, and were of veritable oriental porcelain, and that it was not considered a breach of good manners to drink tea out of saucers.

But even this Eden had its serpent, in the shape of scandal, from which the tea table seemed no freer in the time of Good Queen Anne than our own.[1] "Thus they take a sip of Tea, then for a draught or two of Scandal to digest it, next let it be Ratifia, or any other Favourite Liquor, Scandal must be the after draught to make it sit easie on their Stomach, till the half hour's past, and they have disburthen'd

themselves of their Secrets, and take Coach for some other place, to collect new matter for Defamation."

An anonymous poet of that time sings thus of the tea table :—

"Here we see Scandal, (for our sex too base),
Seat in dread Empire in the Female Race,
'Mong Beaus and Women, Fans and Mechlin Lace,

[1] The Works of Thomas Brown, ed. 1708, vol. iii., p. 86.

> Chief seat of Slander, Ever there we see
> Thick Scandal circulate with right Bohea.
> There, source of black'ning Falsehood's Mint of Lies,
> Each Dame th' Improvement of her Talent tries,
> And at each Sip a Lady's Honour dies;
> Truth rare as Silence, or a Negro Swan,
> Appears among those Daughters of the Fan."

Peter Motteux, in the same reign (1712), wrote "A Poem in Praise of Tea;" but his theme may, after all, only have been taken to advertise his East India Warehouse in Leadenhall Street. He says:—

> " From boist'rous Wine I fled to gentle Tea ;
> For, Calms compose us after Storms at Sea.
> In vain wou'd Coffee boast an equal Good ;
> The Chrystal Stream transcends the flowing Mud.
> Tea, ev'n the Ills from Coffee sprung, repairs,
> Disclaims its Vices, and its Vertue shares.
>   To bless me with the Juice two Foes conspire,
> The clearest Water with the purest Fire,
> Wine's Essence in a Lamp to Fewel turns,
> Exhales its Soul, and for a Rival burns.
> The Leaf is mov'd, and the diffusive Good,
> Thus urg'd, resigns its Spirits in the Flood.
>   In curious Cups the liquid Blessing flows,
> Cups fit alone the *Nectar* to enclose.
> Dissembled Groves and Nymphs by Tables plac'd,
> Adorn the Sides, and tempt the Sight and Taste,
> Yet more the gay, the lovely Colour courts,
> The Flavour charms us, but the Taste transports," etc., etc.

As years went on, the poets still sung its praises; and the following portion of "Tea Drinking" brings us down to 1752, by which time it was a necessity in polite society:—

" Sparkling with Youth's gay Pride, like mirthful *May*
   In the Sedan enclos'd, by Slaves up-born ;
See the Love-darting Dame, swing 'long the Way,
   Or to present the Visit, or return.

The sleek-comb'd Valet trimly trips before ;
   Loud, thro' the gazing Croud, commanding Place ;
With well-tim'd Raps he strikes the sounding Door,
   Thunders in Taste, and rattles with a Grace.

Along the Pavement grates the swift-slop'd Chair,
   Back on its well-oil'd Hinges flies the Gate ;
Behind the high held Hoop, up-springs the Fair,
   Rustling in rich Array, and silken State.

The how d'ye ended, the Contest of Place,
   And all the fashionable flutt'ring Toils,
Down, curtsying, sink the Laughter loving Race,
   And undisturb'd one Moment, Silence smiles.

> Behold! the Beau-complexion'd Porcelain,
>   As Bell turn'd Tulips variegated show,
> In order set among the tittering Train,
>   Replete with Spoils which from *Cathaya* flow.
> The leading Fair the Word harmonious gives,
>   *Betty* around attends with bending Knee;
> Each white-arm Fair, the painted Cup receives
>   Pours the rich Cream, or stirs the sweetened Tea," etc., etc.

But, although some wrote in praise of it, there was a class of people who were opposed to its use, and one of them was the celebrated Jonas Hanway, of umbrella fame. Possessed of a competence, he had nothing particular to do, so he turned philanthrope. He took up the cause of the Marine Society, he was a Governor of the Foundling Hospital, and he founded a Magdalen Hospital, which is now at Streatham. These things, however, did not fully occupy his time, and he scribbled *de omnibus rebus:* among other things, about Tea, against which he had a great aversion. In 1757 he wrote "AN ESSAY ON TEA, considered as pernicious to *Health*, obstructing *Industry*, and impoverishing the *Nation;* also an Account of its *Growth*, and great *Consumption* in these *Kingdoms*."

Judged from our present standpoint, it was a farrago of rubbish and false arguments, and he recommends "Herbs of our own growth in lieu of Tea." He gives a list of plants which he thinks useful for the purpose:—Ground Ivy, plain, or with a few drops of lemon Balm, or lemon Balm alone, or mixed with Sage, and Lavender flowers; Lavender itself; the fresh tops of Thyme; Mint; the flowery tops of

Rosemary, by themselves, or mixed with Lavender; Penny royal and Lavender; Horehound; Trefoil flowers; Sorrel; Angelica; Sage; Cowslips; and recommends a drink, which he occasionally used himself, made of Ground Ivy and stick Liquorice.

This roused the ire of no less a person than Dr. Samuel Johnson, who, as "a hardened and shameless

A TEA GARDEN: *George Morland.*

tea drinker; who has for many years diluted his meals with only the infusion of this fascinating plant; whose kettle has scarcely time to cool; who with tea amuses the evening, with tea solaces the midnights, and with tea welcomes the morning,"[1] could not sit still, and have his favourite beverage abused. So he wrote a review

[1] His friend Tyers parodied the last phrase as "*te* inviente die, *te* decedente."

of Hanway's Essay, and demolished it. Johnson certainly was an immoderate and enthusiastic tea drinker, and somewhat a tyrant over it, as Mrs. Piozzi rather ruefully relates. " By this pathetic manner, which no one ever possessed in so eminent a degree, he used to shock me from quitting his company, till I hurt my own health not a little by sitting up with him, when I was myself far from well ; nor was it an easy matter to oblige him even by compliance, for he always maintained that no one forebore their own gratifications for the sake of pleasing another ; and if one *did* sit up, it was, probably, to amuse one's self. Some right, however, he certainly had to say so, as he made his company exceedingly entertaining, when he had once forced one, by his vehement lamentations and piercing reproofs, not to leave the room, but to sit quietly, and make tea for him, as I often did in London till four o'clock in the morning."

When dining one day with William Scott (afterwards Lord Stowell), Johnson told a little story of Garrick and his tea drinking. " I remember drinking tea with him long ago, when Peg Woffington made it, and he grumbled at her for making it too strong." But the names of worthy and eminent tea drinkers are legion, and its virtues are so patent that even our Legislators have a room set apart in the Houses of Parliament for the discussion of it and other matters.

One or two words only, before concluding the subject of tea, and those are to show how to make a good cup of tea.

The teapot should be thoroughly warmed, and the

tea put into it before the addition of the water, which should *just have come to the boil*, and not have been boiling for any length of time. After standing about three minutes it should be ready for drinking. No second water should be used. A sufficiently large teapot, or teapots, should be provided, and if the quantity required exceeds the supply, then fresh tea should be made.

Tea drinking has been stigmatised by some as slow poisoning; and in one of Hood's works we are treated to a pictorial representation of "Sloe poison."

J. A.

MATÉ.

Its Use in South America—Districts where Grown—Its Manufacture—Early Notice of—The *Maté* Cup and *Bombilla*—Method of Drinking—Its Rapid Deterioration.

YERBA Maté, or Paraguay Tea, which is made from the leaves of the *Ilex Paraguayensis*, or Brazilian Holly, takes the place of *Thea Sinensis* in nearly the whole of South America, where it has been used by the Indians from time immemorial, and by their conquerors and settlers since the seventeenth century.

It grows abundantly in Paraguay, Corrientes, Chaco, and the south of Brazil, forming woods called *yerbales*. One of the principal centres of the Maté industry is the Villa Real, a small town above Asuncion, on the Paraguay River; another is the Villa de San Xavier in the district between the rivers Uruguay and Parana. If let alone, it grows into a tree some fifteen or twenty feet high; but the plants from which the Maté is collected are moderate-sized shrubs, with numerous stems from one root. The leaves are from four to five inches long, and the finest Maté is made from the smallest shrubs. One bush will furnish three different kinds of tea, which are called *caa-cuys*, *caa-miri*, and *caa-*

guaza — *caa* meaning leaf. *Caa-cuys* is made from the half expanded buds; but, although fine in flavour, it has the misfortune of not keeping, and, consequently, is all consumed in Paraguay. *Caa-miri* is prepared in the same way as the Jesuit padres made it, the leaves being carefully picked, and the nerves stripped before roasting them; and the *Caa-guaza*, which is the commonest, is prepared as follows:—

A Maté *yerbal*, or plantation, having been found,

and a sum paid to Government for the collection of its leaves, a party of from twenty-five to thirty Indians settle down there with the intention of passing some five or six months. They make themselves as comfortable as circumstances will permit, by building wigwams covered with palm or banana leaves. Their next care is to beat, with mallets, a good hard and smooth earthen floor, about six feet square, which is called a *tatacua*. Over this is built an arch of poles,

S

on which is spread the boughs of the *Ilex*, and under which a lively fire is kindled, that the leaves may be thoroughly dried without being scorched. This result being effected, the fire is swept off the hearth, and the dried branches being spread thereon, the leaves are beaten off with sticks, which operation reduces them to a coarse powder. Sometimes they are pounded in mortars, made by digging holes in the ground, well rammed; but now-a-days the Maté is generally treated in a more scientific and cleanly manner, the leaves being heated, as tea in China, in large iron pans set in brick work. The dried leaves are then taken to the Maté mill, which may be worked by water power, or by mules; the wooden stampers being worked by teeth placed spirally round the circumference of a revolving cylinder. A good-sized mill will turn out three tons of Maté in a day. The crushed leaves are then tightly packed in bags of damp bullock's hide, sewn up and left to dry, when they become as hard as stones. These sacks generally weigh from 200 to 220 lbs., and this quantity is considered a good day's work for a peon. The collectors suffer terribly during this six months of forest life, and the severe labour of collecting, in those tropical forests, is especially fatal to the unfortunate peons.

Its use is as universal as tea in China. The method of taking it has not varied for centuries; and a description of it in 1713[1] is as good as if written to-day.

[1] *Relation du voyage de la Mer du Sud, aux côtes du Chily, et du Pérou, fait pendant, les en ées* 1712, 13, 14, par Amédée François Frezier. *Paris*, 1716, 4°.

"During the day, they make much use of the Herb of *Paraguay*, which some call St. Bartholomew's Herb, who, they pretend, came into that Province, where he made it wholesome and beneficial, whereas, before, it was venomous. Being only brought dry, and almost in Powder, I cannot describe it. Instead of drinking the Tincture, or Infusion, apart, as we drink Tea, they

put the Herb into a cup or bowl, made of a Calabash or Gourd, tipped with silver, which they call *Maté;* they add sugar, and pour on it the hot water, which they drink immediately, without giving it time to infuse, because it turns as black as ink. To avoid drinking the Herb which swims at the top, they make use of a silver pipe, at the end whereof is a bowl, full of little holes, so that the liquor sucked in at the other end is clear from the Herb. They drink round from the same pipe, pouring hot water on the Herb as it is drank off. Instead of a pipe, which they call *Bombilla;* some part the Herb with a silver separation, called *Apartador*, full of little holes. The reluctance which the French have shown to drink after all sorts of people, in a country where so many are diseased, has

occasioned the inventing of the use of little glass pipes, which they began to use at *Lima*. That liquor is, in my opinion, better than Tea; it has a flavour of the Herb, which is agreeable enough; the people of the country are so used to it, that even the poorest use it once a day, when they rise in the morning."

Frezier gives us an illustration of *Maté* drinking, in

which we see a lady using the *bombilla*, although the *Maté* cup has an *apartador*. The silver kettle for supplying hot water is fed with charcoal at the side, and somewhat resembles the Russian *Samovar*.

We give a modern *Maté* cup and *bombilla;* but this, which is made wholly of silver, is only intended for one person's use.

Sometimes the *Maté* cups are made of the gourds of the Cuca (*Crescentia Cujete*) or Cabaço (*Cucurbita lagenaria*) silver mounted. Indeed, the cup itself is the *Maté*, which gives the name to the Herb, meaning, in the language of the Incas, a *calabash*. The decoction is drank with a little brown sugar or lemon added, never with milk, and if not drank very quickly will turn quite black.

It loses in flavour and aroma by keeping, so that in England it cannot possibly be drunk in perfection, which, of course, can only be done on the spot where it is produced. Its virtues are much vaunted. It is supposed to give nervous vigour, and to enable the system to resist fatigue; but this can scarcely account for the enormous quantity drunk, although to persons unused to it, when taken in large doses it is both purgative and emetic.

Like Chinese tea, it has a volatile oil, which gives it its peculiar aroma; it also contains nearly 2 per cent. of theine, and about 16 per cent. of an astringent acid, resembling tannin, which causes the infusion to turn black after a slight exposure to the air.

There is another variety of *Maté*, called *Gongonha*, which is drunk in Brazil, which is prepared from two other species of holly, the *Ilex Gongonha* and the *Ilex Theezans*. In Chili a tea is made from the leaves of the *Psoralea glandulosa*, and in Central America an infusion of the leaves of the *Capraria bifolia* is drunk.

J. A.

CUCA.

Where Grown—Sustaining Power of Cuca—Early Mention of it, and Methods of Preparing and Using it—Cowley on Cuca—Its Modern Manufacture and Cost—Its Medicinal Properties—Cocaine and its Dangers.

CUCA or Coca (*Erythroxylon Coca*) is now used as a drink, the leaves, hitherto, having been masticated. It has very valuable medicinal qualities, one of the chief being the ability to sustain fatigue by those who use it. It grows in the valleys of the eastern slope of the Andes, in Bolivia, and Peru; wild in many places, but that in use is generally cultivated. It has been known ever since the Conquest of Peru, notices of it being very early; and, considering the length of time this knowledge has obtained, it is marvellous that it is only of very late years that our scientific men have interested themselves in its medicinal properties, and that an infusion of its leaves has not come into common use.

The earliest mention I can find of it is in a [1] translation (1577) of a book written by Dr. Monades of Seville.

"OF THE COCA.

" I was desirous to see that hearbe so celebrated of the Indians, so many yeares past, which they doe

call the *Coca*, which they doe sow and till with muche care and diligence, for because they doe use it for their pleasures, which we will speake of. The *Coca* is an hearbe of the height of a yerd, little more or lesse,

[1] *Joyfull Newes out of the newe founde Worlde*, etc. Englished by Jhon Frampton, *Marchaunt*, 1577, fol. 101 b.

he carrieth his Leaves like to *Arraihau*, somewhat greater, and in that Leafe there is marked another Leafe of the like forme, with a line very thinne, they are softe, and of Coulour a light greene, they carrie the seede in clusters, and it commeth to be so redde when it is ripe, as the Seede of *Arraihau*, when it is ripe. And it is of the same greatnesse, when the hearbe is seasoned, that it is to be gathered, it is knowen in the seede, that it is ripe, and of some rednes like to a blackekishe coulour, and the hearbe beyng gathered, they put them into Canes, and other thinges, that they may drie, that it maie be kepte and caried to other partes. For that they carrie them from some high Mountaines, to others, as Marchaundise to be soulde, and they barter and chaunge them for Mantelles, and Cattell, and Salte, and other thinges whiche doe runne like to money amongest us, they doe put the seede into *Almaciga*,[1] and from that thei do take them up, and set them in another place, into Earth that is wel laboured or tilled, and made as it is convenient for to put them, by their lines and order, as we doe put here a Garden of Beanes, or of Peason.

"The use of it amongest the Indians is a thing generall, for many thinges, for when they doe travail by the waie, for neede and for their content when they are in their houses, thei use it in this forme. Thei take Cokles or Oisters in their shelles, and they doe burne them and grinde them, and after they are burned they remaine like Lyme, very small grounde,

---

[1] Garden beds in which seeds are planted.

and they take of the Leves of the *Coca*, and they chawe them in their Mouthes, and, as they go chawyng, they goe mingling with it of that pouder made of the shelles in such sorte, that they make it like to a Paste taking lesse of the Pouder then of the Hearbe, and of this Paste they make certaine small Bawles' rounde, and they put them to drie, and when they will use of them, they take a little Ball in their mouthe, and they chawe hym; passing hym from one parte to another, procuring to conserue him all that they can, and that beyng doen, they doe retaurne to take another, and so they goe, using of it all the tyme that they have neede, whiche is when they travaill by the waie, and especially if it be by waies where is no meate, or lacke of water. For the use of these little Bawles doe take the hunger and thurste from them, and they say that they dooe receive substaunce, as though that they did eate. At other times thei use of them for their pleasure, although that they labour not by the waie, and thei do use the same *Coca* alone, chawing it and bringing it in their mouthes, from one side to another, untill there be no vertue remainyng in it, and then they take another."

Garcia Lasso de la Vega, who wrote his *Commentarios Reales* in 1609, gives a fine description of Cuca—which I take from his translator, Sir Paul Rycaut.

"*Of the pretious Leafe called* Cuca."

"But above all we must not omit to discourse at large of the Herb which the *Indians* call *Cuca*, and

the *Spaniards, Coca*, being that which is, and hath been a considerable part of the Riches of *Peru*, and such as hath yielded great benefit to the Merchants. And, indeed, the *Indians* did justly esteem it for the rare Virtues and Qualities of it, which the *Spaniards* have not onely approved, but have also discovered several other specifick and medicinal Qualities belonging to it. *Blas Valera*, who was a very curious Person, and one who had resided many years in *Peru*, and came from thence thirty years after my departure, hath wrote Very largely of the many Virtues of this Herb, and such as he hath found out by his own experience. His words are these, ' The *Cuca* is a
' small, tender Tree or Bind, about the height and
' biegness of a Vine ; it produceth not many Branches,
' but is full of delicate Leaves, of about the breadth and
' length of a Man's Thumb ; it is of an excellent smell,
' and very fragrant ; the *Spaniards* and *Indians* do both
' give them the name of *Cuca ;* the which is so much
' esteemed by the *Indians*, that they prefer it before
' Gold, or Silver, or Pretious Stones. They plant and
' manure them with great art and diligence, and gather
' them with great care, pulling them leaf by leaf, and
' then lay them to dry in the Sun, and so the Indians
' eat them dry.

"' The Virtue and Benefit of this *Cuca* is plainly
' observable in labouring Men, who, having eaten it are
' much refreshed, and often labour a whole day in the
' strength of it, without any other nourishment. The
' *Cuca* moreover preserves the Body from many in-
' firmities ; and our Physicians make use of it, being

'dried and beaten to powder, to ease and assuage the
'Inflammation, or swelling of any Wound; it is good
'to strengthen bones which have been broken, and
'expell colds from the Body, and to prevent them; it
'is good also to cleanse great Wounds of Worms, and
'heal them; nor is the Virtue of it less, being taken
'inwardly, than it is by outward applications. Besides
'all which Virtues, it yields a great benefit to the
'Bishop and Canons and other Dependents on the
'Cathedral Church of *Cozco*, the Tithes of the Leaves of
'*Cuca* being their greatest Revenue; it is also a great
'commodity amongst the Merchants; notwithstanding
'all which good Qualities of the *Cuca*, there are many,
'who being ignorant of its Virtues have wrote against
'it; for no other reason, than because the Gentiles, in
'ancient times, did, by their Diviners and Wizards offer
'this *Cuca* to their Gods in Sacrifice; and, therefore,
'having been abused to Idolatry, they conclude that it
'ought for ever to be esteemed abominable and pro-
'phane. This Argument might be available, if it had
'been the custome to offer this Herb onely to the Devil,
'but, in regard that both ancient and modern Idolaters
'have made their Corn, and Fruits, and whatsoever
'grows above or beneath the earth, their Drinks and
'Water, their Wool and Clothing, their Flocks and
'Herds, and all things else, the matter and subject of
'their Sacrifices; we may argue from the same founda-
'tion, that all those things are defiled and rendred as
'abominable and unclean as the *Cuca;* but to the clean,
'all things being clean, let us teach them to abhor and
'forsake their superstitious and idolatrous Worships,

' and let us, using our Christian Liberty, receive those
' Blessings with moderation and thanksgiving.'

"Thus far are the Words of *Blas Valera*. To which
we shall add thus much farther, that this little Tree is
about the height of a Man, in the planting of which
they cast the seed in its green shell, and when it
grows up, they then hoa and open the Earth for it, as
they do for Vines, supporting the tender twigs with
stakes; and in planting, they take great care that the
tender roots be laid streight in the Earth, for with the
least doubling they dry and wither; they take likewise the Leaf of every sprig by itself, and, holding it
between their fingers, they cut it with great care till
they come to the Bud, but do not touch it, for then
the whole branch will wither; both the outside and
inside of this Leaf in the greenness and shape of it, is
like the *Arbuteus*, onely the Leaves are so thin, that
three or four of them, being doubled, are not so thick
as that of the *Arbuteus*. . . .

"When they gather the Leaves they dry them in the
Sun; but care is to be taken that they are not over-
dried, for then they lose much of their Virtue, and,
being very thin, soon turn to powder; nor will they
bear much moisture; for they soon grow musty and
rotten; but they lay them up in Baskets of slit Canes,
of which many fine ones are made in the *Antis*.
With the Leaves of those big Canes, which are about
the third of a yard long, they cover the top of the
Baskets, to keep Moisture from the Leaves, which is
very prejudicial to them; and to consider the great
pains and care which is taken to nourish this *Cuca*,

and the provisions of all things which are made for it, we ought rather to render thanks to God for his abundant blessings in the variety of his Creatures, than to believe or conclude that what we write is fabulous or incredible; if these fruits were to be planted or nourished in other Countries, the charge and labour of them would be more than the benefit.

"The Herb is gathered every four Months, that is three times a year, and in the manuring of it care is taken to weed it often; for the Country being hot and moist, the Weeds grow apace, and the Herb sometimes increases so fast, that the season for gathering of it advances fifteen days; so that sometimes they have four Harvests for it in a year; the which, a certain covetous Tithe-gatherer observing, in my time, farmed the Tithes of all the principal and rich Inheritances and Possessions about *Cozco*, and, taking care to keep them clear and clean from Weeds, he so improved his Revenue, that the year following, the Farmer of the Tithes made two thirds more than what had been made in the preceding years; which caused a Law Suit between the Farmer and the Proprietor, but what the Issue was of it, I that was then but a Boy, did not much remark.

"Amongst many other Virtues of this *Cuca*, they say it corroborates the Gums, and fortifies the Teeth, and that it gives strength and vigour to any person that labours and toils, onely by carrying it in his mouth. I remember a Story which I heard in my own Countrey. That a certain Gentleman, both by Bloud and Vertue, called *Rodrigo Pantoia*, journeying once from *Cozco* to

Rimac,[1] met with a poor *Spaniard* (for there are some poor there, as well as here), travelling on foot, carrying a little Girl of about two years of age in his Armes ; and being an acquaintance of this *Pantoia*, he asked him how he came to give himself the trouble of carrying that burthen ; to which the person that was on foot, replied, that he was poor, and had not money to hire an *Indian* to carry it.

" In this discourse with him, *Pantoia* observed that his mouth was full of the *Cuca ;* and it being, at that time, that the *Spaniards* abhorred all things which the *Indians* did eat or drink, because they had been abused to Idolatry, and particularly they hated the *Cuca*, as a base and stinking Weed, which gave cause to *Pantoia* to ask him farther, why he, being a *Spaniards*, did use those things which the *Spaniards* hated ; for his necessities could never be so great as to compell him to Meats or Customs unlawfull. To which the Souldier replied, that though he abhorred it as much as the *Spaniards*, yet necessity forced him to imitate the *Indians* therein ; for that without it he could never be able to travell and carry his Burthen, for that holding it in his mouth, he found such refreshment and strength, that he was able to carry his Load, and perform his Journey with chearfulness. *Pantoia* wondring at this Report, related to many others, who, afterwards, making the same experiment thereof, found that the *Indians* made use of it rather for their refreshment and necessity, than for any pleasure in the taste, which in itself is not very pleasant or agreeable."

[1] Lima.

A plant having such manifold and beneficent properties must needs have a supernatural origin, and the Indians had a belief that the goddess Varischa first introduced the Cuca plant into Peru, and taught the inhabitants the use thereof. Abraham Cowley sang thereof in his Latin poems, "Sex libri plantarum," and I make use of the translation by Nahum Tate, of the fifth book, published in 1700. The Indian Bacchus challenge the other deities to judge between the fruits of the two worlds.

* * * * *

"But *Bacchus* much more sportive than the rest,
  Fills up a Bowl with Juice from Grapestones drein'd,
  And puts it in *Omelichilus* hand ;
  Take off this Draught, said he, if thou art wise,
  'Twill purge thy Cannibal Stomach's Crudities.
    He, unaccustomed to the acid Juice
Storm'd, and with blows had answer'd the Abuse,
But fear'd t'engage the *European* Guest,
Whose Strength and Courage had subdu'd the *East.*
He therefore chooses a less dang'rous fray,
  And summons all his Country's Plants away :
Forthwith in decent Order they appear,
And various Fruits on various Branches wear ;
Like *Amazons* they stand in painted Arms,
Coca alone appears with little Charms ;
Yet led the Van, our scoffing *Venus* scorn'd
The shrublike Tree, and with no Fruit adorn'd.
The *Indian* Plants, said she, are like to speed
In this Dispute of the most sterile Breed,
Who choose a *Dwarf* and *Eunuch* for their Head.
Our Gods laugh'd out aloud at what she said.
Pachamama defends her darling Tree,
And said the wanton Goddess was too free,

You only know the fruitfulness of Lust,
And therefore here your Judgement is unjust,
Your skill in other offsprings we may trust,
With those Chast Tribes that no distinction know
Of Sex, your Province nothing has to do.
Of all the Plants that any Soil does bear,
This Tree in Fruits the Richest does appear,
It bears the best, and bears 'em all the year.
Ev'n now with Fruits 'tis stor'd—why laugh you yet?
Behold how thick with Leaves it is beset,
Each Leaf is Fruit, and such substantial Fare
No Fruit beside to Rival it will dare.
Mov'd with his Countries Roming Fate (whose Coil
Must for her Treasures be expos'd to toil)
Our *Varicocha* first this *Coca* sent,
Endow'd with Leaves of wondrous Nourishment,
Whose Juice succ'd in, and to the Stomach ta'en,
Long Hunger and long Labour can sustain ;
From which our faint and weary Bodies find
More Succour, more they cheat the drooping Mind,
Than can your *Bacchus* and your Ceres join'd.
Three Leaves supply for six days march afford,
The *Quitoita* with this Provision stor'd
Can pass the vast and cloudy *Andes* o'er—
The dreadful *Andes* plac'd 'twixt Winter's store
Of Winds, Rain, Snow, and that more humble Earth
That gives the small but valiant *Coca* Birth ;
This Champion that makes war-like *Venus* Mirth.
Nor *Coca* only useful art at home,
A famous Merchandize thou art become ;
A thousand *Paci* and *Vicugni* groan
Yearly beneath thy Loads, and for thy sake alone
The spacious World's to us by Commerce known."

Dr. Von Tschudi says that the Coca plant is regarded by the Peruvian Indian, as something sacred and mysterious, and it sustained an important part in religion of the Incas. In all ceremonies, whether religious or warlike, it was introduced, for producing smoke at the great offerings, or as the sacrifice itself. During divine worship the priests chewed Coca leaves, and, unless they were supplied with them, it was believed that the favour of the gods could not be propitiated. It was also deemed necessary that the supplicator for divine grace should approach the priests with an *Acullico* in his mouth. It was believed that any business undertaken without the benediction of Coca leaves could not prosper ; and to the shrub itself worship was rendered.

During an interval of more than 300 years, Christianity has not been able to subdue the deep-rooted idolatry ; for everywhere are found traces of belief in the mysterious power of this plant. The excavators in the mines of Cerro de Pasco throw masticated Coca on hard veins of metal, in the belief that it softens the ore and renders it more easy to work. The origin of this custom is easily explained, when it is recollected that in the time of the Incas it was believed that the *Coyas*, or deities of metals, rendered the mountains impenetrable, if they were not propitiated by the odour of Coca. The Indians, even at the present time,[1] put Coca leaves into the mouths of dead persons, to secure to them a favourable reception on their entrance into another world ; and when a Peruvian Indian, on a journey, falls in with a mummy, he, with timid reverence, presents to it some Coca leaves as his pious offering.

[1] Tschudi travelled in Peru, 1838-1842.

Markham[1] also says, "The reliance on the extraordinary virtues of the Coca leaf, amongst the Peruvian Indians, is so strong, that, in the Huanaco province, they believe that, if a dying man can taste a leaf placed on his tongue, it is a sure sign of his future happiness."

He also gives an account of the modern cultivation of the plant. Sowing is commenced in December and January, when the rains begin, which continue until April. The seeds are spread on the surface of the soil in a small nursery or raising ground called *almaciga*, over which there is generally a thatch roof (*huascichi*). At the end of about a fortnight they come up; the young plants being continually watered, and protected from the sun by the *huascichi*. The following year they are transplanted to a soil specially prepared by thorough weeding, and breaking up the clods very fine by hand; often in terraces only affording room for a single row of plants, up the side of the mountains, which are kept up by small stone walls. The plants are generally placed in square holes called *aspi*, a foot deep, with stones on the sides to prevent the earth from falling in. Three or four are planted in each hole, and grow up together.

In Caravaya and Bolivia the soil in which the Coca grows is composed of a blackish clay, formed from the decomposition of the schists, which form the principal geological features of the mountains. On level ground the plants are placed in furrows called *nachos*, separated by little walls of earth, *umachas*, at the foot of each of

[1] *Travels in Peru*, by C. R. Markham, 1862, p. 237.

which a row of plants is placed; but this is a modern innovation, the terrace cultivation being the most ancient. At the end of eighteen months the plants yield their first harvest, and continue to yield for upwards of forty years. The first harvest is called *quita calzon*, and the leaves are then picked very carefully, one by one, to avoid disturbing the roots of the young tender plants. The following harvests are called *mitta* ("time" or "season"), and take place three and even four times in the year. The most abundant harvest takes place in March, immediately after the rains; the worst, at the end of June, called the *Mitta de San Juan* The third, called *Mitta de Santos*, is in October or November. With plenty of watering, forty days suffice to cover the plants with leaves afresh. It is necessary to weed the ground very carefully, especially while the plants are young, and the harvest is gathered by women and children.

The green leaves, called *matu*, are deposited in a piece of cloth which each picker carries, and are then spread out in the drying yard, called *matu-caucha*, and carefully dried in the sun. The dried leaf is called *Coca*. The drying yard is formed of slate flags, called *pizarra*; and when the leaves are thoroughly dry, they are sewn up in *cestos*, or sacks, made of banana leaves, of 20 lbs. each, strengthened by an exterior covering of *bayeta*, or cloth.[1] They are also packed in *tambores* of 50 lbs. each, pressed tightly down. Dr. Poeppig (writing in 1827-32) reckoned the profits of a Coca farm to be forty-five per cent.

[1] In 1861, the cesto of Coca sold at 8 dollars in Sandia. In Huanaco it was 5 dollars the aroba of 25 lbs.

The harvest is greatest in a hot moist situation; but the leaf generally considered the best flavoured by consumers, grows in drier parts, on the sides of hills. The greatest care is required in the drying; for too much sun causes the leaves to dry up and lose their flavour, while, if packed up moist, they become fetid. They are generally exposed to the sun in thin layers.

The approximate annual produce of Coca in Peru is about 15,000,000 lbs., the average yield being about 800 lbs. an acre. More than 10,000,000 lbs. are produced annually in Bolivia, according to Dr. Booth of La Paz; so that the annual yield of Coca throughout South America, including Peru, Bolivia, Ecuador, and Pasto, may be estimated at more than 30,000,000 lbs. At Tacna, the *tambor* of 50 lbs. is worth 9 to 12 dollars, the fluctuations in price being caused by the perishable nature of the article, which cannot be kept in stock for any length of time. The average duration of Coca in a sound state, on the coast, is about five months, after which time it is said to lose flavour, and is rejected by the Indians as worthless.

Cuca leaves can be bought in London, but up to the present time it has not come into much use as a beverage, yet it is supplied in Roots' Cuca Cocoa, which is a combination of Cuca leaves, and the Cocoa bean.

There is no doubt whatever in Cuca possessing the qualities ascribed to it, and its application in medicine for many "ills that man is heir to," is being diligently pursued by physicians all over the civilized world, with very beneficial results, and it is a valuable addition to our pharmacopœia. Johnston, in *The Chemistry of Common Life*,[1] speaking of the general effects of the Coca leaf, says that it "acts differently according to the way in which it is used. When infused, and drunk like tea, it produces a gentle excitement, followed by wakefulness; and, if taken strong, retards the approach of hunger, prevents the usual breathlessness in climbing hills, and, in large doses, dilates the pupil, and renders the eye intolerant of light. It is seldom used in this way, however, but is commonly chewed in the form of a ball or quid, which is turned over and over in the mouth, as is done with tobacco. In this way its action is more gradual and prolonged than when the infusion only is taken. It is also very different in its character, because the constant chewing, the continued action of the saliva, and the influence of the lime or ashes chewed along with it, extract from the leaf certain other active constituents which water alone does not dissolve, when it is infused after the manner of tea."

It contains at least three different constituents; an odoriferous substance, a bitter principle, and a kind of tannic acid. When Cuca is imported into this country the leaves are coated with a resinous substance, like hops have, slightly soluble in water, but wholly in ether—which, on evaporation, leaves a brownish resin, which is powerfully odorous. This scent vanishes if it is exposed to the air for any length of time, and thus is lost one of the most important ingredients of good Cuca—rendering the leaf useless by keeping.

[1] Ed. 1879, p. 363.

It contains a crystalline bitter principle which can be separated from it by alcohol. Like *Theine*, it is an alkaloid, and is called *Cocaine;* but it is not harmless, as, in many particulars, and in its physiological action upon the system, it resembles *Atropine*, the alkaloid of the deadly nightshade.

It also has a tannic acid, which gives a deep brownish green colour to the *per* salts of iron. So we see in its constituents it closely resembles the *Thea Sinensis*, only it is more powerful in its effects on the human frame, and, consequently, ought not to be taken in the same quantity as we now take tea, but it is invaluable in preventing, or greatly diminishing, the ordinary and natural waste which usually accompanies bodily exertion. J. A.

KOLA.

Whence Kola comes—Early Mention of—Early Trade in—Cure for Drunkenness—The *Cattia edulis*—Substitutes for Tea.

KOLA can scarcely be called a tea, because, as a drink, it is produced from a nut, instead of a leaf, but it is put here because it contains the alkaloid *Theine*. Its botanical name is *Sterculia acuminata*, and it is a native of tropical West Africa, although now introduced into the West Indies and Brazils. The earliest mention of it that I have found, is in "the Sieur Brüe's Journey from Albreda, on the river Gambia, to Kachao, by land, in the year 1700." Shortly after his start from Gambia, he was entertained by a Portuguese lady, and "after a short Compliment, one of her Slaves, a young, handsome Girl, but very immodestly dressed, presented the General a Pewter Basin full of *Kola*, a fruit much valued by the *Portugueze*. It is bitter, and makes the Teeth and Spittle yellow."

Barbot[1] gives a very bad illustration of the nut, and the following description. "The *Cola* is a sort of fruit, somewhat resembling a large chestnut. The tree is

[1] *A Description of the Coasts of North and South Guinea, etc., by John Barbot, etc. Now first printed from his original MS.*, 1732.

very tall and large, on which this fruit grows, in clusters, ten or twelve of them together; the outside of it is red, with some mixture of blue; and the inside, when cut, violet colour and brown. It comes once a year, is of a harsh, sharp taste, but quenches the thirst, and makes water relish so well, that most of the *Blacks* carry it about them, wheresoever they go, frequently chewing, and some eat it all day, but forbear at night, believing it hinders their sleeping. The whole country abounds in this *Cola*, which yields the natives considerable profit, selling it to their neighbours up in the inland; who, as some *Blacks* told me, sell it again to a sort of white men, who repair to them at a certain time of the year, and take off great quantities of it. These white men are suppos'd to be of *Morocco* or *Barbary*, for the *English* of *Bence* island assur'd me, there was a great quantity carry'd yearly by land to *Tunis* and *Tripoli*, in *Barbary*."

So we see that, although a fair trade was done in Kola over 150 years ago, it is only beginning to be known in Europe.

In Congo it is called Makasso, and Guru in Soudan. and the seeds or nuts are used in West and Central Africa to make a refreshing beverage, which is somewhat allied to tea, and which has the same active principle as cocoa, without so much fatty matter. It is refreshing, invigorating, and has digestive properties. In the West Indies it is sometimes used by the negroes to counteract the effects of intoxication. It grows in pods, which contains several seeds, about the size of a horse chestnut. At present it is only used as a tonic. Kola is said to be a cure for drunkenness, and to sober an inebriate in an hour's time; but woe be to him if he returns to his evil courses for three or four days—his punishment will be equal to sea-sickness.

There is a new product, about which, at present, very little is known in Europe. This is the *Cattia edulis*, which is said to be similar in its properties to Maté, Cuca, and Kola, in maintaining animal strength for a time, in the absence of food. It has been used by the natives of Arabia and Abyssinia for centuries. The plant is a shrub with lanceolate leaves of an olive-green colour, and it flourishes in Africa between 15° N. and 30° S. latitude, but it is chiefly cultivated in Arabia, especially in the province of Yemen. From Aden it is exported to the north-east of Africa, and the coasts of Somali land. The leaves are either chewed or infused like tea, and their sustaining virtues have recently been tested by M. Leloups, a French therapeutist. He employed not only the infusion, but the tincture, and an extract of the leaves, finding them all to produce wakefulness and banish fatigue. No definite alkaloid has yet been obtained from the leaves.

In conclusion I may give the following list of substitutes for Chinese Tea and Maté.

Popular Name.	Where collected and used.	Name of Plant.
Arabian Tea.	Arabia. Abyssinia.	Cattia edulis. Cattia Spinosa.
Unnamed.	China.	Sageretia theezans.
New Jersey Tea.	N. America.	Ceanothus Americanus.
Unnamed.	Chili.	Psoralea glandulosa.

DRINKS.

Popular Name.	Where collected and used.	Name of Plant.
Boer Tea.	Cape of Good Hope.	Cyclopia Vogelii.
Sloe and Strawberry Tea.	North Europe.	Prunus spinosa $\frac{1}{3}$ Fragraria collina or F. resca $\frac{2}{3}$.
Long-life Tea.	Bencoolen.	Glaphyria nitida (flowers).
Tea Plants. Tasmanian Tea.	New Holland.	Leptospermum scoparium and L. Thea. Melaleuca genistifolia, and M. scoparia.
Unnamed.	Chili.	Myrtus ugni.
Colony Tea.	Cape of Good Hope.	Helichrysum serpyllifolium.
Mountain Tea.	N. America.	Gualtheria procumbens.
Labrador Tea. James's Tea.	N. America.	Ledum palustre and Ledum latifolium.
Toolsie Tea.	India.	Ocymum album.
Oswego Tea.	N. America.	Monarda didyma and M. purpurea.
Unnamed.	France.	Micromeria thea sinensis.
Sage Tea.	North Europe.	Salvia officinalis.
Ama tsja: Tea of Heaven.	Japan.	Hydrangea thunbergii.
"Burr."	New Holland.	Acœna sanguisorba.
Santa Fé Tea.	New Granada.	Styrax alstonia.
Unnamed.	Central America.	Capraria bifolia.
Cape Barran Tea.	New Holland.	Correa alba.
Capitão da matto.	Brazil.	Lautana pseudo thea.
Faham or Bourbon Tea.	Mauritius.	Angrœcum fragrans.
Brazilian Tea.	Austria.	Stachytarpheta jamaicensis.
Mexican Tea.	Mexico and Columbia.	Chenopodium ambrosoides.
Apalachian Tea.	N. America.	Viburnum Cassinoides, and Prinos glaber.

A tea is also made of coffee leaves, and this infusion has been drunk for an unknown time in the Eastern Archipelago, especially in the island of Sumatra. It is said to be an agreeable beverage, and is preferred by the natives to the berry.

J. A.

COFFEE.

Its Growth and Birthplace—Where most Drank—Legends as to its Origin—Its Gradual Spread—Introduction into Europe and England— Pasqua Rosee's Handbill — The English Coffee Houses—Their Rules—A Poem about Coffee Houses.

NEXT to tea, Coffee is, perhaps, the infusion most drank, its use being universal in Turkey, Egypt, Persia, and most Mahometan countries ; and on the continent of Europe, with the exception of Russia, it is a greater favourite than tea. In Norway and Sweden it is especially drank, whilst tea is comparatively disused.

It is the seed of an evergreen shrub (*Coffea Arabica*) which grows from six to twelve feet high, with a stem of from six to fifteen inches in circumference. When the blossom falls off, there remains, in its room, or rather, springs from each blossom, a small fruit, green at first, but which becomes red when it ripens; it is not unlike a cherry, and is very good to eat. Under the flesh of this cherry, instead of the stone, is found the bean, or berry, which we call coffee, wrapped round in a fine thin skin. The berry is then very soft, and of a disagreeable taste; but as the cherry ripens, the berry in the inside grows harder, and the dried-up fruit being the flesh or the pulp of it, which was before eatable, becomes a shell or pod, of a deep brown colour. The berry is now solid, and of a clear transparent green. Each shell contains one berry, which splits into two equal parts.

In Abyssinia coffee appears to have been used as a drink from time immemorial. Abd-Alkader, a learned native of Medina, writing at the beginning of the seventeenth century, gives us the history of its introduction into Arabia. A certain Sheikh, notorious for his piety and knowledge, named Jemal-Eddin, brought it from Persia to Aden. He was wont to take it as a medicine relieving the headache, enlivening the heart, and preventing drowsiness. This last attribute at once recommended it to the various imams, muftis, and dervishes, who wished to remain awake for the performance of religious exercises at night. The examples of these holy persons had its usual influence upon the people, and coffee drinking soon became a common custom.

Not, however, without considerable opposition did this fashion come into vogue; there were many long and animated disputes about the legitimacy of drinking coffee. Its defenders alleged its medicinal virtues, its opponents declared it to be like wine, of an inebriating nature—indeed, a sort of wine itself; and went so far, in the heat of argument, as to say that all who drank it would appear at the general resurrection with faces blacker than the bottoms of their coffee-pots.

An insult of this sort was surely sufficient to justify a prompt adoption of the severest rejoinder by the other side, and, in replying, they became poetic. Said one :—

"It is a dear object of desire to the collector of knowledge;
It is the drink of the people of God, and in it is health.
It's odour is Musk, it's colour Ink:
The wise man and the good will sip it pure as milk in its innocence,
And differing from it but in blackness."

And another sang—

"Courtesy is the coat of the customers in a Coffee-house.
The Coffee-house itself is as Paradise in its carpets, its company and its tender delights.
When the waiter comes with the Coffee in its cup of porcelain, sorrow disappears, and all anguish sinks under its dominion.
In its water we wash away our impurities, and burn out our solicitudes in its fire.
The man who has looked only on its chafing dish will say, 'Fie upon the Wine and the Wine Vats.'"

Coffee won the day.

There is, however, another story of its introduction —how in the far-off past a poor dervish, who lived in the deserts of Arabia, noticed that his goats came home every evening in a state of hilarity. Unable to account for this, he watched them, and found them feeding on the blossoms and berries of a tree which he had never before noticed. He experimented upon himself by eating them, and soon became as jocund as his goats, so much so, that he was accused of having partaken of the accursed juice of the grape. But he soon convinced his maligners that the source of his high spirits was harmless, and they, tasting, became converts, and the berry became of general use.

From Abyssinia, the use of coffee spread to Persia and Arabia, thence to Aden, Mecca, Cairo, Damascus, Aleppo and Constantinople, whence it found its way to Venice in 1615. But it is hard to say exactly when its use was introduced into England. Robert Burton mentions it in his *Anatomy of Melancholy*, but not in the 1621 edition. He says,[1] "The Turks have a drink called Coffee (for they use no wine), so named of a berry, as black as soot, and as bitter (like that black drink which was in use among the Lacedæmonians, and perhaps the same), which they sip still of, and sup as warm as they can suffer; they spend much time in those coffee houses, which are somewhat like our alehouses or taverns, and there they sit, chatting and drinking, to drive away the time, and to be merry together, because they find by experience that kind of drink, so used, helpeth digestion, and procureth alacrity."

Anthony à Wood says that the first coffee-house was kept in 1650 in Oxford, by Jacobs, a Jew; and it seems generally recognised that the first coffee-house in London was opened in St. Michael's Alley, Corn-

[1] Part 2, Section 5.—Mem. 1, Sub. 5.

hill, in 1652, by one Pasqua Rosee, a Greek, servant to Mr. Edwards, a Turkey merchant. In "A Broadside against COFFEE, or the Marriage of the Turk" (1672), he is thus mentioned :—

> "A Coachman was the first (here) *Coffee* made,
> And ever since the rest *drive on* the trade ;
> *Me no good Engalash!* and sure enough,
> He plaid the Quack to salve his Stygian stuff;
> *Ver boon for de stomach, de Cough, de Ptisick,*
> And I believe him, for it looks like Physick."

Here is Rosee's handbill :—

"THE VERTUE OF THE COFFEE DRINK.

"First publiquely made and sold in England, by *Pasqua Rosee*.

"The grain or berry called *Coffee*, groweth upon little Trees, only in the *Deserts of Arabia*.

"It is brought from thence, and drunk generally throughout all the Grand Seignior's Dominions.

"It is a simple innocent thing, composed into a Drink, by being dryed in an Oven, and ground to Powder, and boiled up with Spring water, and about half a pint of it to be drunk, fasting an hour before. and not Eating an hour after, and to be taken as hot as possibly can be endured ; the which will never fetch the skin off the mouth, or raise any Blisters, by reason of that Heat.

"The Turks drink at Meals and other times, is usually *Water*, and their Dyet consists much of *Fruit;* the *Crudities* whereof are very much corrected by this Drink.

"The quality of this Drink is Cold and Dry; and though it be a Dryer, yet it neither *heats*, nor *inflames* more than *hot Posset*.

"It so closeth the Orifice of the Stomack, and fortifies the heat within, that it's very good to help digestion; and therefore of great use to be taken about 3 or 4 o'clock afternoon, as well as in the morning.

"It much quickens the *Spirits*, and makes the Heart *Lightsome*.

"It is good against sore Eys, and the better if you hold your Head over it, and take in the Steem that way.

"It suppresseth Fumes exceedingly, and therefore good against the *Head-ach*, and will very much stop any *Defluxion of Rheums* that distil from the *Head* upon the *Stomack*, and so prevent and help *Consumptions*, and the *Cough of the Lungs*.

"It is excellent to prevent and cure the *Dropsy*, *Gout* and *Scurvy*.

"It is known by experience to be better than any other Drying Drink for *People in years*, or *Children* that have any *running humors* upon them, as *the King's Evil*, etc.

"It is very good to prevent *Mis-carryings* in *Child-bearing Women*.

"It is a most excellent remedy against the *Spleen*, *Hypocondriack Winds*, or the like.

"It will prevent *Drowsiness*, and make one fit for busines, if one have occasion to *Watch;* and therefore you are not to drink of it *after Supper*, unless you intend to be *watchful*, for it will hinder sleep for three or four hours.

"*It is observed that in Turkey, where this is generally drunk, that they are not trobled with the Stone, Gout, Dropsie, or Scurvey, and that their Skins are exceeding cleer and white.*

" It is neither *Laxative* nor *Restringent*..

"Made and Sold in *St. Michael's Alley* in *Cornhill*, by *Pasqua Rosee*, at the Signe of his own Head."

That it met with opposition at its introduction, we have already seen in "A Broadside against Coffee;" but Hatton, in his "New View of London," 1708, gives a case of clear persecution. "I find it Recorded that one *James Farr*, a barber, who kept the Coffee House which is now the *Rainbow*, was, in the year 1657, presented by the Inquest of St. Dunstan's in the W. for Making and Selling a sort of Liquor, called Coffee, as a great Nusance and Prejudice of the neighbourhood, etc. And who would then have thought London would ever have had near 3000 such Nusances, and that Coffee should have been, as now, so much Drank by the best of Quality and Physicians."[1]

The coffee houses soon became popular, because they filled a social want. There were no clubs, as we know them, although there were limited social gatherings, under the name of club, held at stated periods— and the coffee house provided a convenient place for gossip and news. Here were served alcoholic drinks

[1] For a list of 500 Coffee Houses, see Appendix to *Social Life in the Reign of Queen Anne*, by John Ashton.

as well as coffee; here the newspapers might be seen; here, also, men could indulge in a pipe, and its advantages are well summed up by Misson,[1] who

[1] *Memoirs and Observations in his Travels over England*, etc.

travelled in England in the reign of William and Mary. " These Houses, which are very numerous in London, are extreamly convenient. You have all Manner of News there ; You have a good Fire, which you may sit by as long as you please ; You have a dish of Coffee, you meet your Friends for the Transaction of Business, and all for a Penny, if you don't care to spend more."

"THE RULES AND ORDERS OF THE COFFEE-HOUSE.[1]

" Enter Sirs, freely, But first, if you please,
Peruse our Civil-Orders, which are these.

" First, Gentry, Tradesmen, all are welcome hither,
And may, without Affront, sit down Together :
Pre-eminence of Place, none here should Mind,
But take the next fit Seat that he can find :
Nor need any, if Finer Persons come,
Rise up for to assigne to them his Room ;
To limit Men's Expence, we think not fair,
But let him forfeit Twelve pence that shall Swear ;
He that shall any Quarrel here begin,
Shall give each Man a Dish t' Atone the Sin ;
And so shall he, whose Complements extend
So far to drink in COFFEE to his Friend ;
Let Noise of loud Disputes be quite forborn,
No Maudlin Lovers here in Corners Mourn :
But all be Brisk, and Talk, but not too much ;
On Sacred things, Let none presume to touch,
Nor Profane Scripture, or sawcily wrong
Affairs of State with an Irreverent Tongue :
Let mirth be Innocent, aud each Man see,
That all his Jests without Reflection be ;

[1] *A Brief Description of the excellent Vertues of that Sober and Wholesome Drink called Coffee.* 1674, s. sh. fol.

> To keep the House more Quiet, and from Blame,
> We Banish hence Cards, Dice and every Game:
> Nor can allow of Wagers, that Exceed
> Five Shillings, which, oft-times, much Trouble Breed;
> Let all that's Lost or Forfeited be spent
> In such Good Liquor as the House doth Vent,
> And Customers endeavour to their Powers,
> For to observe still seasonable Howers.
>> Lastly, Let each Man what he calls for *Pay*,
>> And so you're welcome to come every Day."

To know of coffee-houses in their prime, we must turn to the pages of Addison and Steele, to the *Guardian*, the *Spectator*, the *Tatler*, etc., but they are well epitomised in the following poem, which bears date 1667:—

> "NEWS FROM THE COFFEE-HOUSE.
> " In which is shewn their several sorts of Passions,
>> Containing Newes from all our Neighbour *Nations*.

>> "A POEM.

> "You that delight in Wit and Mirth,
>> And long to hear such News,
> As comes from all Parts of the *Earth*,
>> *Dutch, Danes*, and *Turks*, and *Jews*,
> I'le send yee to a Rendezvouz,
>> Where it is smoking new;
> Go, hear it at a *Coffee-house*,
> *It cannot but be true.*

> There Battles and Sea-Fights are Fought,
>> And bloudy Plots display'd;
> They know more things than 'ere was thought
>> Or ever was betray'd:
> No Money in the Minting House
>> Is halfe so Bright and New;
> And, comming from a *Coffee-House*
> *It cannot but be true.*

Before the *Navyes* fall to Work,
   They know who shall be Winner;
They there can tell ye what the *Turk*
   Last Sunday had to Dinner;
Who last did cut *Du Ruitter's* Corns,
   Amongst his jovial Crew;
Or Who first gave the *Devil* Horns.
   Which cannot but be true.

A *Fisherman* did boldly tell,
   And strongly did avouch,
He Caught a Shoal of Mackarel,
   That Parley'd all in *Dutch*,
And cry'd out, *Yaw, yaw, yaw, Myne Here;*
   But as the Draught they Drew,
They Struck for fear that *Monck* was there,
   Which cannot but be true.

Another Swears by both his Ears,
   Mounsieur will cut our Throats;
The *French King* will a Girdle bring,
   Made of Flat-bottom'd Boats;
Shall compas *England* round about,
   Which must not be a few,
To give our *Englishmen* the Rout;
   This sounds as if 'twere true.

There's nothing done in all the World,
   From *Monarch* to the *Mouse*,
But every Day or Night 'tis hurl'd
   Into the *Coffee-house*.
What *Lillie* or what *Booker* can
   By Art, not bring about
At *Coffee-house* you'l find a Man,
   Can quickly find it out.

They'l tell ye there, what Lady-ware,
   Of late is grown too light;

What Wise-man shall from Favour Fall,
   What Fool shall be a Knight;
They'l tell ye when our Fayling Trade
   Shall Rise again, and Flourish,
Or when *Jack Adams* shall be made
   Church-Warden of the Parish.

They know who shall in Times to come,
   Be either made or undone,
From great *St. Peter's-street* in *Rome*,
   To *Turnbull-street* in *London*.
And likewise tell, in *Clerkenwell*,
   What w—— hath greatest Gain,
And in that place, what Brazen-face
   Doth wear a Golden Chain.

At Sea their knowledge is so much,
   They know all Rocks and Shelves,
They know all Councils of the *Dutch*,
   More than they know Themselves.
Who 'tis shall get the best at last,
   They perfectly can shew
At *Coffee-house*, when they are plac'd
   You'd scarce believe it true.

They know all that is Good, or Hurt,
   To Dam ye, or to Save ye;
There is the *Colledge* and the *Court*,
   The *Country*, *Camp*, and *Navie;*
So great a *Vniversitie*
   I think there ne're was any;
In which you may a Schoolar be
   For spending of a Penny.

A *Merchant's Prentice* there shall show
   You all and every thing,
What hath been done, and is to do,
   'Twix *Holland* and the *King;*

What *Articles* of *Peace* will bee
   He can precisely show,
What will be good for *Them* or *Wee*,
   He perfectly doth know.

Here Men do talk of every Thing,
   With large and liberal Lungs,
Like Women at a Gossiping,
   With double tyre of Tongues;
They'l give a Broad-side presently,
   Soon as you are in view,
With Stories that you'l wonder at,
   Which they will swear are true.

The Drinking there of *Chockolat*,
   Can make a *Fool* a *Sophie*,
'Tis thought the *Turkish Mahomet*
   Was first Inspir'd with Coffee:
By which his Powers did Over-flow
   The Land of *Palestine;*
Then let us to the *Coffee-house* go,
   'Tis Cheaper farr than Wine.

You shall know there, what Fashions are;
   How Perrywiggs are Curl'd;
And for a Penny you shall heare
   All Novells in the World.
Both Old and Young, and Great and Small,
   And Rich and Poore, you'll see;
Therefore let's to the *Coffee* all,
   Come All away with Mee. *Finis.*"

                                       J. A.

Different Sorts of Coffee—Its Enemies—Its Composition and Treatment—Methods of Making—Adulterations—Liberian Coffee—Date Coffee and other Substitutes.

THERE are about twenty-two species of coffee, seven of them belonging to Asia, and fifteen to Africa, where it grows in districts widely apart, as in Angola and on the shores of the Victoria Nyanza; yet, although it is so widely disseminated, and comes from so many different places, it is getting commercially dearer without any present prospect of any reduction. Its value in the market is as follows—the first being the highest, and the last the lowest in price. Mocha, Jamaica, Ceylon, Honduras, Mysore, Costa Rica, Guatemala, Brazil, New Grenada, and divers East Indian growths; and its consumption per head in Europe, ranks thus: Holland, Denmark, Germany, Belgium, Norway, Switzerland, Sweden, France, Austria, Greece, Great Britain, Italy and Russia.

Unfortunately the coffee plant has its enemies, in the shape of two fungi which have devastated the plantations of Ceylon and Mysore, one the *Hemileia*

Vastata, and the other the *Pellicularia Kolerota*, whilst an insect called the coffee bug (*Lecanium Coffeæ*) causes great destruction, as does also the coffee, or Golunda rat. Indeed, these enemies so prevailed in Ceylon as to render coffee growing not only unprofitable, but almost impossible, so the planters took to growing tea, with the good results which we have seen.

Raw coffee has very little scent, and a bitter taste, and no one would credit it with the delicious aroma which is developed—like the tea leaf—by roasting, an operation which increases the bulk of the berry, whilst diminishing its weight. It commercial value is in proportion to its aroma; and it is found that, by keeping the raw berry, a chemical change takes place, which very much improves inferior qualities. But this aroma is extremely volatile, and ground coffee should be kept in scrupulously air-tight cases. Indeed, so fugitive is it, that coffee to be drank in perfection should be made from berries roasted freshly every day, as is frequently done in France.

Raw coffee contains an astringent acid, which does not stain iron black. like that of tea, but green; and it also embodies Theine, or, as it is called when applied to coffee, *Caffeine*. This alkaloid does not exist in large quantities as in tea, *i.e.*, the drinker of an equal number of cups of both beverages would have less of the alkaloid if coffee was drunk.

The berries, when roasted, and their flavour developed, are ground—coarse or fine according to taste, and are then ready to be made into a drink. It is here, in conjunction with the use of stale, and consequently, tasteless coffee, that we, in England, go to grief. Of coffee-making machines there are numbers; but if pure coffee is used, they might as well be dispensed with, whilst they are almost necessary if the coffee is adulterated. Another thing that our English housekeepers do not understand is, that coffee, in order to be productive of a good result, should be used large-handedly and generously, and not according to the time-honoured, grandmotherly, but parsimonious method applied to tea, of a teaspoonful for each person and one for the pot. The allowance of freshly ground coffee should be from $1\frac{1}{2}$ to 2 oz. per pint of water, and any less does not make coffee, but only " water bewitched."

With this quantity excellent coffee can be made without the aid of any machine. Warm the coffee pot, or jug, put in the coffee, and then add the water, which, as with tea, should just have come to the boil, and after standing a little time, the coffee is fit to drink. If the coffee is boiled, the extremely volatile aroma is dissipated, and its exquisite flavour lost.

But a good way of making coffee is to make it over night. Put the coffee in a jug, and pour cold water on it. The lighter particles soon get soaked and fall to the bottom. In the morning it has only to be warmed until it just boils, when it should be strained and served at once. This only applies to *pure* coffee.

There are too many adulterants used, and what " French Coffee " and " Coffee as in France " is made of, the Lord and their manufacturers only know. The chief of these offenders in England is the root of the succory, chicory, or wild endive (*Cichorium Intybus*), which, originally wild, is now extensively cultivated in England; whilst on the Continent it is very largely grown in France, Germany, Belgium, and Holland, and both home-grown and foreign chicory are largely in our market, the latter fetching the higher price. It does not taste like coffee, nor has it any aroma; but, when roasted, it gives a dark colour to water, and a bitter taste, as if a great deal of coffee had been used; and for this purpose it must have been first used in the old coffee-houses. But it is a question whether you buy pure roasted and ground chicory. In Germany it is adulterated largely with turnips and carrots, whilst Venetian red is used to give it a colour.

Notice has already been made of the different kinds of coffee, but not the West African species—the Liberian coffee (*Coffea Liberica*)—which has not, as yet, come into common use in England. There are many substitutes for coffee, one of which developed a few years since into a large commercial undertaking, but eventually collapsed. It was Date Coffee, made out of date stones roasted and ground. Among other substances used in lieu of coffee, are the roasted seeds of the yellow water-lily (*Iris pseudocorus*); the seeds of a *Goumelia*, called in Turkey *Keuguel;* roasted acorns and beans, chick peas, rye and other grains, nuts, almonds, and dandelion roots (*Leontodon taraxacum*), whilst in Africa many berries are used in its stead. J. A.

COCOA.

Where Cocoa is Grown—Its Manufacture—Its Use Abroad and in England—Cocoa as a Drink—Chocolate, Edible and Otherwise—Substitutes for Cocoa.

LINNÆUS was so fond of the drink made from the seeds of this plant that he gave it the name of *Cacao Theobroma*, or "Food of the Gods."

As a drink it cannot be classed among the infusions, like tea, nor is it roasted and ground to powder like coffee; but the seeds are crushed and mealed in a mill, and from this oily meal is made the thin gruel which we drink as cocoa.

It seems to have been originally a native of Mexico, and is now cultivated there, in Honduras, Guatemala, Nicaragua, Brazil, Peru, Ecuador, New Granada,

Venezuela, Guiana, and most of the West India Islands. Commercially the different sorts rank in value as follow: Trinidad, Caraccas, Grenada, Guayaquil, Surinam, Bahia, Ceylon, and British West Indies.

It grows, as we see in the illustration, somewhat like a melon, which contains some fifty or more seeds, in rows embedded in a spongy substance, from which the seeds are cleansed and then dried in the sun, when it becomes brittle and of a dark colour internally, eating like an oily nut, but with a decidedly bitter and somewhat astringent taste. To render it fit for food, it is gently roasted to develop the aroma, allowed to cool, deprived of its husk, and then crushed into small fragments called cocoa nibs, which is the purest form in which it is used, but also the one which entails the greatest trouble in making a drink therefrom. The granulated, rock, flake, and soluble cocoas are made by the beans being ground into a paste in a rolling mill; starch, flour, sugar, and other ingredients being used, according to the taste of different manufacturers.

It was used by the Mexicans and Peruvians before their conquest by the Spaniards, and formed an article of barter among them. Columbus brought a knowledge of it to Europe; but those were not the days of non-alcoholic drinks, and it was some time before it came into vogue. Naturally, first of all in Spain, and to this day Spain is the greatest European consumer of cocoa in some shape or other. It was introduced into England about the same time as tea and coffee, but the chocolate houses, pure and simple, as such, were very few compared to the coffee houses. It was taxed as a drink by the same Acts as tea, and paid the same duty. In the eighteenth century it became a fashionable morning drink, especially for ladies, and is perpetually alluded to by the essayists; but it was so expensive as to be only a drink for the upper classes.

CHOCOLATE DRINKING.

Cocoa as a drink is far more nutritious than either tea or coffee, and like those two substances it has a volatile oil which gives the delicious aroma, and an active principle resembling Theine or Caffeine—but not identical with them—called *Theobromine*. It has no tannic acid, but it has what the other two do not possess, it has a peculiar fatty matter, known as cocoa butter, which sometimes amounts to half the contents of the seed. It is this excess of fat which renders it liable to disagree with some susceptible stomachs, but the mixture of farinaceous matter and sugar tend in a great measure to obviate this inconvenience.

In another method of manufacture it is known as Chocolate, which is simply the cocoa bean ground and flavoured with sugar, vanilla, almonds, cinnamon, or what not, according to taste. It is in a dry form the most popular of sweetmeats, although the adulterations practised by low class firms, in order to sell a cheap article, are many, owing to its high price; yet the goods of first-rate firms like Menier, Fry, Cadbury, and others, may be taken without suspicion, and are—good!!!

There are pseudo cocoas, as there are pseudo coffees and teas. The Guarana, or Brazilian Cocoa (*Paullina sorbilis*); a ground nut, the *Arachis hypogeia*, used in South Carolina, Angola, and elsewhere; the *Cyperus esculentus*, or earth chestnut, in Spain, are the chief substitutes; but it is needless to say that none compare with the THEOBROMA. Alas! that it should be adulterated.

J. A.

AËRATED DRINKS.

Ginger Beer—Old and New Methods of Manufacture—Lemonade—Chemicals in Non-Alcoholic Drinks—Fruit Syrups—Non-Alcoholic Cordials and Liquors—Natural Mineral Waters—Their Constituents—Artificial Aërated Waters—Their Introduction into England—Manufacture.

POPULAR among non-intoxicant drinks is the homely Ginger Beer, so dearly beloved of thirsty holiday makers and small children; dear also to the boating man in connection with good ale, as "Shandygaff." And the stone bottle, in which it used generally to be encased, is familiar to every reader. We say, advisedly, *used*, because now-a-days it is also put up in glass bottles; nay, it is sold in casks, like beer, to the publicans and others. The probability is that, in the old days, its somewhat murky colour would not bear inspection through bright glass. The old ginger beer, whose flavour cannot be approached by the modern decoctions, was made of Jamaica ginger macerated in water, with the addition of lemon juice and sugar. It was allowed to ferment, and possessed decided traces of alcohol. It was made after this fashion :—

Take 1 ounce of best Jamaica ginger, and crush

thoroughly with a hammer or suitable crushing machine; boil gently for about an hour in about a quart of water, then add 1 lb. of best loaf sugar, and make up to a gallon with hot water; stir until all is dissolved. Add a small quantity of the soluble essence of lemon, and gum extract, the quantity to be regulated to taste of the maker. Then stir in ¼ ounce of tartaric acid, and, if required for quick fermentation, a very small quantity of yeast. The beer should fine down perfectly clear, and should then be bottled. In from one to three weeks time it is ready for drinking, and should keep good about six months.

This was the old fashion—now for the new.[1]

First incorporate the lemon oil with 1 quart of the thick syrup. (If the oil contains a large proportion of insoluble matter, it may be well to use rather less than 1 quart of syrup in the first place.) Then add the boiling water, and, after that, the remaining syrup; taking care to keep the mixture constantly agitated during the process.

Lastly, add the acid, and ginger tincture according to taste, or the requirements of the public analyst.

[1] *The Mineral Water Maker's Manual for* 1866, from which many receipts are taken with thanks.

    Plain Syrup, from 56° to 60° T.[2] . 3 quarts
    Boiling Water. . . . . 1 quart
    Oil of Lemon . . . . . 24 minims
    Acetic Acid . . . . . 4 fluid ounces
    Ginger Tincture (21, 22, or 23), Q.S.[3]

Use 1 to 1½ ounce of the flavoured spirit to each bottle.

[2] Twaddell's Hydrometer. From 11 to 12 lbs. sugar to the gallon should give something near this specific gravity.

[3] A sufficient quantity.

By adding boiling *syrup* instead of boiling water to the mixture of plain syrup and oil of lemon, and subsequently adding the required quantity of cold water, the whole operation will be brought more thoroughly under control, and a larger proportion of oil may be employed without waste. With some samples of the oil, it may be necessary to heat a larger portion of the syrup; but the oil should always be mixed with *cold, thick* syrup in the first place, unless a perfectly *close, air-tight vessel* is provided for mixing; in this case, hot, thick syrup may be poured on the oil, cold water being subsequently added to give the requisite density.

When it is required to incorporate a maximum quantity of lemon oil with the syrup, it should first be whisked into the *whole* of the thick syrup *cold;* the flavoured syrup should then be carefully heated by means of a steam jacket, or other convenient arrangement, until the suspended oil is reduced to a state of solution. The syrup will then be transparent. Let it be cooled again as quickly as possible.

Gingerade.

Plain Syrup, 42° T.[1] . . .	. 1 gallon
Ginger Tincture (No. 21 or 22).	. 4 fluid ounces
Acetic Acid	. 4 ,, ,,
Bitter Orange Tincture, Q.S.	

Use 1 to 1½ ounce of flavoured syrup to each bottle.

Ginger Ale is a beverage supposed to beguile the artless teetotaller into an idea that he is doing some-

---

[1] About 8½ lbs. loaf sugar to the gallon of water should produce this S. G.

thing naughty, or at all events, placing himself on the very verge of tampering with the accursed thing "Beer." Hence its name, but what a difference in the two drinks! Here are two receipts for making

Ginger Ale.

Plain Syrup, 42° T.	1 gallon
Comp. Ginger Tincture (No. 23)	4 fluid ounces
Acetic Acid	4 ,, ,,
Sugar Colouring	½ ,, ,,

Or

Plain Syrup, 42° T.	1 gallon
Ginger Tincture (No. 21 or 22)	4 fluid ounces
Capsicum Tincture (No. 24)	1 ,, ,,
Sugar Colouring	¼ ,, ,,

Use 1 to 1½ ounce of flavoured syrup to each bottle.

If desired, the *bouquet* may be enriched by the use of one or more of the following ingredients:—

Essence of Vanilla	3 drams (180 minims) per gallon
Butyric Ether	4 minims ,,
Otto of Roses	⅓ ,, ,,

Half an ounce of Spanish liquorice to the gallon will considerably improve the flavour.

Lemonade.

Plain Syrup, 42° T.	1 gallon
Lemon Tincture (No. 19)	4 fluid ounces
Acetic Acid	4 to 5 ,,

Use 1½ ounce of flavoured syrup to each bottle.

When lemonade is required specially for medicinal purposes, and is sold expressly as a genuine fruit preparation, citric acid should be employed instead of acetic. In that case dissolve 1 lb. of citric acid in a pint of boiling water, and use 4 fluid ounces of the clear solution to each gallon of syrup.

Some manufacturers have attained a high reputation for their lemonade by adding a small quantity of *Neroli*[1] to the ordinary syrup. This, if judiciously used, will doubtless be deemed an improvement by connoisseurs generally, provided they are kept in ignorance of the substance employed; but a still greater improvement is produced by adding about 1 fluid ounce of good *orange flower water* to each gallon of syrup,

In the next beverage we are perilously tempting the fiend Alcohol, although it ranks as a Temperance drink.

Champagne Cyder.

Plain Syrup, 42° T.	1 gallon
Butyrate of Ethyl[2]	4 minims
Acetate of Amyl[3]	4 ,,
Nitrate of Amyl.	2 ,,
Acetic Acid	4 or 5 fluid ounces
Sugar Colouring	1 ,, ,,

Use 1 to 1½ fluid ounces of this syrup to each bottle.

But here is a direction which plainly shows the cloven hoof.

"The Ethyl and Amyl compounds are conveniently used by mixing them separately in the first place with nine times their bulk of Alcohol, or strong rectified spirit, adding these mixtures to the Acetic Acid, and this in turn to the syrup."

[1] An extract made from orange flowers.
[2] Or Butyric Ether, known as Essence of Pine-apple.
[3] Jargonelle Ether.

At every turn, in all these drinks, are chemicals used. Do you want the flavour of the luscious Jargonelle pear? hey, presto! There it is for you in a spirituous solution of Acetate of Amyl, made by distilling potato spirit with Oil of Vitrol and Acetate of Potash, at least this gives a fine fruity flavour, but to bring out the true Jargonelle taste it must be mixed with six times its bulk of spirits of wine (*Mem. for Teetotallers*). The taste of apples can be counterfeited by mixing Amylic Ether (potato ether) and Valerianic Acid, which latter is made by substituting Bichromate of Potash for Acetate of Potash, and largely added Alcohol. The delicious aroma of the Pine-apple is made from Butyric Acid, mixed with ordinary ether, and dissolved in Alcohol. Indeed with compounds of the Ethyls, Methyls, and Amyls, all the bouquets contained in wines or spirits can be obtained.[1]

Does your chemical compound look flat and dull when poured out? lo! you can produce a "head," or froth, made out of isinglass, gum arabic, gelatine, white of egg, Irish moss, or soapwort. The latter gives an excellent head; but as these frothing mixtures detract from the keeping of the chemical drink, yet another chemical has to be used as an antiseptic, and Salicylic Acid, made from Carbolic Acid, is recommended. Do you want to colour your decoctions? There is a wide range of tints for you to choose from, from the harmless burnt sugar to the

---

[1] Beware, however, of one compound ether, which gives the taste of cinnamon, and is, Ethyl Perchlorate. This mixture is *explosive!!!*

Acetate of Rosaniline, or Aniline Magenta, of which $\frac{1}{30}$th of a grain will colour a bottleful, a beautiful red.

For the fruit syrups, fruits are very often used, but of course not necessarily. Even milk is not sacred from the chemist. Here are two recipes for making Cream Syrup :—

No. 1.
- Fresh Cream . . . . . $\frac{1}{2}$ pint
- Fresh Milk . . . . . $\frac{1}{2}$,,
- Powdered Sugar . . . . 1 pound

Another formula :—

No. 2.
- Oil of Sweet Almonds . . . 2 ounces
- Powdered Gum Arabic . . 2 ,,
- Water . . . . . . 4 ,,

Make an emulsion, and add simple syrup to make up 2 pints, and there you are, thoroughly independent of the cow!

In these syrupy mixtures the Americans run riot, and a few years since many shops, notably druggists, sold strange and curious frothing mixtures; but there was no call for them in the winter, and they died out as suddenly as they were introduced. The following is a fair list of syrups, some of which, however, are decidedly exciseable. Ambrosia, Apple, Apricot, Banana, Blackberry, Brandy, Capillaire, Cherry, Chocolate, Citron, Clove, Coffee, Cream, Curaçoa, Currant (black or red), Ginger, Grape, Groseille, Gum, Lemon, Limes, Mulberry, Nectar, Nectarine, Noyeau, Orange (bitter), Orange (sweet), Orange (Tangerine), Orgeat, Peach, Pear, Peppermint, Pine-apple, Plum, Quince, Raspberry, Roses, Sarsaparilla, Sherbet, Strawberry, Vanilla, Violets.

And here is a list of Non-Alcoholic Cordials and Liquors (non-exciseable), it is said; but if so, they must be fearfully and wonderfully made. Anisette, Bitters, Caraway, Cherry Brandy, Clove, Curaçoa, Elderette, Fettle, Ginger Brandy, Ginger Cordial, Ginger Gin, Ginger Punch, Gingerette, Lemon Punch, Lime Fruit, Nectar Punch, Noyeau, Orange Bitters, Orange Gin, Peppermint, Pepper Punch, Pick-me-up, Raspberry, Raspberry Punch, Rum Punch, Rum Shrub, Sarsaparilla, Shrub, Spiced Ale, Strawberry, Tangerine, Tonic, Winter Punch.

But enough of these chemical concoctions of man; let us go to Nature, and see what she turns out of her laboratory. Most marvellous combinations of Minerals, Acids, Gases, and Water. Among the Minerals may be named Alumina, Arsenic, Barium, Boron, Bromine, Cæsium, Calcium, Copper, Fluorine, Iodine, Iron, Lithium, Magnesium, Manganese, Phosphorus, Potassium, Rubidium, Silicon, Sodium, Strontium, Sulphur, Zinc, etc. And of Gases we have Ammonia, Carbonic Acid, Hydrogen, Hydro-Sulphuric, Nitrogen, and Oxygen. These materials are mixed in very varying amounts, and from very valuable medical agencies, from the purgative Friedrichshall, to the nauseous Harrogate. But all are not nasty: some are just sufficiently alkaline to be tasty, and, having a briskness imparted to them either naturally, or otherwise, by carbonic acid, make pleasant drinks for table.

These simple waters are abundant on the Continent. In Germany we have the well-known Apollinaris,

Selters, Landskro, Brückenau, Roisdorf, Gieshübel, and Heppingen, whilst in France there are those of St. Galmier, Chateldon, and Pougues, besides some in Italy and many in America.

These, especially the medical waters, are imported into England; but mineral waters are largely manufactured. By mineral waters I do not mean the aerated waters we drink under the names of Soda, and Seltzer, but the medicinal waters.

The effervescing, or aerated waters, which are now so much used all over the civilized world, were first made on a large commercial scale by the firm of J. Schweppe, of Geneva (a name very well known in England, in connection with the manufacture), in 1789; and ten years afterwards, his partner, Mr. N. Paul (whose name yet survives in the firm Paul & Burrows, St. George's Road, S.E.), established an Aerated Water Factory in England. It is somewhat curious how the names last in this trade, for in 1799 a Mr. Thwaites established a factory in Dublin, and the firm still remains as A. & R. Thwaites & Co.

Since its introduction, aerated water has much improved, especially the universal soda water, which is simply ordinary water charged with carbonic acid gas. Vastly improved machinery has been introduced, cleanliness and purity of materials are specially looked after, and the bottles and vessels for holding it wonderfully improved. We have not, in England, taken so kindly to the syphon as they have abroad; but the cork in the bottle has been nearly entirely done away with, and we are no longer compelled to pay for, if we could not drink, the large bottle, which at one time bid fair to be perennial; but which has almost succumbed to its younger brother the "Small" Soda. Year by year, through competition and vastly increased consumption, aerated waters are getting cheaper, and consequently more used.

The ordinary soda water of commerce contains no soda,—it is made by the absorption, under pressure, of carbonic acid gas, which is generally obtained from chalk or whitening, and sulphuric acid, which makes as good a gas for commercial purposes as if it were produced from the purest Carrara marble.

The number of chemical teetotal drinks is legion. They are all calculated according to their concocter's reports, to make the drinker healthier and wiser; nay, even to provide him with extra brain power, as did the vaunted Zoedone, which contained phosphates and iron. They have their little day, and another nostrum takes their place. It has, hitherto, always been so, and probably will continue, only intensified, to the end of time. J. A.

MILK.

First Food of all Mammals—Skim and Butter Milk—Chemicals used in its Preservation — Condensed Milk — Syllabubs — Koumiss —Its Early Use—When first utilized in Medical Treatment— Koumiss from Cows' Milk—Methods of Manufacture—Intoxicating Drinks made from Milk.

MILK is the first liquid food taken by man, in common with all mammals, after his birth and this liquid is so happily ordered, as to contain all the elements of food necessary for him, at this period of his existence. The new-born mammal naturally, and directly after its birth, seeks the fountain of its nourishment, and even that most helpless of all created beings, a baby, is soon taught where to seek its food.

But we have to consider milk as a beverage, more than as a food, and, as a drink, it is comparatively a failure, as to most people it is indigestible, if taken in any quantity. It may, however, be taken with comparative impunity as skim milk, *i.e.* when deprived to a very large extent of its fat, and of a hot day, for a perfect thirst quencher, let us commend slightly acidulated butter milk. Milk has very great disadvantages as a beverage: first, that it will not keep good any time, unless chemicalized by salicylic acid, borax, liquor potassæ, or some other bedevilment, except as condensed milk, which is milk with much of its water evaporated, and sugar added. This, however good it may be as a substitute for fresh cow's milk, where such is not attainable, can hardly be called a drink. Secondly, milk, in common with all fatty animal substances, has a tendency to absorb any odour which may come in contact with it, and is a ready vehicle for the seeds of disease, especially the microbes of fever or cholera.

It is singular that milk has not been made into more *drinks*. Of modern times we have soda and milk, or aerated milk and water, and in the pastoral times of the last century, the times of Corydon and Phyllis, Chloe and Strephon, it was *de rigueur* to indulge in "syllabubs" whenever the nearest approach to rurality, in the shape of a grass field, and a cow, presented itself. Whoever tastes a syllabub now? Ask fifty people—forty-nine at least, will answer that they have never partaken of the delicacy, and the vast majority will be totally ignorant even of its composition. It was made of milk, milked from the cow into a bowl containing mashed fruit, such as gooseberries, and sugar, or else, wine or beer. The great thing was to make it froth, as we may see in the following recipe for an Ale Syllabub, which our forefathers considered as the *ne plus ultra* of a syllabub.

"No Syllabubs made at the milking pail,
But what are composed of a pot of good ale."

"Place in a large bowl, a quart of strong ale or beer, grate into this a little nutmeg, and sweeten with sugar: milk the cow rapidly into the bowl, forcing the milk as strongly as possible into the ale, and against the sides of the vessel, to raise a good froth. Let it it stand an hour, and it will be fit for use. The proportion of milk, or of sugar, will depend upon the taste of the drinker, who will, after a trial or two, be able to make a delightful beverage. Cider may be used instead of malt liquor for those who object to the alcoholic strength of the ale, or a bottle of wine."

The Dutch, who are naturally a pastoral people, make a syllabub of milk, sugar, etc., which they call *Slemp;* but this rustic delicacy has died out owing to the universal use of tea and coffee. Curds and whey used to be much drank, and white wine whey is not to be despised when one has a very heavy cold—but, of course, it can only be drank by the wicked and intemperate; good people confining themselves to hot milk, or treacle posset, either of which served the purpose nearly as well. So, also, the unregenerate have the solace of rum and milk in the early morning.

We have now exhausted all the milk drinks we know of, except " Koumiss," which, although as old as the hills, is of very modern introduction into civilization, and comes to us heralded by a fanfare of medical trumpets as a *panacea* for many evils which the human body has to bear, especially consumption; but Koumiss is decidedly alcoholic.

As a drink made from mare's milk, it has been known for centuries to the Tartars, Khurgese, and Calmucks of the Russian Steppes, and Central and South Western Asia. Perhaps the first mention of it may be found the *Ipatof Annals,* published at St. Petersburg, 1871. " In 1182, Prince Igor Seversky was

taken prisoner by the Polovtsky, and the captors got so drunk upon Koumiss that they allowed their prisoner to escape." The old monk and traveller Gulielmus de Rubruquis, who travelled in Tartary in the middle of the thirteenth century, says : " The same evening, the guide who had conducted us, gave us some *Cosmos*. After I had drunk thereof, I sweat most extremely from the dread and novelty, because I never drank of it before. Notwithstanding I thought it very savoury, as indeed it was." And in another place, he thus refers to it : " Then they taste it, and being pretty sharp, they drink it ; for it biteth a man's tongue like wine of *raspes*,[1] when it is drunk. After a man has taken a draught thereof, it leaveth behind it a taste like that of almond milk, and maketh one's inside feel very comfortable; and it also intoxicateth weak heads." Ser Marco Polo speaks of it. " Their drink is mare's milk, prepared in such a way, you would take it for a white wine ; and a right good drink it is, called by them *Kemiz*."

It remained as a traveller's curiosity until 1784, when Dr. John Grieve, a surgeon, one of the many Scotchmen who have from time to time entered the Russian service, wrote to the Royal Society of Edinburgh (who published his communication in their "Transactions," Vol. I., 1788). " An account of the Method of making a Wine, called by the Tartars Koumiss, with observations on its use in Medicine," and, especially, he thought that, "with the superaddition of a fermented spirit, it might be of essential

[1] Raspberries.

service in all those disorders where the body is defective either in nourishment or strength." And he further proved the benefit of the milk-wine on three patients, two consumptive, and one syphilitic, sending them to the Steppes among the Tartars, whence they returned stout, and in perfect health. From time to time, until the middle of this century, phthisical patients were sent to Tartary to undergo this milk cure; but life among these nomad tribes, with its filth and privations, was hardly congenial to a sick man, so that although some returned cured, others came back only to die.

But in 1858 Dr. Postnikof started an establishment for the cure of diseases by fermented mare's milk, at Samara, in Eastern Russia, and a similar establishment, about forty-five miles distant, was started by the late Dr. Tchembulatof, both of which have been extremely well patronised, as their places were well ordered, and the Koumiss was prepared in a cleanly manner. So successful were they, that the Russian Government, in 1870, started a place of their own for the cure of sick soldiers belonging to the Kazan district. Here are beds for 100 soldiers and 20 officers.

The curative effect of fermented mare's milk set people thinking whether the milk of cows, which is much more easy to procure, would not answer the same purpose. It was tried, and a new drink was given to the civilized world, as also a new name, which was coined expressly for it—GALAZYENE, from γαλα, milk, and ζύμη, a ferment. It can be obtained in London from the large dairies.

Dr. Polubensky gives the following formula for fermenting cow's milk.

"An oak churn, such as is used for churning butter, has a bottle of fermented cow's or mare's milk, five days old, poured into it in the morning. A tumbler and a half of warm milk (of a temperature of about 90° Fahr.), in which half an ounce of cane, still better milk, sugar has been dissolved, and a bottle of skimmed cow's milk, are then added.

"The addition of the sugar is made for the purpose of remedying the small amount of lactine in cow's milk; the water is added to make the milk, which is rich in casein, thinner, and thus to facilitate its agitation and emulsion. Skim milk is used because it contains less fat, an excess of which interferes with fermentation. The mixture is then beaten up during half an hour, to prevent the curdling of the casein, and is then laid aside for three hours. (This is effected at an ordinary room temperature of 60° Fahr.)

"After the lapse of three hours, when the surface of the mixture is covered with a film (of casein and fat in a non-emulsioned condition), it is again agitated for half an hour, and another bottle of skim milk—with or without warm water, according to the thickness of the milk—is added; the whole mass is again churned for an hour and a half, or longer, until the casein is well divided, and small bubbles appear on the surface of the fluid. Then the mixture, having stood for half an hour, has a fresh bottle of milk added to it, and the stirring is again renewed, with short intervals, until the Koumiss is ready, which usually happens by

10 o'clock p.m., if its preparation was commenced at 8 a.m.

"The approaching completion of the Koumiss is known by a thick froth, which sometimes rises very high, forming on its surface; while the full completion of fermentation is recognised by a falling of the froth, and by certain signs detectable by the ear and hand; the process of churning becomes easier, and the splash of the drops during agitation presents a clearer and more metallic sound. The Koumiss is then poured into Champagne bottles, well corked, and left for the night at a room temperature of from 60° to 70° Fahr. Towards morning, the Koumiss is quite fit for use. Left in bottle till the next day, it becomes stronger, but is still drinkable; while, if placed in a cold room, it may be used even on the fifth day.

"In order that the preparation of Koumiss may be carried on successfully, it will be necessary to put aside two bottles of the Koumiss first prepared, and to keep them for three or four days, so as always to have a bottle of four days old Koumiss in store for fermenting new portions of milk, and of replacing the used bottles by new ones."

This seems to be rather a long method of making Koumiss, compared to that given by Dr. Wolff of Philadelphia, which is excessively simple.

"Take of grape sugar $\frac{1}{2}$ oz.; dissolve in 4 ozs. of water. In about 2 ozs. of milk dissolve 20 grains of compressed yeast, or else well washed and pressed out brewer's yeast. Mix the two in a quart Champagne bottle, which is to be filled with good cow's milk to within two inches of the top ; cork well, and secure the cork with string or wire, and place in an ice chest or cellar at a temperature of 50° Fahr. or less, and agitate three times a day. At the expiration of three or four days, at the latest, the Koumiss is ready for use, and ought not then to be kept longer than four or five days. It should be drawn with a Champagne syphon tap, so that the carbonic acid may be retained, and the contents will not entirely escape on opening the bottle."

Be wary in opening a bottle of Koumiss, or you may be thoroughly drenched, and have nothing left to drink, for it generates a large quantity of carbonic acid gas, so much so, indeed, that extra thick bottles should be used.

There is an interesting speculation abroad, that the milk which Jael gave Sisera was fermented, and highly intoxicating, which rendered him in a condition favourable for her purpose.

The Usbecks, Mongols, Kalmucks, and other Tartars not only made milk into Koumiss, but distil a very strong spirit from it, which they call *araka*, conjectured by some, from its high antiquity, to be the true source whence the Indian *Arrack* derives its name. The distillation is generally effected by means of two earthen pots closely stopped, from which the liquor slowly runs through a small wooden pipe into a receiver, which is usually covered with a coating of wet clay. The spirit, at first, is weak, but after two or three times distilling, it becomes exceedingly intoxicating. Dr. Edward Clarke, in his *Travels in Russia*,

Turkey, and Asia, saw this process performed by means of a still constructed of mud, or very coarse clay, having for the neck of the retort a piece of cane.

J. A.

ADDITIONAL DRINKS.

Jewish Prayers respecting various Drinks—Women's Tears—Dew—Oil—Sea Water—Blood—Vegetable Water—Ganges Water—Vinegar—Ptisana—Toast Water—Bragget—Ballston Water—Warm Water—Asses' Milk—Ghee—Milk Beer—Kumyss—Syra—Lamb Wine—Rice Wine—Garapa—Fenkâl—Brandy and Port—Methylated Spirit.

IN the Jewish prayers there is an especial, exclusive and extensive blessing upon wine, which runs in the following wise :—

" Blessed art thou, O Lord our God, universal King, for the vine, and for the fruit of the vine, and for the produce of the field, and for the land of delight and goodness and amplitude which Thou hast been pleased to give as an inheritance to thy people Israel, to eat of its fruit, and to be satisfied with its goodness." Then follow petitions for the divine mercy upon those who say the blessing upon Israel, God's people, and upon God's city, Jerusalem, and upon Zion, the dwelling-place of His glory, and upon His altar, and upon His temple.

The blessing concludes with a prayer for speedy transportation into the holy city ; " Bring us up into the midst thereof eftsoons, even in these present days, that we may bless Thee in purity and holiness. For Thou art good, and the Giver of good to all. Blessed art Thou, O Lord, for the land and for the fruit of the vine."

This beautiful prayer,[1] of which only the roughest sketch has been given here, has been said by pious Hebrews at every meal in which wine has been drunk from time immemorial. But upon wine alone has this honour been conferred. Those who drink *Shecar*, or water, or any other beverage except wine, say before their draught thus much only: "Blessed art Thou, O Lord our God, universal King, by whose word all things were made;" and after it, "Blessed art Thou, O Lord our God, universal King, the Creator of many souls, and their needs, for all which Thou hast created, to keep alive the soul of every living thing. Blessed art Thou who livest everlastingly."

But these two prayers have no especial and necessary relation to drinks. They are also used where aught is eaten which has not grown originally and directly out of the earth, as, for example, the flesh of some beasts, and birds, and fishes, and cheese, milk, butter, and honey.

In the present work particular attention has been given, in the case of alcoholic drinks, to wines, spirits, liqueurs, and beers, and in the case of non-alcoholic, to mineral waters, tea, coffee, and other beverages

---

[1] The form of this thanksgiving is very nearly akin to that said on the occasion of eating any of the five kinds of cooked food from which the *challah* is due.

usually considered non-intoxicant; but under both these widely extended categories a large number of drinks must enter of which no mention whatever has been made in the preceding pages. It remains for us, therefore, to consider in the present chapter the most interesting and important of these drinks which have been hitherto excluded. Of the curious and, in many cases, repulsive liquids which have from time to time been taken, either to assuage the pangs of human thirst, or to gratify the taste of the human palate in health or in disease, the reader who has not devoted some little time and attention to the investigation of this subject will probably have but a very faint conception To go no farther back on the pathway of time than to the age of John Taylor, the water poet, we find so strange a drink as women's tears.

But at a date far earlier than that of the water poet, the date of the Babylonian Talmud, in *Machshirin*, vi. 64, there are seven liquids comprehended under the generic term *drink* (Lev. xi. 34, and therefore liable to ceremonial defilement), dew, water, wine, oil, blood, milk, and honey. Upon every one of these seven liquids something curious and interesting might be written.

About these drinks a question arises in the Talmud, whether under water are included such beverages as mulberry water, pomegranate water, and other waters of fruits which have a *shem livoui*, or compound name. Rambam the great Eagle, more commonly known as Maimonides, seems to exclude these drinks from the general category. By honey is to be understood the honey of bees; the honey of hornets is not to be numbered in the list. In the *Tosephoth* of *Shabbath* it is asked, How do we know that blood is a drink? Because it is said (Num. xxiii. 24), And drink the blood of the slain. How do we know that wine is a drink? Because it is said (Deut. xxxii. 14), And thou didst drink the pure blood of the grape. How do we know that honey is a drink? Because it is said (Deut. xxxii. 13), But He made him to suck honey out of the rock. How do we know that oil is a drink? Because it is said (Isa. xxv. 6), A feast of fat things. How do we know that milk is a drink? Because it is said (Judges iv. 19), And she opened a bottle of milk and gave him drink. How do we know that dew is a drink? Because it is said (Judges vi. 38), And wringed the dew out of the fleece, a bowl full of water. There is a curious addition, reminding us of Taylor, the water poet. How do we know that the tears of the eye are a drink? Because it is said (Ps. lxxx. 5), And givest them tears to drink in great measure. How do we know that the water of the nose is a drink? Because—but the reader has had probably enough of the Rabbinical lucubrations.

A chapter of this book might, were not space a consideration, be devoted to water, which Thales[1] declared to be the first principle of things, and, according to Seneca,[2] *valentissimum elementum*. Iced, it was inveighed[3] against by the Stoic philosopher, as injurious

---

[1] Arist., *Metaph.*, i. 3.
[2] Seneca, *Nat. Quæst.*, iii. 13.
[3] *Ibid.*, iv. 13.

to the stomach. The desire for it was said to proceed from a pampered appetite. Pliny[1] speaks of a wine made from sea water, but considers it, with Celsus, a bad stomachic. In later times sea water has been converted into fresh.

Bory de St. Vincent,[2] in his *Essais sur les Isles Fortunées*, an entertaining description of the archipelago of the Canaries, says that in Fer, one of the Canary Islands, a nearly total privation of running water was compensated by an extraordinary tree. Bacon (*Nov. Scient. Org.*, 412), the father Taillandier (*Lettr. Edit.* vii. 280), Corneille (*Grand Dict.*, under *Fer*) may be consulted about this tree, called the holy one. Gonzalez d'Oviedo (ii. 9) says it distils water through its trunk, branches, and leaves, which resemble so many fountains. The "exaggerator Jakson," says Bory de St. Vincent, being at Fer in 1618, saw this tree dried up during the day, but at night yielding enough water to supply the thirst of 8,000 inhabitants and 100,000 other animals. According to this authority, it was distributed from time immemorial all over the island by pipes of lead. It is nothing to "Jakson" that lead was not known from time immemorial. Viana (*Cant.* i.) speaks of the sacred tree as a sort of celestial pump.[3] Abreu. Galuido says the holy tree was called *Garoe*, and that its fruit resembled an acorn, that its leaves were evergreen, and like those of a

---

[1] Pliny, *Nat. Hist.*, xxiii. 24. [2] p. 220.

[3] Other authorities concerning this remarkable drinking fountain are Nieremberg (*Occult. Philos.*, ii. 350), Clavijo, Cairasio, and Dapper.

laurel. During an east wind the water harvest was the most abundant.

This celebrated vegetable product was unfortunately destroyed by a hurricane in 1625. But even about this date authors disagree. While Nunez de la Pena is an authority for that given, Nieremberg assures us the catastrophe occurred in 1629. Another date mentioned is 1612.

The view of Bory de St. Vincent is that this holy tree was nothing more than the *Laurus Indica* of Linnæus, which is indigenous to the mountain summits of the Canary Islands. His concluding remark is pregnant with common sense: *Si les auteurs que nous ont parlé du Garoé ont dit qu'il était seul de son espèce dans l'île, c'est qu'ils n'étaient pas botanistes, et qu'ils n'avaient pas réfléchi que cet arbre ayant un fruit, devait se reproduire, comme tous les autres végétaux.*

The water of rivers is often clarified in a peculiar manner before drinking. For instance, that of the Ganges is said to be improved by rubbing certain nuts on the edges of the vessel in which it is kept,[1] though how this may be it is as difficult to understand, as how the turtle is affected by a touch of his carapace, or the Dean and Chapter—to borrow Sydney Smith's illustration—of St. Paul's by stroking the cupola of that cathedral. The Nile water is also said to be purified by treating the vessel which holds it in a similar manner to that which holds the water of the Ganges, with bitter almonds. The bitter waters of Marah were made sweet in a far different fashion.

[1] *Harper's New Monthly Magazine*, xi. p. 499.

The *Melo-cacti* of South America have earned for themselves the name of "springs of the desert," owing to their liquor-preserving properties. An ingenious drink is that of the natives of Siberia, a drink prepared of an intoxicating mushroom,[1] in a peculiar and economical manner, by natural distillation.

Vinegar appears as a beverage in a few countries only, and then for special purposes. The Roman soldiers received it as a refreshing drink on their marches, and even in the time of Constantine their rations included vinegar on one day and wine on the other. After all, this vinegar may have been nothing more than what many of us drink at present under the title of wine. That "excellent claret," for instance, "fit for any gentleman's table," which may be had at 1s. 6d. a bottle, may be very like the vinegar of the Roman soldier. Roman reapers used it mixed with water, we are told by Theocritus (Idyl x.), and before that time Ruth was directed to dip her morsel in the vinegar when she gleaned in the field of Boaz.

Ptisana, mentioned by Celsus (iii. 7), appears to have been a mixture of rice or barley water and vinegar.

Toast-water is a drink which may be held by

---

[1] The mushroom used by the Chukchees is described by Lansdell, *Through Siberia*, ii. 269, as "spotted like a leopard, and surmounted by a small hood—the fly agaric, which here has the top scarlet, flecked with white points. It sells for three or four reindeer. So powerful is the fungus that the native who eats it remains drunk for several days. Half a dozen persons may be successively intoxicated by a single mushroom, but every one in a less degree than his predecessor." Goldsmith, *Chinese Philosopher*.

some unworthy of mention, but they may change their minds after reading what Mr. James Sedgwick, apothecary at Stratford-le-Bow, had to say on this subject in the year 1725. The burning of a crust and putting it hissing hot into water has, according to this gentleman, several good advantages. By it, the "raw coldness from nitrous particles are (sic) taken off and moderated, and it becomes more palatable, besides which, from the sudden hissing opposition of temperament, an elevation is made of the heterogeal particles, a motion, an interchanging position is obtained : These Principles during their intercourses will be imbibed and sucked into the bread in order, according to their respective distance and gravities, whereby the liquor will become more pure and almost uncompounded, less foreign than it was under its natural acception." And yet though all these securities are taken to blunt the "frigorific mischiefs" of the water in general, yet in-many constitutions and at particular seasons it is not to be trusted without some "substantial warmth to give and maintain a glowing, e'er it dilutes and disperses." He goes on to say that it is better to add wine to the water, " to prevent the contingent hazards from the limpid element."

Braket or *Bragget* or *Bragwort*, was a drink made of the wort of ale, honey, and spices.[1] Her mouth, says Chaucer, speaking of Alison, the carpenter's pretty wife in the *Mother's Tale*,

"was swete as *braket* or the meth,
Or hord of apples, laid in hay or heth."

[1] Another description is, "Ale mixed with pepper and honey."

And in Beaumont and Fletcher's *Little Thief, or the Night-Walker*, Jack Wildbrain speaks with contempt of

"One that knows not neck-beef from a pheasant,
Nor cannot relish *braggat* from ambrosia."

The opponents of alcoholic drinks are often met by the objection that some of the drinks recommended by themselves are alcoholic, as indeed they often are. Even water appears to possess, in some cases, an intoxicating property. Pliny (*Nat. Hist.*, ii. cvi.) speaks of a *Lyncestis aqua*,[1] of a certain acidity, which makes men drunken. The celebrated *Ballston* waters in the State of New York, are said to be affected with qualities "highly exhilarating," sometimes producing vertigo, which has been followed by drowsiness; in other words, they who drink them exhibit the usual symptoms of drunkenness.

Timothy Dwight, in his *Travels in New England and New York*, says that these waters are considered by the farmers of the neighbourhood as an excellent beverage, and are sent for from a considerable distance for drink to labourers during haymaking and harvesting, a time well known to be full of desire on the part of country people employed in these agricultural pursuits, for alcoholic refreshment. "They supersede," says Dwight, "in a great measure the use of any ardent spirits. But since the result of drinking these waters seems precisely the same, as far as regards

---

[1] Quem quicunque parum moderato gutture traxit,
Haud aliter turbat quam si mera vina bibisset.
—Ovid, *Metam.*, xv. 329.

inebriation, as that of drinking beer or other alcoholic liquor, it is questionable whether any advantage is gained by this supersession.

The properties of the *Saratoga* water, situated some seven miles from that of *Ballston*, are also of a very remarkable nature. They abound to such an extent in a species of gas, that we are told a very nice sort of breakfast bread is baked from them instead of yeast.

The Romans considered warm water an agreeable drink at the conclusion of the chief repast of the day. This may explain why Julius Cæsar was always taken ill after dinner.

Many drinks are derived from animals, either wholly as milk and blood, or from animals and vegetables in common, as oil.

It is said that there are people here in England who like—so strange is the diversity of tastes—a draught of oil from the liver of a cod as much as an Esquimaux approves of a draught of the oil of a porpoise or a seal.

Of milk a large catalogue of drinks can be reckoned. First, there are the different kinds of milk of different animals, as the milk of asses, of women, of goats, of cows, of sheep, of reindeers, of camels, of sows, and of mares. Then it may be swallowed as it is drawn, or in the form of whey, or curdled. *Ghee* is a common favourite throughout all India. It is a stale butter clarified by boiling and straining, and then set to cool, when it remains in a semi-liquid or oily state, and is used in cooking, or is drunk by the natives.

In milk-beer, milk is substituted for water. *Kef* is

a kind of effervescing fermented milk, much resembling *Koumiss* (or rather *Kumyss*), of which the best is probably to be obtained in Samàra. *Youourt*[1] is a favourite drink at Constantinople, made of milk curdled after a peculiar fashion. *Syra*, a form allied with the German *Säure*, a sour whey, was used for drink like small beer in Norway and Iceland. *Aizen* and *Leban* are both sorts of *Kumyss*, one of the Tartars, the other of the Arabs. The latter have also an intoxicating liquor *Sabzi*, made of *Bhang*, a species of hemp. The green leaf from which the drink derives its name is pounded and diluted with sugared water.

Even the warm blood of living animals has been considered suitable for a drink. In the book of Ser Marco Polo the Venetian, concerning the marvels of the East, we are told,—the Tartar will sustain himself in an economical manner, by opening a vein in the neck of the horse upon which he rides, and having taken a sufficient drink will close the aperture, and ride on as before. Carpini says much the same of the Mongols. This appears indeed to have been a time-honoured institution.

Dionysius Periegetes, in the nineteenth chapter of his *Description of the World*, treating of Scythia and other ancient nations situated in what is now known as Great Tartary, says of the Massagetæ that they have no eating of bread nor any native wine, but

$$\H{ι}ππων$$
Αἵματι μίσγοντες λευκὸν γάλα δαῖτα τίθεντο.

[1] The Hindustani يُغٗ, from the Sanskrit   , Bengali   , Marathi   , a corruption of the Turkish يوغرت. *Yughurt*.

> "Or with horses blood,
> And white milk mingled set their banquets forth,"
> *Orbis Desc.*, 578.

And Sidonius, to the same effect,

> "*solitosque cruentum
> Lac potare Getas, et pocula tingere venas.*"
> *Parag. ad Avitum.*

Another strange variety of drink is made by the Peruvians. The ordinary *chica* is mixed with the bloody garments of a slain warrior. Temple (*Travels*, ii. 311).

According to Lobo, the Abyssinians esteem the gall one of the most delicious parts of a beast, and drink glasses of it, as epicures with us drink *Chateau Lafitte*. Pearce (*Adventures in Abyssinia*, i. 95) says that they also drink blood warm from the animal with an extraordinary relish.

The Mantchoos, the conquerors of China, prepare a wine of a peculiar mixture from the flesh of lambs, either by fermenting it reduced to a kind of paste with the milk of their domestic animals, or by bruising it to a pulp with rice. When properly matured, it is put into jars and drawn as occasion requires. It is said to be strong and nutritious, and the most voluptuous orgies of the Tartars are the result of an intoxication from *lamb wine*. Abbé Rickard, *History of Tonquin*.

The only wine in Sumatra, according to Marco Polo, was derived from a certain tree, the *sacred wine*-tree as it might be called, in comparison with the *sacred water*-tree, afterwards known as *Areng Sac-*

charifera, from the Javanese name, called by the Malays *Gomuti* and by the Portuguese *Saguer*. It has some resemblance to a date palm, to which Polo compares it, but is much coarser and more ragged, *incompta et adspectu tristis*, dishevelled and of a melancholy aspect, as it is described by Rumphius. A branch of this tree was cut, a large pot attached, and in a day and a night the pot was filled with excellent wine, both white and red, which, says the Venetian, cures dropsy and tisick and spleen.

The Chinese *Rice Wine* and its manufacture is described in Amyot's *Memoires*, v. 468. A yeast is employed, with which is often mixed a flour prepared from fragrant herbs, almonds, pine seeds, dried fruits, etc. Rubruquis says the liquor is not distinguishable, except by smell, from the best wine of Auxerre, a wine so famous in the middle ages that the historian friar Salimbene went to that town for the express purpose of drinking it. Ysbrand Ides compares it to Rhenish, John Bell to Canary, and a modern traveller, quoted by Davis, "in colour and a little in taste to Madeira." Marco Polo says, "it is a very hot stuff," making one drunk sooner than any other beverage.

From the walnut, which is cultivated to great extent in the Crimea, a sweet clear liquor is extracted in the spring, at the time the sap is rising in the tree. The trunk of the walnut is pierced and a spigot placed in the incision. The fluid obtained soon coagulates into a substance used as sugar. It does not, however, appear that the juice has been converted to any inebriating purpose. Not only, however, from the walnut can a good drink be extracted, but also from the birch, the willow, the poplar and the sycamore.

A sort of birch wine is made in Normandy.

An excellent drink, resembling brandy, has been distilled, it is said, from water melons in the southern provinces of Russia, where consequently much attention is paid to the culture of this vegetable, producing in some cases water melons of thirty pounds in weight.

In the Sandwich Islands a drink is distilled from the root of the *Dracœna*, something like the beet of this country. The root of the *Dracœna* gives a saccharine juice resembling molasses. From this, with the addition of some ginger, a kind of tea is made, also a spirit called by the natives *Ywera*. Their manufacture of this drink is remarkable for its complexity, involving certain mystic operations with an old pot, a leaky canoe, a calabash, and a rusty gun-barrel. It is unnecessary to give a detailed account of the process. We yearn in vain for that absence of entanglement which distinguishes the religion of the Iroquois, who have no other worship than the annual sacrifice of a dog to *Taulonghyaawangooa*, which being interpreted is the "supporter of the Heavens." At this sacrifice they eat the dog.

Sbitena, or Sbetin, is the name of a delightful drink sold in the streets of *St. Petersburg* to the populace. In Granville's *St. Petersburg* (ii. 422) a mention is made of this beverage. It is composed of honey and hot water and pepper and boiling milk.

A drink called *Omeire* is prepared in the South-West of Africa by the aid of some dirty gourds and milk vigorously shaken therein at stated intervals.

In Nubia the crumb of strongly leavened bread made from *dhurra* is mixed with water and set on the fire. It is afterwards allowed to ferment for two days, strained through a cloth, a lady's garment by choice, and drunk. It is called *Ombulbul*, or the mother of the nightingale, because it makes the drinker sing like that bird. *Pulque* is a vinous beverage made in Mexico by fermenting the juice of the *agave*. Its distinctive peculiarity is its odour, which has been compared by an experimentalist to that of putrid meat.

There are four drinks in Madagascar: *Toak*, made from honey and water; *Araffer*, from a tree called *Sater*, resembling a small cocoa-nut; *Toupare*, from boiled cane, a liquid so corrosive as in a short time to penetrate an egg shell; and *Vontaca*, from the juice of the so-called Bengal quince. The last soon produces intoxication, against which another curious drink is mentioned as a remedy by Ovalle, to wit, the sweat of a horse infused in wine.

The aborigines of Australia (Dawson's *Present State of Australia*, p. 60) are inordinately fond of a beverage known by them under the name of *bull*. The recipe for this, as given by Mr. Dawson, runs thus: Get an old sugar bag, steal it if you cannot get it by any other means, and cut it into small pieces. Prepare a large kettle of boiling water, throw into it as many of these pieces of bag as it will hold, and let it simmer for half a day. An excellent *bull* will be the result. This *bull*, says Dawson, they are extremely fond of, and will drink it till they are blown out like an ox with clover, and can contain no more.

Poncet speaks of booza as the usual liquor of the Abyssinans, "vastly thick and very ill tasted," produced from a day's soaking of a roasted berry.

The negroes of Brazil affect a mixture of black sugar and water without fermentation, called *Garapa*, to which heat is sometimes added by the leaves of the *Acajou* tree.

Snow melted and impregnated with the flavour of smoke from the fire upon which it is placed is the common drink of the Lapp. Occasionally he gets a decoction of the herb *angelica* in milk. The maritime Lapp drinks with gusto the oil squeezed from the entrails of fish. Women, it is said, will take a pint and a half of this so-called *tran* at a meal. But the favourite drink is composed of water and meal flavoured with a quantity of tallow, and, if circumstances will permit, the blood of the reindeer.

Taidge or *Tedge* or *Tedj* is a kind of honey wine or hydromel, said by Father Poncet[1] to be a delicious liquor, pure, clarified, and of the colour of Spanish white wine. The process of its manufacture is simple. Wild honey is mixed with water, and set in a jar, with a little sprouted barley, some *biccalo* or *taddoo* bark, and a few *geso* or *guécho* leaves. A superior kind is made by adding *kuloh* berries. This is called *barilla*. The taste of *tedj* has been described as that of small beer and musty lemonade. The women commonly strain it through their shifts.

Besdon is made like *tedj*, with honey, and is highly valued in some parts of Africa. *Ladakh* beer has the

[1] Lockman's *Travels of the Jesuits*, i. 218.

merit of portability. It is made of parched barley, rice, and the root of an aromatic plant, and pressed into a cake. A piece of this is broken off and cast into water. It resembles in taste sour gruel.

Pombe is a liquid brewed of fruit, furnishing a common sort of cider known well in Eastern Africa.

In Tonquin[1] on the annual renewal of allegiance, they drink chicken's blood mixed with arrack. They make a sort of cider from *miengou*, a fruit like a pomegranate. An extract of wheat, rye, or millet is mixed with *peka*, consisting of rice flour, garlic, aniseed, and liquorice. After fermentation it is distilled and becomes the celebrated *Samchou*.

In Sweden, with the *smör-gås*, or fore taste[2] at a side-table a glass of *fenkål*, sometimes very good, sometimes very bad, is given to him who is about to dine. It is made from fennel—a form perhaps of *fœniculum*—growing wild and abundant, as at Marathon[3] the celebrated deme on the east coast of Attica, the field of the famous battle.

In addition to strange compounds known in various parts of this country, such as Gin and Lime Juice, Whiskey or Rum and Milk, Brandy and Port, a drink said to have originated in Lancashire, and very many others, may be mentioned Ethyl or Methylated

[1] P. Alex. de Rhodes, *Voyages et Missions.* P. de Marini, *On the Kingdom of Tonquin.*

[2] A word which, according to the *Glossarium Suiogothicum*, originally meant simply bread and butter. It now comprehends anchovies and other antepasts.

[3] So called probably from its being overgrown with fennel (μαραθρῶν in Strabo, 160).

A A

Spirits, a beverage which, like ether in Ireland, has of late years advanced considerably in public estimation. It has the two advantages of being cheap and heady. An Act of 1880 imposed penalties on any retail tradesman selling it for the purpose of drink. A better method perhaps to prevent its being poured down the throats of Her Majesty's liege subjects would be to take steps to ensure its being mixed before sold with a strong emetic. The palate can be trained, but the stomach is far less docile.

INDEX.

	PAGE		PAGE
Absinthe	162-166	Brandy	115
Adulteration of Beer	199	" German Legend	115
Aërated Drinks	324	" Origin of the name	123
" Waters, Introduction of	332	" and Port	361
African Beers	200	Braket	352
" Wines	58	Brewers' Company	220
Aix-la-Chapelle Council Decree	158	Brick Tea	243
Aizen	355	Bull	359
Alcohol in Wine	53	Burgundy	80
" Effects on different Races	51	Burns, Robert	148
" Origin of the word	116	Burton (Robert) and Coffee	306
Alcoholic strength of Gin	140	Burton-on-Trent	219
Ale Conners	200-220	Burton Brewery, early mention of	209
" Syllabub	335	Cæcuban Wine	30
" and Wine drinkers, social difference in	93	Caffeine	317
		Capnian Wine	26
" Early mention of	39	Canaries Wines	62
" Origin of the word	196	Caravan Tea	243
" Various	226	Cassis	166, 175
American Beers	201	Catherine de Medicis	164
" Drinks	180	Cattia Edulis	298
" Terms, explanation of	180-181	Ceylon Tea	243
" Wines	59	Champagne Country, The	64
Aminean Wine	26	Champagne Cyder	328
Analysis of Tea	246	Champagne Manufacture	65
Anglo-Saxon Liquors	44	Chemicals used in non-alcoholic Drinks	329
Animals' Blood	355	Chinese Beers	204
Anisette	165	" Tea, Substitutes for	298
Aqua Vite Composita recipe	120	" Tea Trade	243
" Early esteem of	117	" Natural Beverage	237
Arrack	113, 343	Chocolate	323
Araffer	359	Cider	45, 110
Artificial Wines	157	" The finest, where made	113
Assur-ba-ni-pal's List of Wines	19	Claret	69
Assyrian Wines	18	Clergy Drinking	46
Athenæus on Egyptian Wines	15	Cobbler, The	180, 181
Athol-brose	148	Coca	279
Auld Man's Milk	185	" Cultivation of	291
Augustus' favourite Drink	30	" Early mention of	280
Australian Wines	60	" Leaf, Medicinal qualities	294
Austrian Beers	202	Cocaine	295
Bacon's value of Cider	111	Cocks' Wines of Bordeaux	75
Baga Wine	17	Cocktail	181
Ballston Waters	353	Cocoa	320
Barbot's description of Kola	296	" Substitute	323
Barley Wine	198	" Tax	322
Bastard Wine	48	Cocoa, Its Manufacture	321
Bavarian Beers	202	" Where grown	320
Beer	49	Coffee	303
" Adulteration of	199	" Adulteration	319
" Antiquity of	197	" Legend about	304, 305
" Belgian	202	" Species of	316, 319
" English, The Metropolis of	219	" Prosecution for the Sale of	309
" English, Popularity of	207	" Value of different Species	316
" Egyptian	16	" Its Growth	303, 304
" Manufacture of	195-196	" Its Medicinal qualities	308
" Origin of the word	196	" How to make	318
" The Inventor of	197	" Where most drunk	303
" Various	226	Coffee-Leaf Tea	300
Beowulf	37, 38, 45	Coffee and Liqueur	159
Besdon	360	Coffee Houses, A Poem on	312
Biliousness, Liqueur Specific for	176	" Rules and Orders of	311
Black Jack Jug	213	" Popularity of	309
Bon Gaultier Ballads	149	" The first	306
Bordeaux Wines	69	Columella's Wine Receipt	31
Borneo Beers	203	Continental Liqueurs	165
Bottled Beer, origin of	219	Cooked Wine	157
Bottling, Italian mode of	97	*Cordial Makers' Guide*	167

	PAGE
Cordials (Non-Alcoholic)	331
Cornish Drink	124
Corsican Wines	82
Cowley's Poem on Cuca	288
Cow's Milk, Formula for Fermenting	341
Cream Syrup	330
Crème de Noyau	175
Croker's Irishman and Whiskey	144
Crusta, The	181
Cuca	279
Curaçoa	165, 177
Curious Records	132
Cuttach	20
Danish Drinking Vessels	49
Dantzig Liqueurs	171
Date Coffee	319
Definition of Wine	52
Distilling Brandy, Mode of	126
Drinking Cups	49
„ „ Mode of Keeping	34
„ Health, Origin of	33
„ Horns	41
„ Vessels	213-214-216
Drinks, Pliny's List of	33
Drunkards, Punishment of	51
Drunkenness, Common Cause of	132
„ Cure for	298
Duty on Gin	133
Eau Clairette de Framboises	176
„ „ Chamberri	177
„ de Cerises	176
Ecbolada	16
Egg-nogg	185
Egyptian Process of Wine Making	14
Egyptians' Early Use of Wine	13, 16
Eichhoff	156
Elixir, Derivation of	166
English National Drink	207
„ Wines	62
Falernian Wine	31
Fall of Madame Geneva	134
Fathers of Brandies	160
Fenkâl	361
Fermenting Cow's Milk	341
Ferrintosh	148
Flannel	182
Flip	181
"Food of the Gods"	320
Francatelli's Service of Wine	55
„ on Gin Sling	188
French Beers	228
„ Liqueurs	172
„ Wines	64
Fruit Syrups	330
Garapa	360
Garway's Tea Advertisement	253
Garoe	349
Gartmore Estate Tea, Sale of	244
Galazyene	340
Gallebodde Estate Tea, Sale of	244
Ganges Water	350
Generous Wines	57
Geneva (Gin)	128, 130
Gerard and the Use of Cider	111
German Beers	228
„ Liqueurs	170
„ Wines	83
Ghee	354
Gill-house	130

	PAGE
Gin	128
„ Lane	138
„ Sling	140, 188
„ Alcoholic Strength of	140
Ginger Ale	327
Gingerade	326
Ginger Beer	324
„ Recipes (old & new fashions)	324-325
Glenlivet	149
Goethe's Opinion of Wines	89
Gongonha	277
Gout, Accredited Agent	104
Grecian Wines	26, 90
„ Dessert Wines	32
„ Process of Wine Making	27
Gregory of Tours	157
Greybeard Jug	216
Grieve (Dr. J.) and Koumiss	339
Guru	297
Hanway's Essay on Tea	266
Harrison's (Gen.) Favourite Beverage	185
Haynau (Gen.) & Brewer's Draymen	225
Heather Beer	227
Hebrews and Wines	22
Heidelberg Tun	83
Helbon, The Wine of	18
Herb Wine	157
Hervey (Lord) and Drunkenness	132
Hippocras	158
Hippocrates and the Virtue of Wines	33
Hittites and Wines	20
Hock	85
Hogarth's Gin Lane	138
Holy Tree, The	349-350
Homer's Wine of Thrace, &c.	25
Hunding, King, Death of	48
Hungarian Wines	93
Hydromel	48, 158
Hypoteques	177
Indian Beers	231
„ Tea	245
Irish Whiskey	146
Italian Mode of Bottling	97
„ Wines	94
Japanese Beers	232
Jekyll, Sir Joseph	133
Jerry Thomas	180
Jewish Prayers respecting Wine	345
Johnson (Dr.) on Tea	267
„ „ The Gin Act	137
„ „ Different Liquors	124-267
Julep	181-182
Kef	355
Kirsch	178
Kola	296
Koumiss	336-355
„ Its Curative Properties	339
„ Its Manufacture	341-342
Kümmel	165-174
Kvas	112
Ladakh Beer	360
Ladies' Tippling	121
Lamb Wine	356
Lapps, The Common Drink of	360
L'Eau Clairette de Groseilles	176
„ „ Grenade	177
„ „ Coings	177
Leather Bottel, The	214
Leake's Description of Grecian Wines	93

Leban 355	Pomeranzen 178
Lemonade 327	Pope 129-130
Liqueurs 156	Popularity of Tea 237-238
„ (Non-Alcoholic) 331	Populo 164
Liqueur Makers' Guide 167	Port Wines 99-100
Lovage Receipt 168	Portugese Wines 99
Madeira Wines 97	Private Brewing 209
Mahogany Drink 124	Procope 175
Maimonides 347	Psithian Wine 26
Makasso 297	Ptisana 351
Malmsey Wine 100	Pulque 359
Maraschino 175	Pulteney's Duty on Gin 133
Markham on the Coca Leaf ... 291	Punch 181-185-187
Marryatt, Capt., and Mint Julep ... 182	Punishment of Drunkards 51
Maté 272	Pusey Horn, The 42
„ Production of... 273	Raspail 178
Maturing Spirits, New Process ... 151	Ratafia 166-175-176
Mead... 41-48	Recipes (Drinks):—
Mead-hall 40	A Yard of Flannel 190
Mead-horns 41	Archbishop 192
Medicinal Quality of Tea 255	Black Stripe 193
Médoc Wines 72	Blue Blazer 192
Melo-cacti 351	Bimbo Punch 191
Methylated Spirits 362	Bishop 192
Metropolis of English Beer ... 219	Bottled Velvet 191
Milk 334, 354	Champagne Cyder 328
„ Beer 355	Cardinal 192
„ As a Beverage, Disadvantages of 334	Ginger Ale 327
Mineral Waters 331	Gingerade... 326
Mint Julep 183	Ginger Beer 324-325
Misson on Coffee Houses 310	Lemonade... 327
Monastical Liqueurs 160	Locomotive 192
Montaigne 159	Pope 192
Moonshine on American Drinks ... 193	Pousse l'Amour 192
Morat 45-158	Rumfustian 191
Morewood and Birch Wine ... 63	Sleeper 191
Motteux's Poem in praise of Tea ... 264	Stone Fence 191
Mulder, Professor 54	White Tiger's Milk 190
Mulls... 181-183	Recipes (Liqueurs):—
Murrey 158	Amiable Vainqueur 173
Murrhine Cups 34	Eau Aerienne 172
Mushroom Drink 351	„ d'Amour 170
Nantz 123	„ de Pucelle 171
Negus 181-185	„ de Scubac 173
Nile Water 350	„ de Sultane Zoraide 170
Nogg... 181-185	„ de Yalpa 170
Non-Alcoholic Cordials & Liqueurs 331	„ Divine 171
Northern Love of Drinking ... 47-50	„ Miraculeuse 171
Noyau 175	„ Nuptiale 170
Olaus Magnus 47	Elixir de Garus 173
Old Falernian 156	Guignolet d'Angers 173
Old Tom, Origin of... 141	Huile des Jeunes Mariés... ... 173
Ombulbul 359	Vespetro 172
Omeire 358	Recipe for Cream Syrup 330
Oporto Wine Co. 99	„ Fermenting Cow's Milk 341
Osiris... 197	Redding, Cyrus ... 60-83-85-94-107
Paraguay Tea 272	Redi's *Bacco in Toscana* 95
Parfait Amour 177	Reis' Classification of Wines ... 56
Pepys 209-260	Reland 55
Pereira 169	Rhine Wines 83
Perry 114	Rhodes, Father, on Tay 249
Persian Wines 97	Roman Wines 30-32
Perlin's description of English society 209	Roots' Cuca Cocoa 293
Peter's Pence 162	Rosee's Handbill on Coffee ... 307
Pigment 45, 158	Rossolio 164
Pliny's List of Drinks 33-197-349-353	Roussillon 81
Poem on Tea 261	Rubruquis and Koumiss 339
Polo (Marco) ... 339-355-356-357	„ „ Rice Wine... ... 357
Pombe 361	Rice Wine 357

	PAGE		PAGE
Rules & Orders of the Coffee House	311	Tea Poems on	261-263-264-265
Rum	153	„ The Finest	243
Russian Beers	233	„ When First Used	240
„ Wines	104	„ Where Grown	239
Sabzi	355	Teas, Various	242
Sacred Wine Tree	356	Thales	348
St. Vincent and the Holy Tree	349, 350	The Brown Jug	216
Saguer	357	Theine	295, 296
Samchou	361	Theobromine	322
Sangaree	181, 188	Thudicum, Dr.	150
Saprian Wine	26	Toak	359
Saratoga Water	354	Toast Water	351
Säure	355	Toby Philpot	216
Sbitena	358	Toddy	189
Scandal and the Tea Table	263	Tokay Wine	94
Schiedam	139	Toupare	359
Scotch Whiskey	147	Trade Rum	154
„ „ Earliest Account of	148	Transition Wines	57
Sea Water Wine	349	Tree Water	349
Setine Wine	30	Tschudi on the Cuca Plant	289
Shandy-gaff	324	Ulph's Horn	43
Sherries	106	Usquebath, Recipe for	146
Shrub	181, 188	Varieties of Wines	53
Sicilian Wines	105	Vega's Description of Cuca	282
Silent Spirit	151, 154	Vermuth	178
Sir John Barleycorn	210	Village Ale-house, The	225
Slemp	336	Villeneuve	161-163-164
Sling	181, 188	Vine, Cultivation of	39-99
Sloe Poison	271	Vine's Treatise on Home-made Wines	62
Small Still Whiskey	150	Vinegar	351
Smash	181, 189	Vizitelly and White Wines	76
Social difference in Ale & Wine drinkers	39	Vontaca	359
Soda Water	332	Waller's Poem on Tea	261
Spanish Wines	106	Walnut Liquor	357
Sparkling Wines	57	Walpole, Sir Robert	133
Spirit Beading	167	Ward, Edward, and Ladies' Drinking	122
Spruce Beer	233	Ward's Dialogue : Claret & Darby Ale	212
"Still Room"	119	Warm Water	354
Strabo	55	Wassail Song	206
Substitutes for Chinese Tea	298	Water	348
Surrentine Wine	31	Water Melon Drink	358
Swedish Beers	233	Water of Life	144
„ „ Drinking Vessels	49	Whiskey	144
Swiss Wines	108	„ Distillation	146
Syllabub	335	„ Manufacture	145
Syra	355	„ Maturing	151
Syrups, List of	330	„ Duty on	149
Table Wines	56	Whistling Shop	143
Taidge	360	White Ratafias	177
Tartary Beers	234	White Wines of the Médoc District	75
Tatler, The	262	Wine Making by Greeks & Romans	27
Tay	250	„ Vessels	24
Tea Advertisement, Garway's	253	„ Alcohol in	53
Tea	237	„ Definition of	52
„ Duty	238	„ Distinguishing Qualities	52
„ Houses	237	„ Origin of	54
„ Statistics	245	„ Oldest Records of	13
„ Trade, Centre of	238	„ Egyptian Process of	14
„ Plant, Growth of	241	„ Varieties of	53
„ Value in time of Queen Anne	262	„ and Beer, Merits of	197
„ Analysis of	246	Wines, Assyrian	18
„ Earliest mention of	248, 249	„ Francatelli's Service of	55
„ Early Duty on	253	„ Goethe's Opinion of	89
„ High Prices for	244, 245	„ Reis' Classification of	56
„ How to Make	268	Wolff's Description of Kirsch	178
„ Introduction to England	253, 260	Women's Tears	347
„ Largest Consumers of	239	Youourt	355
„ Legendary Origin of	239	Ywera	358
„ Medicinal Qualities of	255	Zythum	16

www.ingramcontent.com/pod-product-compliance
Lightning Source LLC
Chambersburg PA
CBHW020227240426
43672CB00006B/441